America's Waterfront Revival

Lee,

I HOPE YOU WILL FIND AT LEAST
ONE OR TWO NEW IDEAS IN THIS BOOK
THAT WILL HELP YOU IN YOUR CITY-
BUILDING EFFORTS.

— PETER.

THE CITY IN THE 21ST CENTURY

Eugenie L. Birch and Susan M. Wachter, Series Editors

A complete list of books in the series is available from the publisher.

America's Waterfront Revival

Port Authorities and Urban Redevelopment

PETER HENDEE BROWN

PENN

University of Pennsylvania Press

Philadelphia

Published by
University of Pennsylvania Press
Philadelphia, Pennsylvania 19104–4112

Printed in the United States of America on acid-free paper

10 9 8 7 6 5 4 3 2 1

A Cataloging-in-Publication record is available from the Library of Congress

ISBN 978-0-8122-4122-8

For Magnus

Contents

Chapter 1

Port Authorities and Urban Redevelopment

A Philadelphia Story

In Philadelphia during the 1990s a handful of independent units of local government called "public authorities" engaged in a wide variety of coordinated activities in support of Mayor Ed Rendell's tourism-, arts-, culture-, and entertainment-based economic development plan for the city. But many of these activities appeared to be only peripherally related to the purposes of the authorities that were implementing them. The Philadelphia Authority for Industrial Development, for example, financed a number of entertainment-, tourism-, and sports-related projects including two new stadiums, a major airport expansion, the conversion of a number of old office buildings into new hotels, and numerous new tourist attractions on Independence Mall and elsewhere throughout the city. The Philadelphia Parking Authority, which the state had created to finance and develop public parking lots and garages, supported these projects by building a major new parking facility at the airport and providing both parking facilities and partial financing for many of the office-hotel conversions that were intended to add rooms and boost the city's growing convention business. The parking authority also played a leading role in attempting to develop an urban entertainment center and a major movie theater project, both of which were to be supported by its new parking garages. Rendell's successor, John Street, reawakened the city's long-dormant redevelopment authority in order to advance his own agenda. In 2001 the agency sold $300 million worth of revenue bonds for the purpose of demolishing thousands of abandoned and blighted houses and creating new development parcels throughout the city as part of the mayor's Neighborhood Transformation Initiative.

Finally, the region's bistate port authority, created in 1911 for the purpose of building one bridge, expanded over the years, entering into a number of other business lines. By the early 1990s the Delaware River Port Authority was operating four toll bridges, a commuter rail service, intermodal cargo facilities, and a cruise terminal. But the port had also made a change in course, reenvisioning itself as a new kind of economic development engine and engaging in a major program of real estate development and urban revitalization projects focused on dramatically transforming the urban waterfront into a regional center for tourism. In 2005 the Delaware River Port Authority remained primarily a transportation agency, with 70 percent of its $1.25 billion in debt backed by tolls and fares and committed primarily to its four bridges and commuter rail system. But between 1995 and 2005 the port also invested nearly a half-billion dollars, $378 million of which remained outstanding debt in 2005, in more than forty major economic development projects, more than half of which were built on or near the Philadelphia-Camden waterfront.

As in Philadelphia, politicians, administrators, and private interests in cities throughout the country view existing public authorities as flexible tools that are waiting to be picked up, dusted off, and used for new and different purposes. When faced with the choice between creating a new agency and reusing an existing one to accomplish a policy goal, a politician or legislator will usually find the latter alternative to be more expedient, less visible, and less costly. In other cases authority leaders and administrators will choose to engage in new functions to replace lost revenues and ensure future growth, often following examples set by their peer organizations. Sometimes a combination of external political influence and internal aspirations will push an authority into a new activity or line of business. This process—how preexisting, industrial-era public authorities diversify into new lines of business and transform themselves into new, postindustrial urban redevelopment agencies in American cities—is the subject of this book.

Public Authorities, Port Authorities, and Urban Redevelopment

Since the early part of the twentieth century, public authorities have been providing an enormous and ever-increasing share of the public infrastructure in the United States, shaping the urban environment in powerful ways. Growth in the number of local general-purpose governments and school districts has been in decline since the 1950s, but politicians and local leaders have continued to create new public authorities. At the same time, older authorities have learned to adapt to changing trends, technologies, and constituent demands by entering new lines of business. Academicians have studied authority origins, character, growth, use, and administration, but current knowledge does not adequately explain how these existing authorities change as they diversify into new functional areas.

In this book I examine the experiences of four port authorities that diversified beyond maritime cargo operations and into waterfront rede-velopment, and then I consider three questions. First, how did external and internal forces encourage and impede these port authorities as they engaged in new functions? Next, how did the port authorities transform themselves as organizations in order to implement waterfront redevel-opment? And finally, do real public authorities change as institutions as they diversify into new functional areas, and, if so, do abstract theoretical models of public authorities adequately account for this institutional evolution?

Drawing on a wide range of sources including enabling legislation, annual reports, financial statements, strategic business plans, land use plans, audits, media accounts, and interviews, this book offers important new insights into the opportunities and challenges existing authorities face when they engage in new functions. Specifically, these port authori-ties all demonstrated the ability to change as organizations, becoming more innovative and entrepreneurial as they engaged in waterfront redevelopment. Increasing challenges and competition from other pub-lic and private interests, however, led to conflict that influenced and often hampered their efforts. Most important, these four port authori-ties all changed as institutions, devolving over time and becoming more representative as waterfront land controlled by a historically narrow and well-defined interest group was opened up to a new, broader, and more diverse set of constituencies.

This last finding calls into question previous characterizations of authorities as being politically insulated, financially independent, auton-omous, and stable over time. Together, these findings contribute to planning literature and practice by providing empirical research into how public authorities change as they engage in new functions and, more specifically, how port authorities change as they implement water-front redevelopment. More important, these findings will also serve pub-lic officials, port administrators, planning and design consultants, and the public as they continue to collaborate in the real work of redevel-oping our nation's waterfronts.

PUBLIC AUTHORITIES

The public authority is a form of special purpose or special district government. Special district governments differ from general-purpose governments, such as cities, counties, and townships, in that they con-centrate their efforts in only one functional area. General-purpose gov-ernments are responsible for a host of services and products ranging from police protection and trash pick-up to parks, libraries, and street repair, but special district governments provide only a single facility or service, such as an airport or transit system. Public authorities are differ-

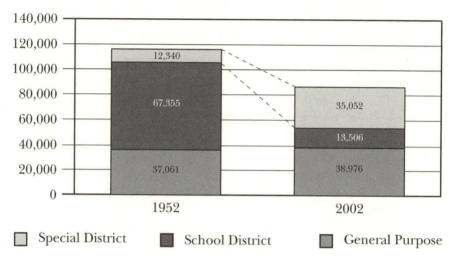

Figure 1.1. Changes in numbers of local units of government, 1952–2002.
Source: *2002 Census of Governments:* Volume 1, *Government Organization.*

ent from special district governments because they do not tax and are governed by appointed rather than elected boards.[1]

A product of the Progressive Era and the Wilsonian ideal of a separation between politics and professional administration, public authorities proliferated during Roosevelt's New Deal as mechanisms through which to funnel federal funds to local projects. Over the second half of the twentieth century, as growth in other forms of local government including municipalities, counties, and school districts flattened or declined, growth in special district governments continued at a rapid rate. The number of special district governments nearly tripled between 1952 and 2002, by which time there were 35,052 special district governments operating in the United States, representing nearly 40 percent of all local governments. Approximately 10,000, or 29 percent, of these special district governments were public authorities. But while the rate of creation of new special district governments and public authorities is of interest, so is the fact that, once operational, authorities rarely go out of business. Many industrial-era authorities continued to grow and expand vigorously, diversifying into new lines of business as their original projects were completed and their purposes were made irrelevant by a combination of new technologies and global economic trends.[2]

Indeed, the public authority has proven over time to be one of the most enduring, resilient, versatile, and adaptable forms of government ever created. These characteristics stem from two factors that are unique to the design of the authority as a form of governmental institution and that together give it freedoms that other special district and general-purpose governments lack. First, authorities are not subject to debt limits or voter referenda. Second, they are not subject to the same employment and procurement restrictions that constrain cities. As a result, authorities are politically insulated from public scrutiny and are therefore able to finance and develop major public facilities and infrastructure systems more quickly and flexibly than a city agency. In many cases authorities serve as both a new line of credit for cities that have reached their own debt limits and a work-around to avoid ossified city bureaucracies. The enabling legislation that creates and empowers an authority is usually general enough to allow for the broadest possible interpretation of its purposes by politicians, administrators, civic leaders, and interested private parties. In those cases when an enabling act is not worded broadly enough to permit a new function, legislators can quickly and easily amend it to do so. For these reasons politicians and administrators have often used existing public authorities for new and different purposes.

Public authorities represent an increasingly dominant form of local government in the United States. Because of their tremendous heterogeneity and mixed public-private character, however, current knowledge of the behavior of governmental bureaucracies and private corporations does not adequately explain how public authorities change as they age, evolve, and diversify into new lines of business. This book remedies this condition by comparing four port authorities in the United States that have engaged in a new and very different line of business from that for which they were originally created: waterfront redevelopment.

FOUR PORTS

The Tampa Port Authority, the Port of San Francisco, the Port of San Diego, and the Delaware River Port Authority—along with their respective waterfronts and cities—serve as the moorings for this book. Each port is located at the heart of a major United States Metropolitan Statistical Area (MSA), with 2006 size rankings and populations in descending order from Philadelphia, ranked fifth (population, 5.8 million); to San Francisco, twelfth (4.2 million); San Diego, seventeenth (2.9 million); and Tampa, nineteenth (2.7 million). Located on Florida's Gulf coast, Tampa was first discovered at the end of the sixteenth century but began to boom in the late 1900s with the discovery of the mineral phosphate and the rapid expansion of the railroads and the port. The explosive growth of the cigar manufacturing industry fueled by Cuban and Spanish immigrants gave Tampa the nickname "Cigar City." By the 2000s Tampa was at the heart of a rapidly growing region and a center for many retail, finance, real estate, tourism, and service businesses. The Spanish first settled San Francisco's Golden Gate in 1776, but rapid growth came with the gold rush of 1848, as the port became the major transportation hub for all of northern California. Cargo and industry began to decline in the 1960s, and by the end of the twentieth century the region had become a major center of culture, finance, and business as well as home to the Bay Area's entrepreneurial high-tech industry, located in nearby Silicon Valley. The Spanish also discovered San Diego, but Americans claimed it as a naval outpost in 1846 during the Mexican War, and by the mid-twentieth century it had grown to become the United States' largest naval installation. Less industrial than Los Angeles to the north, San Diego became home to a thriving biotech and biosciences industry as well as a center for finance, business, and tourism that relied on the region's beautiful beaches and Mediterranean climate. The largest of the four regions, Philadelphia, was once the second-largest city in the British Empire; briefly the largest and most important city in the United States culturally, politically, and financially; and one of the nation's first capitals. After the federal government moved to Washington, D.C., Philadelphia remained an important industrial power through the mid-twentieth century, when it was known as the "workshop of the world." In the 1960s Philadelphia suffered the fate of many Rust Belt cities as industry moved abroad and job losses and "white flight" led to declines in population and tax base. A renaissance that began in the 1980s led to the city's reemergence as a major commercial, educational, medical, and cultural center.

These four cities' port agencies have many similarities. First, legislators originally created each for a single purpose: the development and operation of maritime cargo facilities in the case of the first three. The Delaware River Port Authority was originally created to build a toll bridge, but maritime operations soon became a primary purpose of this agency as well. But over the years the four agencies diversified and expanded beyond their primary purposes. Each became a large and regionally influential multipurpose special district government engaged in a combination of maritime, transportation, and urban redevelopment activities. And beginning in the 1980s all four ports assumed the primary responsibility for waterfront revitalization in their respective cities, becoming deeply involved in real estate development in support of nontraditional maritime and nonmaritime public and commercial uses.

These four ports also differ in many ways. First, because they are located in different parts of the country, they grew at different times and were shaped by different commodities and markets. The cities they serve also developed unique characters and political cultures, which act as additional forces on the ports. Until the 1960s, however, the four ports shared one very important characteristic: simple, labor-based cargo-handling technologies. But during the past half-century, dramatic technological innovations, globalization, and the consolidation of the shipping industry have resulted in tremendous growth at just a few major shipping hubs worldwide. Many other, older ports, including these four, grew at slower rates or began to decline as a direct result of geographic location. For example, because it is not located on the Atlantic or Pacific coasts, Tampa's cargo business diminished steadily, although its location on the Gulf coast of Florida and its proximity to the Caribbean fueled a dramatic expansion into the cruise business. San Francisco's location on a congested peninsula virtually ended its role as a cargo port, although it controlled beautiful waterfront real estate in the form of abandoned maritime piers and facilities. Similarly, a remote location, poor rail access, and a shallow bay long ago conspired to stunt San Diego's cargo aspirations. And because the ports of Philadelphia and Camden lie at the end of a 135-mile shipping channel, only 90 miles south of the enormous Atlantic Coast-based Port Authority of New York and New Jersey, they attract primarily niche and bulk cargoes, such as petroleum products that are distributed locally and within the region.

The physical characteristics of the four waterfronts are also quite different, with Tampa bounded on three sides by narrow shipping channels. San Francisco and San Diego facing broad, scenic bays that open into the Pacific Ocean; and Philadelphia and Camden facing one another across a wide, tidal river. Coastal form influenced cargo operations at the four ports in the past, and it continues to influence waterfront redevelopment strategies today. Finally, these four ports are representative of many others throughout the United States that experienced declines in cargo in the wake of the container revolution and sought to generate new sources of revenues by diversifying into new lines of business.

In their business operations, the Tampa Port Authority remained a cargo port, the Port of San Francisco became a real estate development agency, and the Delaware River Port Authority remained a toll-crossing operation. The Port of San Diego combined equal parts aviation and real estate until 2003, when state legislators transferred its airport to a new authority, halving the port and reducing it to a real estate development agency. The scale and importance of cargo operations at the four ports varied, and while none were major container ports, all four diversified into specialty niche, break bulk, and container cargoes. Philadelphia and Tampa ranked among the largest bulk ports in the country in total gross tonnage because they are both regional oil ports while Tampa also exports aggregates and phosphate products. Conversely, cargo con-

TABLE 1. AGENCY CHARACTERISTICS

	Tampa Port Authority	Port of San Francisco	Port of San Diego	Delaware River Port Authority
Revenues, expenses, debt (in thousands)				
Net assets	$337,944	$297,422	$427,177	$1,074,669
Operating revenues	$34,949	$57,519	$112,924	$219,863
Primary source/%	Maritime/50%	Rents/60%	Rents/68%	Tolls/75%
Secondary source/%	Cruise/23%	Maritime/20%	Maritime/21%	Transit/8%
Third source/%	Rents/23%	Parking/15%	Other/11%	Maritime/1%
Total revenues	$57,447	$59,217	$121,362	$254,931
Operating expenses	($29,631)	($53,753)	($112,865)	($154,154)
Total expenses	($43,126)	($54,941)	($123,740)	($239,663)
Outstanding debt	$156,347	$19,084	$102,182	$1,245,209
Number of paid staff (approx.)	125	217	600	850
Governance/commission				
Total commissioners	7	5	7	16
Appointed commissioners	5	5	7	14
Ex-officio commissioners	2	0	0	2 (PA)
Appointing authorities	1 governor	1 mayor	5 city councils	2 governors
Jurisdictions represented	State, county, city	City	5 cities	2 states
Commissioners per jurisdiction	5/1/1	5	3/1/1/1/1	8/8

TABLE 1 (CONTINUED)

	Tampa Port Authority	Port of San Francisco	Port of San Diego	Delaware River Port Authority
Jurisdictions				
Location	1 county	1 city/county	5 cities in 1 county	13 counties (5PA/8NJ)
Land area (square miles)	1,053	46	4,212	5,840
Land control				
Type of land control	Ownership	Trusteeship	Trusteeship	Ownership
Land area	1,400 acres	645 acres	2,103 acres	NA
Length of urban waterfront	1.75 miles	7.25 miles	27 miles (SD)	3.0 miles (2 sides)
Port rankings				
Cargo value (2003)	41	Not ranked	36	17
Container volume (2005)	Not ranked	Not ranked	37	27/46[a]
Total cargo tonnage (2005)	14	113	98	21/63[a]

Sources: Financial figures are taken from the FY 05 Delaware River Port Authority Comprehensive Annual Financial Report, the FY 04–5 Port of San Francisco Annual Report, the FY 05–6 Port of San Francisco Audited Financial Statements, and the FY 05 Unified Port of San Diego Annual Report. Jurisdiction and land control figures are from the individual agency's Annual Reports, Strategic Plans, and Land Use Plans. Port Rankings are by the American Association of Port Authorities.

[a]Philadelphia/Camden are individually ranked.

tinued to account for only a small share of business at the two California ports.

The four agencies are all financially large as ports in the United States go, varying in size from approximately $35 million in total annual operating revenues at the Tampa Port Authority to $220 million at the Delaware River Port Authority in 2005. To put financial size in perspective, only a couple of ports in the world can compete with the Port Authority of New York and New Jersey, which realized nearly $3 billion in revenues in 2005 from combined operations including port, aviation, toll crossings, commuter rail, and rents from real estate. By comparison, this is about seven times larger than the Port of Seattle and eight times larger than the Port of Los Angeles, two of the largest ports in the United States, which earned revenues of $416 million and $369 million, respectively, each in the same year.[3]

The four agencies were also similar in organizational structure and institutional character. At some point each fit the traditional definition of an independent public authority: a special district government with an appointed board and no power to tax. Three ports originally lacked taxing power, although the Florida Legislature granted the Tampa Port Authority this power in 1989. Conversely, while the Port of San Diego always had taxing power, it ceased using it in the late 1960s, effectively operating like a self-sustaining public authority ever since. In 1968 the California Assembly transformed the Port of San Francisco from a state public authority into a city enterprise department, although its finances were to remain separate from those of the city and it did not receive general fund revenues. Finally, appointed commissions governed all four agencies, although there were subtle but important variations between them in terms of commission structure, composition, and method of appointment.

The Public Authority in Theory and Practice

Types of Public Authorities

Public authorities provide a wide variety of products and services including mass transit, ports and airports, housing, public facilities, economic development, and urban redevelopment. The two basic organizational types are operating and financing or "lease-back" authorities. Operating authorities sell bonds to finance the projects they develop, own, and operate and then use revenues from tolls, fares, rents, and other charges to repay the debt. Port, aviation, water, bridge, and highway authorities are usually of the operating variety. Financing authorities provide conduit financing to the local municipal government that actually develops and operates the project. Many economic development authorities are based on this model, as are authorities that fund the construction of public housing, health care, educational, and general-use facilities.

Financing authorities sell revenue bonds to fund the development of major public projects, but because they do not directly own or operate these projects, they are typically very small organizations. Some financing authorities are unstaffed organizations that are operated under contract by other agencies and effectively exist only on paper. For example, many housing and economic development authorities are actually operated by city planning and economic development departments whose staff serve both agencies simultaneously. In contrast, operating authorities own substantial assets in the form of land, facilities, systems, and infrastructure. Because they also operate these facilities and systems, they typically employ large work forces that serve the public directly with transportation, housing, and other goods and services.

In a case-based study of governments involved in urban regional development in the New York metropolitan area, Danielson and Doig found that, despite variations in geographic scope, function, and constituency demands, these large operating authorities or "functional agencies" share several important and interrelated characteristics. First, the combination of a narrow functional approach to each task, a small and known constituency, and policy decisions made through low-visibility negotiations ensures effectiveness over long time frames. This narrow functional perspective attracts strong leadership while insulation from civil service regulations and patronage helps to attract quality staff and maintain organizational flexibility. Functional agencies also demonstrate strong planning capabilities, and unlike many general-purpose governments, they produce measurable results in the form of completed projects. These characteristics are not independent but rather reinforce and strengthen one another. A functional agency with insulated revenue sources combined with a narrowly defined and statutorily protected mission that gives it legitimacy discourages competition from other political actors and agencies. Finally, this type of organization attracts leaders who seek "public influence unencumbered by the need for wide consultation and compromise" while at the same time encouraging these leaders to act "vigorously and decisively."[4]

WHO CREATES AND USES AUTHORITIES AND WHY

State legislatures create public authorities because they offer distinct advantages over other governmental agencies in their efficient and effective implementation of certain types of functions, projects, and programs. The state of Pennsylvania department of community affairs, for example, outlines the three categories of advantages typically promoted by governments, politicians, and authority administrators: financial, administrative, and jurisdictional.[5]

Financially, the creation of an authority allows a municipality to borrow outside of its constitutional debt limits while at the same time avoiding the need to raise taxes. This advantage was largely responsible for the dramatic growth in authorities during the 1930s, when they were the only vehicles available to municipal governments to raise matching funds required for federal public works grants. Because raising taxes has become ever more difficult politically, the avoidance of debt limits remains an important advantage, and it partially explains the continued growth in the number of authorities since the 1950s.[6]

Administrative advantages stem from the single-purpose character of the authority, which allows for the concentration of energies on just one problem. Because they are insulated from close public control, authorities can make decisions that may be unpopular in the present but that may benefit the public in the long run. This political insulation also allows public authorities to attract higher-quality board members and staff who can be paid more than those in other units of government that are constrained by civil service systems. Finally, authorities have a greater incentive to operate efficiently, because they must succeed as financially self-sustaining independent entities and cannot operate as loss-makers.[7]

The jurisdictional advantages of using an authority are related to the size, location, and natural features of the service area as well as the nature of the service that is to be provided. Many public services can be administered efficiently only if a large service area is covered, but political boundaries and the boundaries of the ideal service area do not always coincide. A joint authority, therefore, is a separate entity created by a number of municipalities that can efficiently provide a specific service for a larger area. A rare but important variation is the bistate authority, which allows for a single jurisdiction that encompasses areas of two states, often for the purpose of creating a bridge, tunnel, or other transportation facility that will serve both.[8]

But there are other advantages to using authorities that go beyond the efficiency and effectiveness arguments that are typically proffered by governments and politicians. In a study that compared cases of authorities operating in New York City, Walsh found three slightly different sets of incentives for authority creation and use: financial, managerial, and political. Financial incentives are most important because authority financing allows a city to exceed its debt limit by financing public projects off-budget with debt that is not backed by taxes and is therefore not subject to voter referenda. However, Walsh found that neither theory nor experience supports the contention that authorities operate in a more efficient and businesslike fashion. Rather, the primary incentive for authority creation from a management standpoint is to avoid the rules, laws, practices, and personnel and procurement constraints that impede the ability of general-purpose governments to act quickly in the implementation of projects. Former Philadelphia Parking Authority director Rina Cutler put it even more bluntly: "The beauty of the authority structure is that it gets you out of the bureaucratic horror show surrounding procurement and employment."[9]

The original concept behind the authority was that its unique financial and governance structure would insulate it from politics, but in practice authorities rarely operate free of external political influence. Instead, Walsh confirmed that an important conclusion from Sayre and Kaufman's 1960 book *Governing New York City* continued to hold true: that authorities merely change the "arena within which the political contests over their decisions take place." This new arena enhances the influence of bankers, consultants, developers, and other private interests in city business. Activist mayors and governors recognize the political advantages of authorities, using them to "break through some of the obstacles to action and create specialized pockets of efficacy, even at the expense of giving up some administrative control." They also know that it is often easier to create a new authority than to fix an old general-purpose government, for as Mayor Ed Koch of New York City said, authorities are often "the path of least resistance." Perhaps most important, Walsh concluded that the continued popularity of public authorities, particularly among elected officials, is a reflection of the larger issue of how hard it is to manage, control, and use general-purpose government in the development of large, costly, nonroutine projects.[10]

New and Innovative Uses for Authorities

Once operational, authorities are subject to a variety of ongoing pressures that influence them over time, from new technologies to global economic trends. Transportation technologies have been changing constantly since the internal combustion engine led to trucking and busing over roads, making railroads largely obsolete. Containerized cargoes soon made traditional finger piers and their stevedores redundant; jet air travel replaced ocean liners, leading, in turn, to the birth of the cruise industry; and, more recently, electronic toll collection systems replaced toll collectors on roads, bridges, and tunnels. At the same time, the globalization of financial markets increased the mobility of capital and the role played by foreign investment in fueling real estate development on authority-owned land.

Many authorities have been coerced by superior governments into managing or subsidizing loss-making operations, from social and economic programs to environmental cleanup, habitat restoration, and the provision of non-revenue-generating facilities such as parks. Others have been forced to seek intergovernmental revenues, federal funds, and taxing power in order to pay for these new functions. In some cases authority corporate and financial structures have changed fundamentally in order to match new uses with diverse sources of funds. Together, these trends led to reduced financial independence and autonomy for public authorities.

Because the number of authorities continues to grow and existing authorities rarely go out of business, authority leaders and politicians continue to seek new and innovative uses for existing authorities. The New Jersey Turnpike Authority added new lanes in order to keep growing, while over the years the Port Authority of New York and New Jersey added bridges, tunnels, airports, bus facilities, container ports, and even communications facilities in a constant attempt to integrate new technologies into its mission. Other authorities added new services that responded to political and social concerns, such as the New York Metropolitan Transportation Authority's provision of a police force for crime prevention in the subways. A particularly innovative example was the Battery Park City Authority's transfer of surplus revenues to the New York Housing and Preservation Department for use in developing low-income housing in Harlem and the South Bronx.[11]

Finally, while some cities created agencies like the Battery Park City Authority to redevelop their waterfronts, in many others existing port authorities stepped in, diversifying into new lines of business and developing new types of facilities, from ferry and cruise terminals to cultural facilities, entertainment centers, and public parks.

Waterfront Redevelopment

THE EVOLVING WATERFRONT

Brian Hoyle identifies five stages of waterfront development, beginning with the period from antiquity to the mid-nineteenth century, when the "primitive cityport" served as the physical, social, and economic nerve center of the city. But during the second half of the nineteenth century and the first half of the twentieth century, rapid commercial and industrial development forced many ports to expand by increasing land areas and constructing artificial harbor facilities to accommodate growing trade. New forms of communication and transportation that were affected by geography, particularly railroads and the telegraph, greatly influenced the locations of these port expansions.[12]

Late nineteenth-century trends, including increasing ship size and draft and increasingly specialized industrial growth continued through the mid-twentieth century. The development of new industries, particularly for crude oil and ore extraction, resulted in the need for larger sites, which pushed port facilities farther downstream toward available land and deeper waters. The development of container technology, which also required large sites, further reinforced these trends. In addition, the public's increasing sensitivity to environmental issues led many people to question the appropriateness of industry on the waterfront, so close to inhabited urban areas. Continued technological advances, ever-larger ships, growing land requirements, and the migration of the port downstream culminated in the abandonment of the urban waterfront and the complete separation of the port from the city.[13]

Urban waterfront redevelopment began in the 1970s. As ports moved away and manufacturing and industrial businesses relocated to the suburbs, the deserted waterfront offered large sites that soon became attractive to nonmaritime interests, including developers of housing, offices, and restaurants, and to the public for recreational uses, including parks and marinas. At the same time, the environmental movement was gaining momentum, leading to pollution controls that sought to clean up old industrial sites like those on the waterfront to make them appropriate for these new uses.[14]

These trends created enormous challenges for port authorities. Growing ports were confronted with the difficulties of land acquisition, planning, and development of new port areas and facilities on a much larger scale than ever before. But more important, all ports were faced with the enormous challenge—and opportunity—that surrounds the redevelopment of huge, abandoned land areas, including the old port and the original waterfront in the heart of the urban core.[15]

REDEVELOPMENT CHALLENGES

Urban waterfront redevelopment presents a number of unique opportunities and obstacles to cities that seek to revitalize their downtown cores. First, waterfront sites are typically very large, numbering in the tens, hundreds, and even thousands of acres, but they lack basic modern street, power, and sewer systems. Further, waterfront infrastructure, including piers, pilings, bulkheads, and seawalls, requires constant and costly maintenance whether or not the property is in use.

The issues revolving around the control and ownership of waterfront property are also complex. The existence of many property owners, including a distressed port authority, multiple city agencies, private individuals and companies, and the federal government in the case of naval shipyards and other military installations, makes for a patchwork of interests on the waterfront. The transference and acquisition of waterfront property can also be challenging, especially when there are preexisting environmental conditions that stem from former industrial and military uses. Furthermore, a web of federal and state laws and regulatory agencies increases this complexity by restricting and controlling the use of coastal lands.

Another major issue related to the scale of these sites is timing. Waterfront sites may present a tremendous redevelopment opportunity for a city, but they are often so large that the supply of land far exceeds demand. As a result, the up-front improvement of such large sites does not guarantee the total redevelopment of the waterfront within a brief time frame. Rather, the redevelopment of large waterfront sites often takes decades to substantially complete.

Finally, the issues of scale and timing together complicate the financing of redevelopment. Local leaders expect large waterfront sites to pay returns in the form of rents and fees to authorities and taxes or payments in lieu of taxes to cities. However, as Gordon demonstrated in a study of the finances of large-scale waterfront redevelopment in four cities, the up-front costs of providing infrastructure improvements that are required as a precondition of development can be exorbitant, and it can take decades before the debt on these investments is repaid and the first returns are realized. As a result, one of the most difficult balancing acts in waterfront redevelopment is financing enough infrastructure to stimulate development while at the same time matching these costs with anticipated revenues on an incremental, project-by-project basis.[16]

Uses on the New Waterfront

The biggest challenge in urban waterfront redevelopment is balancing the new uses, which typically include some combination of residential, commercial, tourism, or recreational anchors. Condominium towers, for example, anchor Toronto's waterfront, which also has a continuous promenade lined with public uses including retail shopping, restaurant, and recreation facilities. New York relied on commercial development at the World Financial Center to stimulate residential, tourist, and recreational development along the Hudson River at Battery Park City. At South Street Seaport in New York and in other older port cities, such as Baltimore and Boston, local leaders concentrated on developing tourism-based anchor projects. In these cities the redeveloped historic district on the old waterfront served as a framework that was then augmented with heritage ships, aquariums, museums, entertainment facilities, festival marketplaces, and a variety of other attractions.

All anchor types stimulate public debate over access to the water's edge, equity in the provision of housing, the obstruction of views, and the overall character, purpose, and use of the waterfront. For example, residential anchors typically create tension because they threaten to privatize the waterfront for wealthy residents, blocking access to the public. Politicians are torn by the pressure to provide low- and moderate-income housing on these sites and the knowledge that high-income housing promises greater financial returns not only to private developers but also to the city in the form of property taxes. The public typically opposes high-rise housing, hotel, and commercial developments that will block views as well as proposals that threaten to turn the waterfront into a place for out-of-town tourists rather than local residents. At the same time, cities and waterfront redevelopment agencies resist low-density, park- and recreation-based anchors because they simply do not generate the revenues required to cover the costs of building and maintaining their facilities. For all of these reasons, most waterfronts combine a mix of uses. However, the choice of primary anchor depends on a city's location, history, economic base, political culture, and regulatory climate with respect to land use. As Gordon concluded in a study of implementation at the Battery Park City Authority, the choice of uses, the quality of design, and the speed of implementation together play a crucial role in determining the success of waterfront redevelopment, both in financial terms and in the eyes of politicians and the public.[17]

In short, the waterfront redevelopment problem is characterized by a lengthy time frame for development, very large up-front investments, and enormous scale: the very type of problem that the progressives envisioned the public authority solving.

Charting a Course

What We Know

Research on public authorities is concentrated in two areas: quantitative studies explaining authority proliferation, distribution, size, and purpose, and historical and theoretical studies that examine authority origins, character, governance, and administration based on case studies of individual authorities and their projects. While the quantitative research offers a relatively balanced picture of the numbers and activities of authorities, it fails to capture their operating character, in part because of the great variety that exists among authorities. The case study research on public authorities addresses issues of operating character more directly but is subject to bias, as it concentrates on just a handful of very large, old port, transportation, and redevelopment authorities in the northeast and principally in New York City.[18]

Indeed, an enormous share of the scholarship on public authorities is based on the Port Authority of New York and New Jersey. As a result, public authority research and port authority research are closely interrelated, and both are dominated by New York's famous port.[19] The knowledge of waterfronts is even less developed, and there is no comprehensive theory of waterfront redevelopment.[20] As with public authorities and port agencies, the waterfront redevelopment research also covers just a handful of large agencies and projects in world cities, primarily New York and London.[21]

This book remedies these deficiencies and adds to our knowledge base in three key areas. First, it compares the experiences of four port authorities in the United States with the prevailing Port Authority of New York and New Jersey–based public authority model. Second, by examining four other port agencies, this book adds both breadth and depth to the port agency literature while offering a corrective to the Port Authority of New York and New Jersey's past dominance. More generally, this study also serves as a corrective to the bias toward large agencies in the Northeast, and in New York specifically, that permeates the public authority, port authority, and waterfront redevelopment literature. Third, this is the first study of its kind to specifically address the role of agency type in waterfront redevelopment by examining what happened when development was implemented by preexisting port authorities rather than by specially created waterfront redevelopment authorities, existing redevelopment authorities, and other types of agencies.

PORT AUTHORITIES

Port authorities form the core of this study because they are the oldest and most studied type of modern authority still in operation. Indeed, no public authority has been studied more than the Port Authority of New York and New Jersey. Moreover, because many port authorities are so old, they have roots in an industrial era that is now past, but they continue to survive and adapt as they engage in new, postindustrial functions, making them perfect subjects for this book.

Public authorities are also central to this study because of their growing influence as urban redevelopment tools. The tax revolt in combination with the era of devolution, during which the federal government reduced its financial commitment to cities, caused mayors and other politicians to seek new, nontax forms of revenue for the revitalization of urban areas. Public authorities that were once created to serve industrial purposes have proven to be an important source for these new revenues.

Politicians, administrators, and private interests have used authorities to address a wide variety of new, postindustrial purposes including arts, culture, entertainment, tourism, and convention business. While cities of the past competed for industry and jobs, postindustrial cities compete for convention and tourism business as well as for white-collar service jobs and residents. Today's competitive city is characterized by a collection of urban projects that constitute Judd's "tourist bubble" and "mayor's trophy case" and that Frieden and Sagalyn call "showpieces." A list of these projects includes a festival marketplace, atrium hotel, aquarium, convention center, historic district, ballpark, arena, stadium, performing arts center, entertainment center, gambling casino, farmer's market, museums and cultural institutions, and importantly for this study, a revitalized urban waterfront comprising a mix of commercial office space, residential development, parks and recreation facilities, and tourist attractions.[22]

The Plan of the Book

This book is divided into two parts. As this introductory chapter has framed the issues and questions, the next four chapters introduce the four ports—Tampa, San Francisco, San Diego, and Philadelphia/Camden—and their waterfronts and cities.

The first three chapters in the second half of the book consider the questions posed in the introduction by looking at crosscutting analyses of the four cases through different sets of theoretical lenses. Chapter 6, "The Changing Waterfront," relies on theories of change on the waterfront, the politics of urban redevelopment, and the challenges of implementation to consider how a variety of forces influenced each of the four ports in their attempts to engage in waterfront redevelopment. Chapter 7, "The Rise of the Diversified Port," takes the port's point of view by looking from the inside out and focusing on theories of innovation and organizational change in private companies, government bureaucracies, and public authorities to explain how the four agencies evolved as business organizations as they engaged in new functions. Chapter 8, "Devolution and the End of Autonomy," focuses on theories of the character, governance, and administration of public authorities to illuminate how external forces reshaped these four authorities as institutions.

These three chapters weave together the findings from the four cases, demonstrating that these port authorities were capable of innovating, adapting to new functions, and diversifying into new lines of business, including waterfront redevelopment. As they did so, however, their moral and legal authority was often challenged, creating a power struggle on the waterfront. Emboldened by the port's apparent weakness, other organizations and politicians began to compete for control over land and projects, reducing the port's autonomy as well as the speed, consistency, continuity, and quality of development. As the four port authorities diversified into multiple lines of business, they became more prone to a variety of external forces, losing both autonomy and independence over time. Through this process of devolution, they all became more representative and responsive to broader constituencies. Indeed, over two decades these ports each became more akin to the general-purpose governments that they were originally created to augment, losing a share of the autonomy they had possessed in the past, when they had more closely fit the traditional public authority mold.

The last chapter, "The Price of Diversification," reframes these findings into ten lessons. These lessons build upon one another to create a new framework through which port leaders, public officials, developers, and private citizens may better work together to help their ports grow, their waterfronts redevelop, and their cities thrive. The chapter concludes by reconsidering the role, meaning, and importance of public authorities today, both in practice and in theory, and by asking the question "Do authorities really matter anymore?"

Chapter 2
Tampa

Waterfront History and Geography

The story of the Port of Tampa began in the late nineteenth century when phosphate, a major ingredient in fertilizer and other agricultural products, was discovered in surrounding Hillsborough County. In 1883 the first channel was dredged to the Port of Tampa, and the resulting boom in phosphate mining coincided with the rapid growth of the railroads. Expanding trade with Cuba further fueled port growth, and by the early 1890s, 280 tons of phosphate per hour were being loaded at the Port of Tampa, along with fruit and Cuban tobacco destined for Ybor City's cigar factories. In 1905 a second channel was dredged, connecting the Hillsborough River through Hillsborough Bay to Tampa Bay. The dredge spoils from this project were used to create Seddon Island, where in 1925 construction was completed on five elevators for the loading of phosphate from trains onto boats.

In the early twentieth century, the port's shipbuilding business expanded from building schooners and yachts to include cargo and warships for the navy during World War I. Shipbuilding in Tampa boomed during World War II when more than twenty-three thousand workers built and repaired or refitted hundreds of warships at Hooker's Point. The port has since served as a center for bulk cargo exports and imports including phosphate, petroleum, and chemical products; for shipbuilding and ship repair; and, until 1960, as Cuba's primary trading partner.

Tampa Bay, which opens to the south, into the Gulf of Mexico, is split in half by the Interbay Peninsula, which runs from the north to the south, leaving Old Tampa Bay to the west and Hillsborough Bay to the east. Hillsborough County is comprised of the Interbay Peninsula, also called South Tampa, and the area surrounding and to the east of Hillsborough Bay, with downtown Tampa located at the northern edge of the bay.

Tampa's urban waterfront is an approximately three-and-a-half-mile stretch of land wrapping around a peninsula that forms the southern end of the city's central business district. The western edge of the peninsula fronts on the Hillsborough River, which flows south for about a mile and a half before emptying into Hillsborough Bay. The southern side of the peninsula is a one-mile stretch that fronts on Garrison Channel, an old shipping channel that is no longer in use. The east side of the peninsula fronts onto Ybor Channel, an active shipping channel that runs north for a little less than a mile and dead-ends.

Tampa's central business district, which includes several high-rise office buildings, an art museum, and a performing arts center, fronts on the east side of the Hillsborough River, facing several large parks, the landscaped grounds of the H. B. Platt Museum, and the University of Tampa campus on the west side. Across Garrison Channel to the south but connected by several bridges is Seddon Island, which served as a major terminal for the phosphate trade for forty years before it became uninhabited in the 1960s. In 1980 the Beneficial Corporation bought Seddon Island, renamed it Harbour Island, and in 1984 initiated the development of a gated residential community. Across Ybor Channel to the east are large industrial port facilities on Hooker's Point including grain elevators, chemical and petroleum tanks, and a shipbuilding company with floating dry docks. The streets in the waterfront area are laid out on a grid pattern, but several major elevated highways, the Crosstown Expressway and Kennedy Boulevard, cross the peninsula from east to west, making traffic more confusing and separating the port area visually from the rest of downtown, which lies just to the north.

The Tampa Port Authority

At the end of World War II, Florida legislators acted to consolidate what had become a fragmented port by creating the Hillsborough County Port District. The new district was comprised of uplands and submerged lands within an area that is roughly coterminous with Hillsborough County. The legislature also created the Hillsborough County Port Authority, now the Tampa Port Authority, as the district's governing body.

Legislators structured the port as a typical public authority with a governing commission comprised of five gubernatorial appointees and the power to sell revenue bonds. The port used this power to finance the purchase of the marine holdings of the port's major shipbuilder, McCloskey and Company, along with those of another smaller shipbuilding company and 131 acres of waterfront land on the west side of Hooker's Point. In 1947 the legislature granted the Hillsborough Board of County Commissioners the power to levy taxes on behalf of the port, although this power was used infrequently over the years.

By the early 1980s, the Tampa Port Authority was facing several daunting challenges. At the time, private terminal operators owned virtually all of the property on the urban waterfront except for the banana docks on Ybor Channel that were owned by the port. But the global forces that affected many ports during the second half of the twentieth century, including the container revolution and the consolidation of steamship lines, caused declines in cargo volumes, and the situation in Tampa was further exacerbated by the cessation of trade with Cuba in the early 1960s. These declines caused financial hardship for the private terminal operators who stopped maintaining their facilities. As these facilities slid into decay, the port began to lose its ability to compete with other, more modern ports, and the urban waterfront became an eyesore. The port was also becoming increasingly concerned because bulk phosphate and petroleum products accounted for virtually all its cargo, and the corresponding lack of revenue diversity exposed the port to potentially traumatic economic shocks. This concern was intensified by anticipated gradual declines in phosphate cargoes due to depleted mines and environmental concerns. In the 1970s the local maritime community began to pressure the port to enter the container cargo business, but while a study was done nothing would come of it, and another potential source of cargo and revenue bypassed the port.

At all ports the cost structure of cargo operations is based on a combination of the "port tariff," which includes charges paid to the port for dockage, wharfage, rents, and water, in addition to charges paid for piloting, tug services, fuel, stevedoring operations, and demurrage, or warehousing facilities. But according to Port Director Emmett Lee, "In Tampa this formula was skewed towards lower labor rates that discouraged competition from outside stevedoring companies, which was a recipe for stagnation rather than the growth of the port." The Tampa Port Authority had always operated as a landlord port, leasing property and facilities to stevedoring companies and other tenants but not operating any facilities directly. But rents typically account for only a small share of total cargo revenue, with the lion's share going to the terminal operators. The port was realizing only a small share of revenue from cargo operations, and by the 1980s these revenues had dwindled to less than $5 million a year.[1]

At the same time, the very lucrative cruise business had been growing at an exponential rate in the United States and worldwide. Because the potential for growth in number of passengers and number and size of ships appeared to be limitless, Lee and the members of the Port Commission began to envision Tampa as a future home port for the older, smaller cruise ships that would be displaced as the more mature Florida cruise ports of Miami and Everglades became congested. "So in 1981, the port hosted a big cocktail party and dinner at the Tower Club for Holland America Cruise Lines," recalled Lee. "During the party I was approached by several executives of Holland America who drew a sketch of a basic cruise terminal on a paper napkin, so at a hastily assembled press conference the next morning the chairman and I agreed to build it and Holland America agreed to come to Tampa." The port quickly used all of its available resources to finance the fast-track construction of a temporary, convertible structure on the east side of Hooker's Point, in the center of the industrial port, that would house both the new terminal and a cargo transit shed. In 1982 the Holland Cruise Terminal (this area of the port had long been called Holland Terminal, named after former Florida governor and United States senator Spessard Holland, not the cruise lines) was completed, and Holland America began operating their *Nieuw Amsterdam* cruise ship out of Tampa. But the port also recognized that if it was to grow its cruise business it would have to develop larger and more attractive passenger terminal facilities, and Port Commission chair Joseph Garcia began pushing the idea of developing a major, permanent cruise port on Tampa's urban waterfront.[2]

By the late 1980s, Lee, Garcia, and other port leaders were searching for ways to create a more competitive cost structure for cargo operations and stimulate the growth of the greater port as an important regional economic development engine. To do so they would have to increase the Tampa Port Authority's operating revenues, diversify its revenue base, fund the improvement of cargo facilities, and accommodate the long-term growth of the cruise business downtown.

The port developed a two-part strategy to address these interconnected problems. First, it would enter the operating business by acquiring Garrison Terminals, a large operator that occupied twenty-three acres of dilapidated terminal facilities on Ybor Channel whose owners were interested in selling. The port would create a new operating entity and retain Garrison's owners to run the new operation under contract. Second, in a simple land swap, the terminal facilities would be relocated to Hooker's Point, freeing up the land on Garrison Channel for the development of cruise facilities.

But while the port had a forty-month option to acquire Garrison, it did not have any money, having recently financed the new Holland Cruise Terminal. So Lee and Garcia took members of the Hillsborough County Commission on a boat tour of the harbor to make the case for the value of the Garrison property to the port's future as both a cruise port and a larger economic engine for the region. Lee, Garcia, and the Port Commission convinced the county to levy taxes on behalf of the port in 1986, and they used the proceeds to acquire Garrison and a second terminal operator and to pay for the conversion of a warehouse facility on Garrison Channel into Cruise Terminal 1, which opened in 1987. Regency Cruise Lines began to call at the new facility, which became known as the Garrison Cruise Ship Terminal. The remaining proceeds were used to pay for the conversion of the temporary Holland Cruise Terminal on Hooker's Point into a split facility, half of which would house the port's new operating unit, Tampa Bay International Terminals, which was created in 1989.

This initial set of transactions laid the groundwork for the Tampa Port Authority's transformation into an operating port and, more important, for the creation of a major new cruise port and waterfront destination in downtown Tampa.

Redevelopment Begins

In 1985 a Clearwater businessman began to promote the idea of a Florida state aquarium; however, the project ran into opposition in Clearwater, so in 1987 aquarium backers began planning for a site on Harbour Island, in Tampa. In 1989 the city of Tampa agreed to back the project with up to $84 million in bonds, and when plans for the Harbour Island site fell through in 1990, Tampa mayor Sandy Freedman, who was a major aquarium advocate, proposed locating the new facility on the other side of Garrison Channel, on the port's new waterfront property. "I had reservations," recalled Lee, "and so did Joe Garcia and the other commissioners, but attendance projections showed that the project would be financially viable." Garcia concluded that, "despite my own reservations, I recognized that an aquarium would serve as an appropriate first anchor attraction, stimulating both additional development and the growth of the cruise industry on Garrison Channel."[3]

In negotiations with the aquarium over the ground lease for the 4.3-acre site, the port was able to obtain a seat on the board and $4.0 million for the construction of a new seawall and cruise ship berth adjacent to the site. In exchange, the port agreed to a $1.0 million loan to the aquarium and a loan guaranty of up to $10.0 million, which was later increased to $14.3 million. The 120,000-square-foot Florida Aquarium was completed and opened in the spring of 1995, but attendance was significantly below the projected numbers, and the aquarium soon faced financial difficulties. In January of the following year, the aquarium asked the city for financial assistance and in March announced that attendance for the first year was 1.0 million rather than the projected 1.8 million. In the fall of 1996, the city acquired the failing aquarium. As part of the bailout, the port relinquished 7.8 acres of land to the city, including the building site and an adjacent parking lot, in exchange for a reduction in their loan guaranty from $14.3 million to a maximum limit of $1.67 million.

Although the city absorbed most of the financial losses in the aquarium bailout, the port lost a valuable, strategically located piece of property, and it also took a financial hit, as it was required to make substantial annual payments to pay off its loan guaranty. Yet the completion of

Cruise Terminal 6 in 1987 for Holland America, the reconstruction of two seawalls and ship berths, one by the port in 1990 and the other by the aquarium in 1993, and the opening of the aquarium in 1995 together signaled the beginning of both urban waterfront redevelopment and the expansion of the cruise business in downtown Tampa.

In the mid-1980s and prior to the port's acquisition of the Garrison site, Port Director Emmett Lee brought in a team composed of a marketing firm from San Diego and an architect and planner from San Francisco to develop a master plan for the property. According to Lee, "The plan relied on private developers to finance the port's purchase of the Garrison property, which in the end was a reach too far, that failed." After acquiring the property with tax revenues in 1986, the port developed another master plan, which formed the basis of a request for proposals "seeking a developer-lessee to design, construct, finance, and operate public and private improvements including two cruise terminals serving three ship berths alongside a new 2,200-foot bulkhead; 1.5 million square feet of office space; two, 600-room hotels; 40,000 square feet of retail; new Tampa Port Authority offices; and 3,700 parking spaces." The request for proposals did not elicit any responses, and Lee deemed the plan "another reach too far, because the site was not close enough to the downtown core to attract such dense development at the time. Further, the cruise terminals placed an excessive burden on an already economically challenging project because they were to be subsidized by rents from the other uses."[4]

In July 1990, and partially in response to the suddenness of the spring 1990 aquarium site selection decision, the Port Commission hired Prime Interests, Inc., a development management firm, to create a site development master plan for the sixty-three-acres of land that the port either owned or controlled along Garrison and Ybor channels. In March 1991 the commission expanded Prime Interests' contract to include a major update to the port's strategic plan. The *Strategic Plan Update*, which was completed in January 1992, was a unique, comprehensive, and far-reaching document that also incorporated broad input from the Port Commission and staff. According to Richard Gehring of Prime Interests, "The plan sought not only to identify and refine the port's new business goals and strategies, but also to reshape the Tampa Port Authority itself as a business organization in order to best implement the new goals and strategies and to integrate them with the development master plan."[5]

In 1994, Prime Interests and Cooper Carry & Associates completed the *Seaport District Plan*. The plan was based on three simple objectives: "Create an efficient and attractive cruise ship facility that can be successfully combined with non-maritime uses; open the waterfront up to public use by creating opportunities for a unique mix of recreation and maritime activities at the water's edge, and extending the visual amenity of the waterfront inland; and create an attractive and marketable private development opportunity that is integrated with and enhances the cruise ship and other public facilities and takes advantage of the unique waterfront location."[6]

The plan envisioned extending the existing street grid to the edge of Garrison and Ybor channels and creating a new, dense, urban entertainment destination. The terminals would be embedded in new blocks of mixed-use development that would in turn be bordered by new "destination streets," "water streets," and public plazas. The plan also included design guidelines for the new buildings and a kit of parts for street furniture that together would be used to create an architecturally coherent urban environment where none had existed before. "The overall idea behind the plan," according to Gehring, "was to develop cruise terminals as a primary source of revenue while at the same time generating additional ground rents, or 'secondary dirt revenue' from the remaining land by using private mixed-use development to create the framework for a waterfront destination."[7]

But most important, the plan hinged on attracting three large and strategically sited anchor projects to provide the level of investment needed to jump-start development and create the street energy necessary to make the seaport a lively destination. Conceptually, the plan did not require specific types of anchors; however private developers had already independently proposed three major projects for the area, so these were incorporated into the plan. The $84 million Florida Aquarium, which was already financed and in development, was to be the first. The second anchor, initially proposed in 1991, would be a $25 million MusicDome concert venue, with huge hanger doors that would open onto the water, giving concertgoers views of the channels and bay. The third anchor, announced in the fall of 1992, would be a $70 million pirate museum based around an old pirate ship, the *Whydah*.

By early 1993 the aquarium was under construction, and the other two projects appeared ready to go. But then the development team for the *Whydah* pirate museum, led by Roland Betts, the successful developer of Chelsea Piers in New York City, faced charges from Tampa's African American community of having concealed the fact that the *Whydah* had been a slave trading ship. The developers sought to ameliorate these concerns by establishing an advisory board made up of local African American leaders and agreeing to make the ship's slave history part of the attraction. But the race issue would not abate, so in June 1993 Betts and his partners pulled out and the port announced that it would proceed without the *Whydah*.

Then, in November 1993, after considering several sites, including one on Harbour Island, the city of Tampa announced that a new arena for the Tampa Bay Lightning hockey team would be built on Garrison Channel, adjacent to the MusicDome site, despite concerns that the two projects would be in unhealthy competition with one another for music events. The developers of the MusicDome quickly sought to reconfigure their project to ensure its financial viability, first considering the addition of a treasure-hunting-based museum or other themed museum to replace the lost *Whydah* project. Between December 1993 and July 1995, the project's developers considered adding a variety of components to the program including a comedy hall of fame, Imax theater, laser tag game facilities, flight simulator, theme restaurants, a "dinosaureum" and history museum, business conference facilities, nightclub, music superstore, and a sound recording studio. Finally, in summer 1995, after four years of delays, the frustrated Port Commission severed its ties with the MusicDome developers and selected another developer, the Hogan Group, to proceed with what by that point had become an urban entertainment center.

By 1994 the number of cruise passengers crossing the docks in Tampa had grown to more than three hundred thousand. In 2005 the port demolished interim Cruise Terminal 1 and built two new passenger facilities on Ybor Channel, Cruise Terminals 2 and 6, to accommodate increasing traffic. Holland America relocated to Terminal 2 from its facility on Hooker's Point in 1995 and then moved again to Terminal 6 in 1996. After only a decade, the port was well on its way to achieving its primary strategic goal of attracting the cruise business to Tampa. But its secondary goal of creating a supporting waterfront destination had still not been achieved. The aquarium was up and running, but the second anchor was dead, the third was foundering, the *Seaport District Plan* was fast becoming a dead letter, and the port's planning leadership was moving on. In May 1995 port director Joe Valenti, who had been the driving force behind the plan at the port since 1990, left to take a position with a major cruise line. The port's deputy director, Robert Steiner, succeeded Valenti, but while he had an impressive background in cargo he had no real estate development experience and showed little interest in pursuing a comprehensive approach to waterfront redevelopment. Steiner allowed the port's contract with Prime Interests to expire, and then in December 1997 Charles Towsley, the deputy port director for real estate who had been the other driving force behind the plan, left to take the position of port director in Miami. By 1997 the leadership and senior staff of the port had lost all interest in a comprehensive plan, opting instead for a more incremental and opportunistic style of development on the waterfront.

In January 1997 the port approved the Hogan Group's plan for a 180,000-square-foot entertainment and retail center with a twenty-one screen movie theater. The project was to be completed in December 1998, yet the lease alone took a year to finalize, and the developers received several extensions that were needed to line up all the partners for the project, including the movie theater company. The $49 million building was completed in spring 2001, by which time it had grown in size to 230,000 square feet of retail space, restaurants, and a smaller theater complex with an Imax theater and nine screens.

In June 1997 the port decided to move out of the dilapidated World War II–era building on Hooker's Point that had served as its administrative office for more than forty years. According to Joe Garcia, "The Port Commission debated for a long time about where to locate the new building, ultimately rejecting locations on Hooker's Point and choosing instead a prominent site on the west side of Ybor Channel. There, the new facility would introduce the public to the new, bigger, better, more visible, more public, and more entrepreneurial Tampa Port Authority while at the same time stimulating further private development on port property along Ybor Channel." The port's new, eighty-thousand-square foot International Headquarters building was dedicated to longtime commissioner Garcia and opened in 1999.[8]

The cruise business was booming, so the port continued to expand its passenger terminal facilities on Ybor Channel. In 1999, Cruise Terminal 2, which was originally designed around the unrealized entertainment anchor planned for Garrison Seaport Center, was remodeled and expanded. In 2000 the port announced that it would spend $6 to $10 million dollars to improve Cruise Terminal 6, the Holland America terminal, and another $20 million to build a brand new facility, Cruise Terminal 3, just to the north of the aquarium. The new terminal opened in 2002 and began serving Celebrity Cruise Lines and Royal Caribbean Cruise Lines. In 2001 the port unveiled a new ten-year plan for the entire Channelside area that was designed to further expand cruise capacity on Ybor Channel by adding two new terminals, numbers 4 and 5, between Terminals 3 and 6. The plan also included an expansion to the aquarium, a hotel and condominium complex with a "cyber center" and conference center located on the site of the old banana docks, as well as restaurants, parks, and a thoroughfare designed to connect the waterfront with downtown.

Finally, the blighted industrial area west of Channelside Drive became a nascent residential neighborhood as pioneers seeking an urban lifestyle bought up old warehouse buildings and converted them into residences and offices while larger developers built new loft-style condominiums. In 1999, Mayor Dick Greco targeted the new Channel District for growth by recognizing it as a development district, and in 2003 the city council created a tax increment financing (TIF) district to increase infrastructure spending in the area. By 2006 the neighborhood had largely filled in with low and mid-rise residential buildings while a handful of high-rise condominiums, hotels, and conference centers were in various stages of planning and construction on the ribbon of land on the other side of Channelside Drive, along Ybor and Garrison channels. The other major, nearby urban development district, the Latin quarter called Ybor City, had a head start by virtue of its historical architectural character and the support of its patron, Mayor Dick Greco, but the Channel District finally began to grow too. A new vintage-style trolley line running 2.4 miles from the convention center along Channelside Drive to Ybor City was opened in 2002, linking the two districts and further stimulating the growth of each. The city and the business community jointly financed the trolley, and the Port supported it with operating grants. But the fortunes of the two districts soon reversed. Ybor City became a weekend destination characterized by heavy-drinking, younger crowds and related nuisance crime, and by 2006 the area was suffering and the city had to bail out its centerpiece entertainment project, Centro Ybor. Meanwhile, the Channel District had started to mature into a true, mixed-use neighborhood with residential, office, and retail uses and a busy and vibrant adult dining and entertainment zone, all anchored by the Channelside Shops.

Challenges and Opportunities for the Future

By the time it celebrated its sixtieth year in operation in 2005, the Tampa Port Authority had succeeded beyond its wildest dreams in transforming itself into a major cruising homeport, and in 2006 nearly nine hundred thousand cruise passengers crossed its docks. But despite the sweeping visions contained in the *Seaport District Plan*, the development of a waterfront destination in support of the cruise business on Ybor Channel was slower, more incremental, and less consistent than originally hoped for. That so many of the projects proposed for the seaport area between 1986 and 2006 went unrealized suggests that until the mid-2000s there simply was not enough demand for a major waterfront destination in Tampa. Indeed, the Channelside Shops project that opened in 2001 remained only 60–65 percent leased for almost two years, and most of its restaurants and bars were only open on weekend evenings. However, by late 2003 more than 80 percent of the building had been leased, and by 2006 the center was nearly full. But as Joseph Garcia points out, "The only development of any kind in downtown Tampa for more than ten years was on the waterfront and was stimulated by the

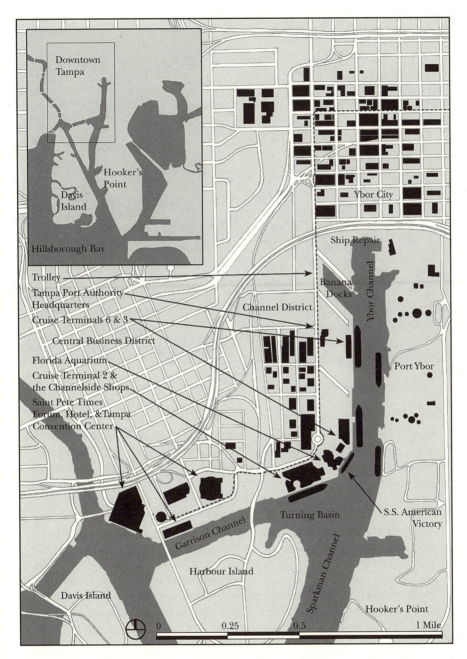

Figure 2.1. The Tampa waterfront. Map by Whitney Parks.

Figure 2.2. Ybor Channel in 1954. Courtesy of the Tampa Port Authority.

Tampa Port Authority." Indeed, by 2006, demand finally appeared to be catching up with the supply of land on Tampa's waterfront, as indicated by the numerous competing proposals for new condominium towers, supermarkets, hotel and conference facilities, and commercial office space on Ybor Channel and in the neighboring Channel District.[9]

So while the 1994 *Seaport District Plan* may have come before its time, a decade later its impact had been felt despite the fact that many of its original underlying components went unrealized. As it found that demand would not support its grand master plan of financially linking cruise terminals and private development, the port's approach to waterfront redevelopment became more opportunistic and piecemeal. Its waterfront redevelopment strategy was simplified to a two-part program of increasing capacity for the expanding cruise industry as a primary goal and supporting the development of a wider variety of major private development projects that would provide the port with ground rents and participation from sales. In retrospect, this incremental approach was simply more realistic, although the comprehensive vision for an

Figure 2.3 Cruise Terminal 3. Photo by author.

Figure 2.4 The Channel District neighborhood. Photo by author.

entertainment-themed waterfront experience was lost. In its place, however, blossomed a more integrated and authentic urban neighborhood that combined tourism and entertainment facilities with retail, services, and new housing, both in waterfront condominium towers and throughout the Channel District.

One element of the seaport area experience that was diminished by these successes, however, was public access to the water's edge. Paradoxically, despite city and port plans for a riverwalk, the growth of the cruise business made the waterfront less accessible to the public. New terminals and increased cruise ship calls meant that more ships were tied up at any one time to the bulkheads along Garrison and Ybor channels. Florida port security law had already constrained public access to the water's edge at cruise terminals when ships were in port, but the events of 11 September 2001 and subsequent additional requirements of the Department of Homeland Security made stretches of the promenade along the waterfront a gated and inaccessible place for much of the week. Access was destined to become even more limited as several condominium towers proposed for Ybor Channel began to move ahead, although Mayor Pam Iorio's administration was hoping to use the city's regulatory powers to compel private developers to incorporate public space into these waterfront projects.

In 2003, former Tampa Port Authority managing director Charles Towsley thought that "development in the seaport area will work out in the end, but that the seaport is in a difficult position because it has to compete with Ybor City." By 2006 this had already started to happen as the seaport pulled ahead of Ybor City in the competition for growth and the development of a true mixed-use district. But more important, former port director Joe Valenti offered the reminder that "both the strategic business plan and the master plan were always about the cruise business, not about the waterfront, and despite slower than hoped-for development on the waterfront, the port's strategy for growing the cruise business in Tampa was tremendously successful."[10]

And by growing its cargo business and diversifying beyond bulk cargoes and shipbuilding into break bulk, autos, containers, and contract cargoes such as steel, as well as cruise and related waterfront real estate development, the Tampa Port Authority also expanded and diversified its revenue base and became a much healthier and more financially stable organization than it had been in the 1980s. The agency experienced dramatic growth in its operating revenues, from less than $5 million in 1981 to $35 million in 2005, 50 percent of which was generated by maritime cargo despite the lackluster performance of its general cargo operation, Tampa Bay International Terminals.

The port's greatest success was indeed the growth of the cruise business. Between 1996 and 2005 the number of passengers crossing the docks in Tampa swelled from 192,230 to 771,550, and almost 1 million passengers were expected in 2007. During the same period cruise revenues grew from $1.7 million to $7.9 million, and they also became a larger share of the port's revenues, growing from 11 percent to 23 percent of total operating revenues. Financial stability was further enhanced by the addition of annual tax revenues that became a dependable share of the port's total revenue base beginning in 1986. But the port's second greatest success, according to Joe Garcia, "was the cleaning up of Tampa's urban waterfront, which set the stage for the completion of the aquarium, the ice hockey arena, now called the Saint Pete Times Forum, and the Channelside Shops, all of which together primed the pump for the residential and commercial development that began to follow in the 2000s."[11]

The decision to rely on tax revenues led to several other important changes to the Tampa Port Authority's institutional structure and character. First, when the port gained the power to tax independently in 1989, the local legislative delegation reacted to concerns about "taxation without representation" by passing legislation in 1991 that changed the Port Commission's composition to make it more representative. Gubernatorial appointees were reduced from five to three, and two new ex officio seats were added for the mayor of Tampa and one Hillsborough County commissioner. But this change also led to improved intergovernmental relations as the port and the city and county all began to work more closely together and coordinate their efforts, particularly around improvements to transportation infrastructure. Second, when it issued revenue bonds in 1993, the port persuaded the Hillsborough County Commission to back its bonds in exchange for a role in reviewing port plans and projects. Because its bonds were now supported both by project revenues and by the county's taxing power, Wall Street's rating services upgraded the port's credit rating, dramatically increasing its bonding capacity. While the port surrendered some autonomy by giving the county a greater role in its decision making, in financial terms it benefited tremendously and as a result became a much stronger organization.

But beginning in the 1980s, perhaps the most important influence operating on the Tampa waterfront was the growing tension and conflict between maritime interests, private developers, downtown residents, and the port. By 2006 the Tampa Port Authority had succeeded in attracting the cruise industry, revitalizing the waterfront, growing its cargo business, and strengthening its own finances. It also invested new revenues from the cruise business, ground rents, participation, and parking throughout the entire port on maritime facilities and land

Figure 2.5. The fountain and courtyard at the Channelside Shops. Photo by Eric Taylor, © EricTaylorPhoto.com.

acquisition, and in 2005 it spent $40 million to build a new container port on the east side of Hooker's Point. But speaking for Tampa's industrial maritime interests, shipping company owner Arthur Savage argued that "the port's priorities were misplaced and that its successes were at the expense of the larger port as a regional economic development engine and provider of jobs." At the same time, nearby residents in the Channel District criticized the port for promoting large waterfront projects that would block views and restrict public access to the waterfront. The epicenter of this conflict was Ybor Channel, where new cruise terminals, tourist attractions, and residential projects along the west side of the channel faced ship repair operations, an industrial distribution center, and petroleum tanks to the east.[12]

Arthur Savage and other maritime business owners protested that "the development of land alongside deepwater berths for non-maritime uses like the hotel and conference center proposed for the Banana Docks and the condominium tower proposed for the site south of the Channelside Shops would permanently reduce the port's cargo capacity." For its part, the port sought to acquire other land and port facilities with deepwater access throughout the greater port area for the purpose

Figure 2.6. Channelside Drive by night. Photo by Eric Taylor, © EricTaylor Photo.com.

of relocating industrial uses away from the urban waterfront and providing for future maritime growth. In 1995 the port acquired privately owned Port Redwing, and in 2005 it bought a parcel of land adjacent to the shrimp docks to preserve as industrial port land rather than allowing it to be developed for housing, which would soon have led to conflicts between the existing port users and the new residents. The port paid a substantially higher residential price for the parcel, but it preserved good port land with access to deep water while protecting maritime businesses from the threat of being pushed out in the future by higher value uses. Even the waters became contested territory as cruise ships and petroleum tankers competed for priority in the port's congested Sparkman shipping channel.[13]

In 2005 the simmering conflict between the port and its industrial tenants erupted when the port announced plans for a twelve-lane security gate and other improvements on Hooker's Point that maritime companies viewed as unnecessary and bad for business. About a dozen companies formed a lobbying group called the Port of Tampa Maritime Industries Association, which succeeded in promoting state legislation passed in 2005 that changed the Port Commission's composition once

Figure 2.7. Aerial view of Ybor Channel. Courtesy of the Tampa Port Authority.

again. The amendment increased the number of commissioners from five to seven, adding two with direct maritime experience or interests, despite concerns that the port would come to be dominated by knowledgeable but self-interested and conflicted commissioners who would have undue influence over their lay peers.

But as Joe Garcia concludes, tension between maritime interests and the port is the norm rather than the exception: "There is nothing more constant in the history of ports than change and there are never enough resources, so there is always conflict over priorities and spending on the waterfront." Indeed, it was the Tampa Port Authority's relative success and balanced growth in multiple competing lines of business—cruise, waterfront redevelopment, and cargo—that sustained and at times even heightened this tension. The next chapter will explore how relations between the port, maritime interests, developers, and the public played out in San Francisco, where by the 1980s cargo had all but abandoned the commercial waterfront.[14]

Chapter 3

San Francisco

Waterfront History and Geography

As in Tampa, a variety of forces at the global, national, and local levels influenced maritime operations at the Port of San Francisco. However, steeper declines in cargo volumes, a historically powerful longshoremen's union, a labor-friendly culture, a very restrictive regulatory environment, and an activist citizenry together led to quite different outcomes on this city's waterfront.

The city of San Francisco occupies a forty-six-square-mile rectangle located at the northern tip of the peninsula that forms the western edge of San Francisco Bay. The city and its port are both products of the gold rush of the mid-nineteenth century, which attracted ships and immigrants from around the world and fueled the initial growth of all of northern California. The commercial waterfront and harbor developed along the eastern side of the peninsula, fronting on the bay, and in 1863 legislators created a state commission for the purposes of improving the harbor. The Port of San Francisco continued to grow rapidly throughout the remainder of the nineteenth century.

The Ferry Building, located at the foot of Market Street and completed in 1898, came to serve as the center of the commercial waterfront. As the Harbor Commission developed new finger piers, they assigned them odd numbers ascending to the north, beginning at the Ferry Building, and even numbers ascending to the south. The piers terminated at bulkhead buildings that fronted on the city's most important industrial thoroughfare and rail corridor, the Embarcadero. The port grew steadily throughout the first half of the twentieth century, and the outbreak of World War II further fueled this growth as San Francisco became a major West Coast logistics center, shipping troops, equipment, and supplies to the Pacific theater and causing a boom in the city's shipbuilding and ship-repair industries.

By midcentury San Francisco boasted more than seventy finger piers as well as supporting railroad terminals and warehouses, all densely packed along a busy commercial waterfront that stretched nearly eight miles from Pier 45 at the northern end of the city to Pier 98 in the south.

The Port of San Francisco

San Francisco remained the West Coast's premier cargo port until the 1950s, when the Port of Oakland, on the east side of the bay, succeeded in securing a steady stream of federal grants for harbor improvements. Oakland used these funds to invest in the revolutionary shipping technology of containerization, transforming its mud flats into a new, high-tech container port. Oakland inaugurated its containership service in 1962, and by 1965 its cargo tonnage equaled that of San Francisco's. By the late 1960s, worldwide, Oakland was second only to Rotterdam in container tonnage and second only to the Port Authority of New York and New Jersey in its terminal acreage.

Across the bay, political leaders in San Francisco grew alarmed as their port continued to lose business to Oakland throughout the 1960s while the state Harbor Commission sat by and did nothing. San Francisco leaders felt that the commission, which was comprised of five gubernatorial appointees, was out of touch with the needs of the city and the port and ineffective at securing the state funding for the harbor improvements needed to ensure San Francisco's future competitiveness, so they began to advocate for local control of the port. These efforts led to the California Assembly's 1968 passage of the Burton Act, which transferred control of the port from the state to the city. This act replaced the old, independent San Francisco Port Authority with the Port of San Francisco, a new city enterprise department that would be governed by a port commission comprised of five mayoral appointees.

In 1969, the new agency sold $19 million in revenue bonds to finance improvements at Pier 96, gambling on a new cargo technology called "lighter-aboard-ship," or LASH. But LASH proved to be an ineffective competitor to containerization, and the port's new facilities on the southern waterfront went unused. In 1971 the port sold another $20 million in bonds and used the proceeds to build a modern container terminal at piers 94 and 96. By this time, however, Oakland had already signed leases with the major containership lines, so these facilities went largely unused as well. But the port had more serious problems that couldn't be solved with money or technology. Its location on a peninsula, poor rail access, lack of rail competition, and the uncomfortable fact that all of its inbound cargo had to be shipped by rail around the bay to Oakland—adding two days to the trip—before it could be shipped into the hinterlands, meant that San Francisco faced a dim future as a cargo port.

Nonetheless, in 1984 the port issued another $42.5 million in revenue bonds and used the proceeds to improve its container facilities. In 1986 the port claimed to be "on the comeback trail" as a cargo port, although critics suggested otherwise, pointing to the fact that Oakland now handled 90 percent of the container traffic in San Francisco Bay. A 1986 management audit conducted by the San Francisco Board of Supervisors further criticized the port for plans to spend $7.9 million to acquire three new container cranes and to refurbish an existing crane when the seven existing cranes went unused 95 percent of the time. Still, the port's cargo aspirations did not abate. In 1987 the Port Commission spent another $3 million to develop an intermodal container transfer station that went unused and considered spending $215 million for a new container terminal and $88 million for rail tunnel improvements and other work required to accommodate double-stack container cars.

But despite the port's cargo aspirations, by the mid-1980s much of the industrial waterfront had been largely abandoned. Commercial fishing operations and seafood restaurants occupied Pier 45 and Fisherman's Wharf, at the northern end of the waterfront, while the city's one remaining ship-repair yard and the port's modern container terminals anchored the southern end of the waterfront, between piers 70 and 98. The bond covenants for the San Francisco Bay Bridge, which became effective when the bridge was completed in 1939, severely restricted ferry service, rendering the Ferry Building largely obsolete. For more than four decades this symbolic center of the waterfront was allowed to deteriorate and suffer from an insensitive, nonhistorical renovation and shoddy deferred maintenance. By the 1980s the Ferry Building—the only office space actually on the water in San Francisco—could only command class B and class C rents despite its stunning views and an unmatched central location for ferry, transit, and commuter rail service. Finally, many of the obsolete finger piers that comprised the large remaining areas of the central waterfront had fallen into decay and been abandoned while cargo revenues had dwindled to less than 20 percent of the port's total revenues.

Redevelopment Begins

Dianne Feinstein was the first mayor to attempt to assuage the fears of maritime interests by angrily asking the question "Are we or are we not a port?" Feinstein, however, had also come to realize that the port's future could no longer be based on maritime uses alone, so in 1986 she backed a proposal to erect a hotel on Pier 45, the revenues of which would be used to help improve facilities at Fisherman's Wharf. But anger over the thought that the city might displace commercial fisherman led the public to kill the idea.[1]

In this case, and in many to come, the public saw the support of commercial fishing as well as cargo, shipbuilding, and other traditional mari-

Figure 3.1. Busy finger piers on the San Francisco waterfront, circa 1950. San Francisco History Center, San Francisco Public Library.

time uses as the port's primary purpose. Yet these uses were already well into decline, and maritime operations, which accounted for only a small share of the port's revenues, were heavily subsidized by rents from other commercial uses. By the late 1980s the restaurants at Fisherman's Wharf were paying more in annual rent, more than $5 million, than all other maritime tenants combined, with the highest grossing restaurant, Scomas, accounting for nearly a third of this amount. The Port Commission and senior staff concluded that the port's future lay in the development of new types of nonmaritime, revenue-generating commercial projects on its valuable waterfront property. Over the next four years it considered a number of proposals for major projects at three specific sites.

First, in June 1986, the Port Commission signaled its intent to grow its cruise business by hiring a local architect to develop proposals for expanding the port's passenger terminals. In March 1988 the commission entered into agreement with a group of Danish investors to develop a $60 million mixed-use complex at piers 30 and 32 on the southern waterfront that was to include a cruise terminal as well as a Scandinavian cultural center and a fisheries center. By 1990 the project had grown to $128 million, and the program had expanded to include an exhibition

Figure 3.2. Rotting finger piers, with Oakland's container cranes in the distance, in 2003. Photo by author.

hall, a 360-room conference hotel, four restaurants, a retail pavilion, an enclosed arcade, a small marina, and a five-story office building on the inland side of the Embarcadero. The office of Jørn Utzon, the architect of the world famous Sydney Opera House, was to design the project. Second, in February 1987, the port decided to try again to develop a project on the pier 45 site near Fisherman's Wharf. This time it considered four proposals for a hotel and convention center. The revenues from this project would be used to finance new fishing boat berths and modern fish-processing facilities at other areas on the wharf. Third, in December 1989, the Port Commission considered three schemes for a second hotel and mixed-use complex based around a "sailing center," to be located at piers 24 and 26 on the southern waterfront. This last project attracted the attention of the press, resulting in a critical editorial from the *San Francisco Chronicle* that questioned the port's selection process because it emphasized revenue-generating capacity over design quality. Members of the nonprofit environmental group San Francisco Tomorrow followed by threatening a ballot initiative designed to further regulate development on port-controlled waterfront property.

In August 1989 the port hired a management consulting firm to draft a new strategic plan and a waterfront master plan. But while the planning process was underway nature intervened: On Tuesday, 17 October 1989, the Loma Prieta earthquake struck. The quake caused billions of dollars of property damage in the Bay Area and it weakened the elevated double-decker Embarcadero Freeway that ran along the waterfront. Mayor Art Agnos recalled how, "after considering studies that recommended both repairing and demolishing the freeway, I finally decided to tear it down."[2]

In April 1990 the port released its new strategic plan, which not only proposed improvements to cargo facilities but also contained the long-awaited master plan for the redevelopment of the waterfront. The plan included a convention center, a seafood center, and at least one hotel, although by this time the port had already decided to build the other two cruise terminal and sailing center–based hotel and mixed-use projects. In presenting the plan, port director Michael Huerta acknowledged that while "tradition is very important in San Francisco," the port must develop innovative new methods to finance projects and accommodate not only maritime uses but also new uses, using port land in a "balanced and diverse" way.[3]

Immediately after the port released its plan, San Francisco Tomorrow announced detailed plans for a ballot initiative that would ban all hotels on the waterfront. The group feared that the development of the two hotels proposed by the port would cause a chain reaction leading to the erection of a "wall of hotels" along the waterfront that would block public access and views of the bay. A history of projects such as Fisherman's Wharf, Ghirardelli Square, and the Cannery that politicians and developers touted as being for the citizens but that actually catered to out-of-town tourists fueled the concerns of many San Franciscans. The public also saw these two projects as cynical attempts to slip through much larger commercial developments by cloaking them in maritime wrappers to satisfy existing regulations limiting land uses on port property.

In a May 1990 meeting, the Port Commission attempted to assuage the public's fears by passing a motion that called for capping the number of new hotels on port property at two. The public, however, did not trust the port to stick to its own resolution, so San Francisco Tomorrow president Andy Nash assumed a lead role in drafting the ballot initiative that became known as Prop H. This initiative sought to ban the development of hotels on the waterfront and to place a moratorium on waterfront development of any kind until the port completed a comprehensive waterfront land use master plan through a process that ensured maximum feasible public involvement. The San Francisco Labor Council, the Chamber of Commerce, and the *San Francisco Chronicle* editorial board all opposed Prop H. Together they criticized it as a drastic threat to the port that would wipe out the financial base for two developments proposed for little-used sites on the southern waterfront, cost the city in jobs and tax base, and threaten the financial health of the port. Port tenants also opposed Prop H, claiming that it would constrain the port and threaten the new projects that would serve as sources of revenue for the improvement of their own decaying facilities. But despite this vocal opposition, on 6 November 1990, San Francisco voters approved Prop H by a slim majority, freezing all waterfront development, banning waterfront hotels, and killing the two major projects under consideration.

Prop H added another layer of complexity to what was already a fragmented system of land use regulation on the San Francisco waterfront. As a trustee of public lands, the Port Commission controls three types of property, including submerged lands and the piers over them, tidal lands, and filled lands on the inland side of the Embarcadero. The use of this property is regulated by three different agencies with overlapping jurisdictions: the State Lands Commission, the San Francisco Bay Conservation and Development Commission, and the city and county of San Francisco.

Many of the submerged, tidal, and filled coastal lands in California are owned by the public and held in trust by the state, which reserves them for uses that promote navigation, fisheries, waterborne commerce and that enhance natural resources or attract people to enjoy the water. The State Lands Commission usually administers public lands, although in certain cases the state entrusts these lands to other public entities while allowing the commission to retain its power to review and approve land use decisions. In 1968, the Burton Act transferred public trust lands on San Francisco's waterfront to the Port of San Francisco as grantee and trustee. The State Lands Commission identifies three categories of use for public trust lands: acceptable long-term uses, unacceptable long-term uses, and acceptable short-term uses. Acceptable long-term uses include traditional maritime as well as a wide range of public uses such as museums, aquariums, water-based recreational uses, and specialty retail and commercial uses designed to draw people to the waterfront, such as restaurants. Unacceptable long-term uses include office, residential, and non-water-related industrial uses. Finally, acceptable short-term uses include some unacceptable long-term uses, such as parking, that do not preclude conversion to acceptable long-term use in the future.

The San Francisco Bay Conservation and Development Commission is an independent state commission that regulates land use around the entire San Francisco Bay. The commission is charged with ensuring that uses on waterfront property around the bay provide maximum feasible public access to the waterfront and with preventing filling in the bay except for specific water-oriented uses. The commission has regulatory jurisdiction over port property on the bay side of the Embarcadero within one hundred feet of the water's edge. Finally, the city and county of San Francisco's *General Plan* and Planning Code regulates building height, bulk, and use on waterfront property. The code's forty-foot maximum height limit for waterfront buildings was the requirement that most affected the development of port property.[4]

In spring 1991 the port initiated the land-use planning process mandated by Prop H by convening a citizen's advisory committee, whose twenty-seven members represented diverse interests including maritime businesses, port tenants, labor unions, neighborhood organizations, and architects, planners, and other professional interest groups. The first phase of the process was to determine existing land uses. According to former port director Michael Huerta, "The port and maritime interests for many years hewed to an unofficial agreement that all waterfront property south of the San Francisco Bay Bridge, about two thirds of the total waterfront, would remain dedicated to traditional maritime uses." But according to Paul Osmundson, the former director of planning for the port, "The first phase of the public planning process led to the determination that only one-third of the waterfront was used for maritime anymore, so the second phase was determining what to do with the remaining two-thirds of the unused waterfront." Osmundson concluded that "Prop H was actually a godsend for the port, because it focused attention on the most important yet unaddressed and fought-over issue: the future of waterfront land use." Huerta recalled how "the port embraced the plan as a good thing to do and the right thing to do" and agreed that "the plan was a watershed that paved the way for good development."[5]

Although the purpose of the plan was to clarify the uses for the port's property, plan implementation remained a potential challenge, as each proposal and lease would be subject to negotiations between the port, the city, the Bay Conservation and Development Commission, and the State Lands Commission. According to Will Travis, the Bay Conservation and Development Commission's executive director, port director Dennis Bouey "was particularly concerned that working out the details for each project with Travis's commission would make development too time-consuming, costly, and difficult." So Bouey met with Travis and asked, "What do you want, what do I want, and what can we agree on?" "I wanted public access and a bigger bay," recalled Travis, "and Bouey wanted flexibility on the development of piers, so together we struck a deal that the port would remove some deteriorated piers and develop public access and parks in exchange for the Commission['s] agreeing to the overall parameters of the land use plan and giving up the power to micromanage the details of individual waterfront redevelopment projects." Although Bouey had a number of successes during his tenure, when he left the port in the fall of 1996, he cited this agreement as his most important achievement.[6]

Many thought the plan would take no more than a year or two to complete, but voters did not actually approve the final document until seven years later and nine months after Bouey's departure, in June 1997. The port finally had the power to develop again.

Redevelopment Begins—Again

Prop H effectively stopped all development until voters approved the land-use plan in 1997, but several projects began to take shape before the moratorium was lifted. First, in 1994, voters passed Prop P, exempting two projects from the freeze on development: the renovation of the Ferry Building, which had been attempted six times previously, and a small project at Pier 52. Next, in 1996, the voters passed Prop B, exempting a new waterfront ballpark from the moratorium. By then even Andy Nash, the former president of San Francisco Tomorrow and the principal author of Prop H, supported the waterfront ballpark, admitting that "enough planning had been done to demonstrate that there were are no longer enough maritime uses available." AT&T Park, which was built by the city's redevelopment authority on port property with private financing, was completed at a cost of $319 million and opened in 2000.[7]

In 1998 the port issued a request for proposals to developers interested in the $70 million redevelopment of the Ferry Building. But because their own offices were in the building and would have to be relocated, the port also issued a request for proposals to redevelop Pier 1, to the north, as a new commercial office building that would house its own new headquarters along with a handful of other tenants. The port occupied its new space in February 2001, and new tenants began moving into the Ferry Building in spring 2003. In both cases, the port sold no bonds, relying instead on private developers to finance the projects in exchange for ground rent and, in the case of the Ferry Building, additional participation from office rent and retail revenues. The State Lands Commission and the Bay Conservation and Development Commission considered the two projects to be acceptable uses because the commercial components were required to finance the historic preservation and adaptive reuse of the buildings. Seeing this model as the future of waterfront redevelopment, in 2000 the port announced plans for a sweeping historic district along the waterfront that would allow for the redevelopment of all pier and bulkhead buildings.

In January 2000 the port awarded to a consortium of developers, led by the Australian real estate development company Lend Lease, the right to develop a $270 million cruise terminal, hotel, and office complex at piers 30–32, on the site of the project originally proposed by the Danish investors in the 1980s. In June 2000, Malrite, a Cleveland-based developer with ties to Mayor Willie Brown, won the right to develop an entertainment attraction at Pier 45, beating out a more popular local proposal for a nonprofit Bay Center. The finances and organization behind the Bay Center proposal were flimsy at best, and the Malrite project made more financial sense from the port's perspective, but tenants at Fisherman's Wharf and the public decried the attraction as a "plastic tourist outlet." After Mayor Brown was unable to block a nonbinding ballot measure in November 2000 in which voters favored the Bay Center project over Malrite, the port dismissed the mandate and signed an agreement with the developer anyway, although political opposition soon killed the project in 2001. And in December 2000, the owners and operators of New York's Chelsea Piers (the same developers who proposed the *Whydah* pirate museum for Tampa) proposed a plan for a major recreation complex at piers 27–31, on the northern waterfront. The mayor initially supported the Chelsea Piers proposal, but then another national developer that he had ties to, the Mills Corporation, quickly proposed a project for the same site that had a recreational component and for which the YMCA signed on as a tenant but that was largely dominated by commercial office space. In a very controversial decision, in April 2002, the Port Commission voted 3–2 for the Mills project despite reports by independent consultants and port staff that strongly recommended Chelsea Piers over Mills. In a testament to the mayor's influence over the port, one commissioner and union business manager who was undecided prior to a call from the mayor's office admitted that "the Mayor convinced me what was the best project for working people."[8]

By 2006, and largely as a result of the Loma Prieta earthquake, San Francisco's waterfront had been dramatically transformed. The removal of the Embarcadero Freeway had led to the redevelopment of the Embarcadero roadway, sidewalks, and the plaza in front of the Ferry Building and the city's installation of a new rail line that served Market Street and the northern waterfront with vintage trolleys. The earthquake also spurred the temporary and then permanent return of ferry service to the Bay Area, which the port supported with improved facilities at the Ferry Building, which by 2007 was handling eleven thousand passengers a day. The San Francisco Redevelopment Authority's development of AT&T Park for the San Francisco Giants baseball team on port property and Muni's installation of a new light-rail line running along the southern waterfront further stimulated the growth of San Francisco's newest neighborhood, Mission Bay. The port, too, had much to be proud of, beginning with the successful completion of the waterfront land use master plan that signaled the beginning of waterfront redevelopment in San Francisco. At the same time, the port's development of Rincon Park and other public access spaces at piers 7 and 14 increased access to the waterfront and bay views and further encouraged pedestrian traffic along the southern waterfront, particularly on Giants game days. The reopening of the Ferry Building at the heart of the waterfront for mixed-use retail and office, combined with a vibrant new farmer's market, all located at a transit hub that integrated Water Transit Authority ferries, Bay Area Rapid Transit, and Muni commuter stations further increased activity and foot traffic on the central waterfront. Together, the successful Pier 1 and Ferry Building redevelopment projects brought vibrant commercial uses and public access to the waterfront while establishing a new model for the redevelopment of historic waterfront structures that was financially viable and acceptable to regulatory agencies. The redevelopment of piers 1 1/2 through 5 was completed in the fall of 2006, and the creation of several waterfront historic districts would allow the port to propagate this model further.

The port as an organization also changed tremendously in the late 1980s and the early 1990s, beginning with its first-ever strategic plan and organizational analysis and then in response to Prop H, which caused the dramatic expansion of the planning and development and real estate departments. The port also greatly improved its image in the eyes of the public throughout the 1990s as it evolved from an insular and aloof organization with a single-minded focus on maritime operations into an open, engaged agency leading a successful public process for the reuse of the city's waterfront property. Three entrepreneurial port directors, Michael Huerta, Wally Abernathy, and Dennis Bouey, together led this revolution by bringing new business, analytical, and political skills to the job and by hiring similarly skilled and like-minded senior staff. Former finance director Ben Kutnick remembered that "Mike Huerta was the first Port Director to require the finance staff to learn how to calculate net present value, internal rates of return, and return on investment for port properties and projects, and he hired the Port's first true planners and finance experts." Abernathy, who served as interim director for only eight months between Huerta and Bouey, "was the first to recognize that the port owned underutilized real estate assets that could and should be generating more revenue." And Bouey not only picked up where Abernathy left off but also "was the first to use analytical methods to seek the answers to specific questions and determine whether proposed projects with popular support—such as the rail

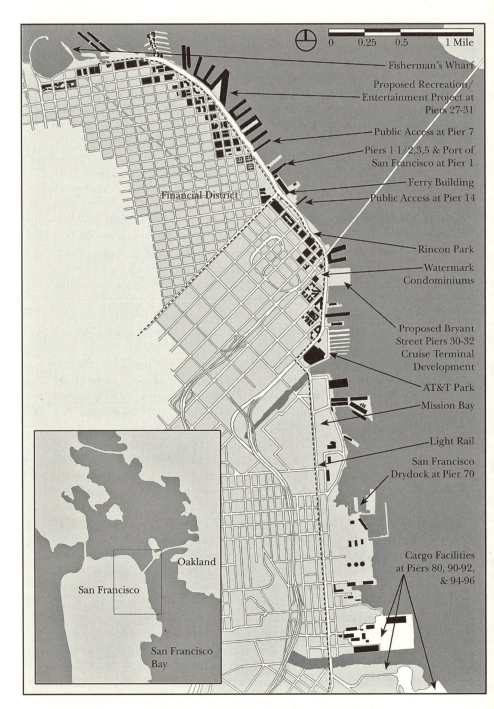

Figure 3.3. The San Francisco waterfront. Map by Whitney Parks.

Figure 3.4. The Embarcadero Freeway and the Ferry Building in 1964. Photo by Larry Moon. Courtesy of the San Francisco History Center, San Francisco Public Library. Reprinted by permission of the family of Larry Moon.

Figure 3.5. The plaza in front of the Ferry Building in 2003. Photo by author.

Figure 3.6. Rincon Park. Photo by author.

Figure 3.7. Public access space at Pier 7. Photo by author.

tunnel improvements—would actually have the desired effects." Finally, Prop H forced the port to develop planning expertise, and this emphasis on planning led to changes in both staff composition and attitudes throughout the organization.[9]

By 1997 the port was also better off financially than it was in the late 1980s, thanks in large part to the efforts of Bouey, who signed a record number of leases that increased rents to market levels, moved the port from the red to the black, and accumulated substantial surpluses. Unfortunately, the Port was unprepared for the downturn in the economy following the bursting of the tech bubble in the spring of 2000. Having grown accustomed to surpluses after six years of constant growth, the Port Commission continued to approve new positions even as revenues fell, payroll increased, and surpluses dwindled. In 2002 the port's revenues were essentially flat, and by 2004 the port was bleeding red ink. Finally, several questionable developer selections stemming from the patronage-driven influence of Mayor Willie Brown and culminating in the Mills decision damaged the image of the port, the credibility of its administration and commission, the morale of its planning staff, and the

Figure 3.8. The Embarcadero on the northern waterfront. Photo by author.

agreement with the Bay Conservation and Development Commission. According to former port planner Alec Bash, these decisions proved that, "for a big, important project, the port couldn't deliver on the fair process it promised in the land-use plan and that, in the end, the mayor got what he wanted."[10]

The last major legislative amendment to affect the port was the 1968 Burton Act, but the agency continued to evolve after this change, slowly becoming more integrated with the city. Former city planning director Dean Macris recalled that "the intent of the Burton Act was to make the port a part of the city, yet for many years the port and its commission remained independent, autonomous, and aloof. It took Prop H and the land-use planning process to force the port to work with the citizens in integrating its land and development goals with those of the city." Further, while the Burton Act required that the port's finances be kept entirely separate from those of the city, the Board of Supervisors found ways to continuously increase charges to the port for city-supplied departmental services. It also used its budget review power to influence port decisions, and while port directors and staff have questioned

Figure 3.9. New housing and light-rail service along the Embarcadero in South Beach. Photo by author.

whether or not this power would stand up in court, it is unclear who would ever bring such a challenge.[11]

During this period, the stability and independence of the port was based largely on the character and personality of the mayor, who had the power to appoint the entire commission and the prerogative to influence hiring decisions for the port director and senior staff. Mayor Art Agnos empowered the Port Commission and encouraged it to hire a qualified executive director, Michael Huerta, and, despite his own lack of interest in the port and waterfront issues, Mayor Frank Jordan did the same when he approved the appointment of Dennis Bouey. But Mayor Willie Brown wanted to play a more direct role in port affairs and waterfront redevelopment, so he sought to control the port from the mayor's office. He appointed a Port Commission that he could influence—a port director, Doug Wong, who would follow his orders—and he filled a number of executive staff positions at the port with patronage hires. In 2003 San Francisco voters elected Gavin Newsome to replace Brown, who had reached his two-term limit and was ineligible to run again. Recognizing the need for fiscal discipline, the new mayor took immediate

Figure 3.10. The commercial fishing fleet at Fisherman's Wharf. Photo by author.

steps to right the listing port by appointing Monique Moyer, the city's former public finance chief, as port director.

Challenges and Opportunities for the Future

By 2006 deep budget cuts, layoffs, and reductions in senior staff salaries proposed by Moyer and her finance director, Tina Olson, and approved by the Port Commission had barely put the port back in the black with revenues exceeding expenses by only 1.4 percent, or approximately $800,000 of an annual operating budget of $57.5 million.

There were even bigger financial problems to come. The port had made repairs to several of its piers but was facing $1.2 billion in repairs to as many as fifteen more, although it only had the capacity to finance a third of this amount. The source of revenue for the balance of the repairs was to be ground rents and participation from private projects on its piers and other waterfront property. But by 2006 the three major development projects that the port was looking to for new revenues were dead or mortally wounded. First, a hotel that had been proposed on a difficult site at the foot of Vallejo Street and that had little support fell to an ordinance proposed by Supervisor Aaron Peskin that capped the height of the building at forty feet rather than the proposed fifty-eight feet, rendering it economically infeasible. The developers let their agreement with the port expire in November 2005. Second, although Mills finally sold its interest in the recreation and mixed-use facility at piers 27–31 to another development team led by Shorenstein in the spring of 2006, the project still lacked entitlements and public support. So, by mid-2006, the port was pinning all of its hopes on one project: the fully entitled cruise terminal and mixed-use project at piers 30–32. In 2003 Lend Lease partnered with the port of Singapore and renegotiated their contract with the Port of San Francisco to allow them to develop the project in two phases rather than one, as previously agreed. The first phase would be a twenty-two-story condominium tower with 136 units, located on a parcel on the inland side of the Embarcadero. Construction started on the Watermark in 2004, and new homeowners started occupying the building in 2006. Phase two would be a major mixed-use project incorporating offices, retail space, parking, a new public park called Brannan Street Wharf, and the cruise terminal, which would be named for James R. Herman, the legendary longshoreman and labor leader who also sat on the Port Commission and conceived the idea of the cruise terminal in the 1980s. In 2005, port director Moyer confessed that the cruise terminal was "the only entitled development project we have to upgrade our piers—it's our beacon."[12]

If all proceeded according to plan, the port could expect to begin earning rent from the facility in 2010, at which time it could issue bonds backed by these rents to pay for maintenance and improvements to a number of the other dilapidated piers. But then the developers of several projects determined that the pilings and substructures below the piers upon which their projects were to be built had been deteriorating more rapidly and needed much more restoration than originally anticipated. A proposal for an International Museum for Women at Pier 26 foundered, and the developers of the recreation center issued a revised plan that doubled the amount of office space in their project and reduced the recreation component to a mere token in order to generate the rents required to cover the increased costs of improving the piers. And finally, the costs to repair the piers at the cruise terminal had risen from $49 million to $81 million. In 2007, Lend Lease and the port of Singapore exercised their option to abandon phase two of the project, the cruise terminal, after completion of the Watermark condominiums.

With this last remaining source of potential revenue apparently dead, the port changed tack once again. Relying on state legislation passed in 2005 that allowed it to collect a share of the taxes generated by developments on port property, in 2006 the port agreed to subsidize $60 million in substructure repairs required to make the recreation center project "pencil out." The port would obtain these funds by issuing tax increment financing, or TIF bonds, that would be paid off with a share of the incremental revenues from future property taxes earned by projects within a designated port infrastructure financing district.

But while the structural financial problem of how the port would fund needed infrastructure improvements when it lacked the revenues required to pay their debt service remained unsolved, the bigger question for San Francisco was whether or not it even wanted its port agency responsible for waterfront redevelopment. Politicians, regulatory agencies, neighborhood and nonprofit groups, and citizens had been ambivalent about the port's role since the 1970s, demanding that it use its land in specific ways, tying its hands in others, and often misunderstanding its finances as well as the powers and constraints under which it operated. Even after the successful development and implementation of the waterfront land use plan—which was based on maximum feasible participation—and the many other successful port-sponsored projects that followed on its heels, San Franciscans continued to harbor a deep mistrust of their port. Some, including Board of Supervisors president Aaron Peskin, suggested nothing less than the complete dismantlement of the port. Long a critic, in 2005, Peskin considered introducing a ballot initiative that would amend the city's charter, dissolving the port commission and reconstituting it with a new group that had to meet minimum qualifications. By 2006, San Franciscans were facing a mixed future of their own making as they continued to politically micromanage and financially hamstring their port. And while it struggled to remain afloat, no one else seemed to have a plan that would ensure the funding required to allow it to develop new, revenue-generating facilities on the waterfront while preventing San Francisco's remaining piers from sliding into the bay. Five hundred miles to the south, in San Diego, where cargo had always played a secondary role to waterfront redevelopment, the outcomes couldn't have been more different.

Port of San Francisco
Project Map
April, 2007

(Completed Projects)

(Hyde Street Harbor)

(Plazas and Ferry Arch)
(Pier 1)

1) Piers 27-31 Mixed-Use Recreation Project

2) Piers 15-17 Exploratorium

Jefferson St.

8) 360

3) Piers 1 1/2 - 5 Project

(Ferry Building Rehabilitation)

(Downtown Ferry Terminal)

(Rincon Park)

(Ballpark & Ferry Landing)

4) Rincon Park Restaurants Project

5) Bryant Street Piers Piers 30-32 Cruise Terminal Development

(Mission Creek Park)

(China Basin Shoreline Park)

6) Brannan Street Wharf

7) Pier 70 Area

On-Going Projects

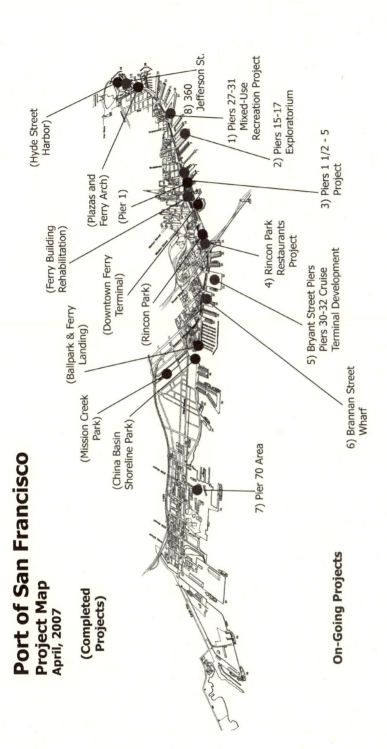

G:\Png&Dev Project Status\Full Port Monthly Map

Figure 3.11. Port of San Francisco project map. Courtesy of Port of San Francisco.

Waterfront History and Geography

San Diego shares some characteristics with San Francisco, including its location on a big blue bay that opens out into the Pacific Ocean and the great, natural beauty of its tidelands. But San Diego was always a naval port first, and it never had the powerful, labor-based pride in its maritime heritage that came to hinder its northern cousin. San Diego is also different from the other three port agencies under discussion in one important respect: it was explicitly created to promote not only maritime operations but also recreation on and around the bay.

San Diego Bay is approximately twelve miles long, running from the northwest to the southeast, with its only opening to the Pacific Ocean at the northwestern end, between Point Loma on the mainland and the peninsula of Coronado. The bay is surrounded by five cities. Beginning at Point Loma and moving clockwise, San Diego surrounds the northern and eastern sides of the bay, followed by National City, Chula Vista, and Imperial Beach, which wraps around the southern end of the bay. Coronado, to the north, is attached to the mainland by the Silver Strand, a thin strip of land that runs north from Imperial Beach, separating the Pacific Ocean from the bay.

Portuguese navigator João Rodrigues Cabrillo originally discovered San Diego Bay in 1542 when he was looking for China, but the modern history of the city began in 1846 when the United States Navy warship *Cyane* sailed into the bay. The crew of the *Cyane* claimed the five-hundred-person settlement of San Diego as an American outpost in the Mexican War, and the navy's presence has been the primary engine of growth for the city and region ever since. In 1919 the navy established Naval Base San Diego, and the base expanded dramatically during World War II, playing an important role in provisioning the South Pacific theater. Fleet support activities in San Diego remained at a very high level throughout the Korean conflict, the Vietnam War, and the Cold War. The navy's presence in San Diego Bay began to decline following the end of the Vietnam War, but Naval Base San Diego still remained the largest United States Navy installation in the world, with bases in San Diego, National City, Coronado, and Point Loma, which together served in 2006 as the homeport for sixty-six active submarines, surface ships, and aircraft carriers as well as a large reserve fleet. In the same year, approximately three hundred thousand sailors, marines, reservists, civilian workers, military retirees, and military family members lived in the San Diego metropolitan area, more than 10 percent of the total population of San Diego County, estimated at 2,941,454.[1]

But San Diego was a "cul-de-sac city," located in the very southwestern corner of the United States with inadequate rail service to the north and no direct rail link to the east. Cargo unloaded in San Diego therefore had to go north by rail through Los Angeles before heading inland. San Diego also had little manufacturing and produced no outbound cargo, so ships that unloaded cargo in San Diego left the port empty, which was a cost disadvantage for shippers, who preferred their boats to be full for backhauls. And also San Diego Bay was shallow. The navy maintained a fifty-foot-deep channel that accommodated aircraft carriers as far as North Island Naval Station, but the channel diminished to the south. Tenth Avenue Marine Terminal had berths with drafts ranging from thirty to thirty-six feet, and National City had berths with thirty-five-foot drafts. By 2003, fruit arriving via container ships that stopped at Tenth Avenue Terminal and autos transported on shallow draft car carriers that steamed as far south as National City accounted for most of San Diego's inbound cargo. For many years the port planned only to build business up to a level that used the capacity of these existing facilities, recognizing that cargo would always be subsidized but that increased business would reduce the size of the subsidy. Otherwise, the port's cargo aspirations remained limited by a poor geographic location, a shallow bay, inadequate infrastructure, landlocked terminals, and a lack of competitive rail service.[2]

The Port of San Diego

In 1919 the city of San Diego established a semi-independent harbor department for the purpose of developing both the waterfront along Harbor Drive, in support of industry and the navy, and the region's airport, Lindbergh Field. But San Diego is well known for its 1917 Smokestacks versus Geraniums debate, and San Diegans have always claimed that they never wanted their city to be like Los Angeles: large, overdeveloped, congested, and industrial. But whether or not San Diego had big industrial-maritime aspirations, during World War II it remained a closed harbor, and naval operations pushed cargo out. San Diego missed a window of opportunity for growth while other West Coast ports such as Long Beach and Los Angeles remained open and were able to expand throughout the 1940s and 1950s and even more rapidly in the 1960s as they adopted container technology. John Bate, who served as port director from 1948 through 1968, said in 1980, "I didn't try to make it a great port. . . . I never wanted to be like Los Angeles: What I wanted was enough business and industry to make it self-sufficient." Local leaders credited Bate with pushing for the development of two spoils islands, Shelter Island and Harbor Island; the consolidation of maritime industry south of the Embarcadero; and the restoration of the polluted bay. But more important, Bate played an instrumental role in the consolidation of the tidelands surrounding the bay. Until the 1960s the city of San Diego managed its waterfront through its Harbor Department, but the other four cities surrounding the bay had no apparatus in place for managing their own waterfronts. Bate lobbied several local politicians, convincing them that the cities and the region would benefit from coordinated management and development of the tidelands. His efforts resulted in state legislation that created the San Diego Unified Port District, also known as the Port of San Diego, effective 1 January 1963.[3]

The purpose of the new port district was to fulfill the need for a regional agency within San Diego County that could "operate effectively in developing the harbors and port facilities." The enabling act also gave the port the power to acquire, build, operate, and maintain harbor, rail, water, and air terminal facilities within a jurisdiction comprised of the tidelands and submerged lands within the five cities surrounding San Diego Bay, for the "promotion of commerce, navigation, fisheries and recreation" on the bay. A commission of seven would govern the new district, three from San Diego and one each from the other four cities, all appointed by their respective city councils.[4]

Bate retired in 1964, and his chief assistant, Don Nay, succeeded him. Nay, too, saw the future of the port not in cargo and maritime operations but in recreation and tourism through the development of new marinas, yacht repair yards, waterfront hotels, restaurants, and other tourist attractions. Within a decade, general military force reductions in the post-Vietnam era began to affect San Diego as the navy's presence diminished. According to former naval captain and San Diego Port Tenants Association director Pete Litrenta, "The vitality in downtown went away and Navy Field, which had been a major recreational area on the waterfront, became a blighted area."[5]

Redevelopment Begins

Downtown redevelopment in San Diego officially began in 1972 when the city council approved a plan supported by then-mayor Pete Wilson to redevelop a fifteen-block area as an urban mall and festival marketplace. The city selected a developer in 1974, and in 1985 the nearly nine-hundred-thousand-square-foot Horton Plaza opened, signaling the beginning of what was to become an enormous wave of business and residential growth in San Diego's previously vacant and deteriorated downtown. Wilson also sought to stimulate the region's convention business, but San Diego had only a small, basic convention center downtown that attracted little business while most conventions took place in a conference hotel in Mission Valley. Wilson twice pushed ballot initiatives that would have given the city the power to finance a new downtown convention center, and both times tax-averse San Diegans voted down the measures.

In 1980 the port took its first steps toward participating in downtown redevelopment with the completion of Seaport Village, a Western-themed waterfront dining and retail complex. The port improved and then leased waterfront property to the private developers who built Seaport Village and who paid ground rents and participation to the port in return. In the same year, the port solicited proposals from developers for the first major new waterfront hotel in San Diego, to be located just south of Seaport Village on Navy Field. Developer Doug Manchester was selected and agreed to develop the first of two hotel towers on the site. The port would make infrastructure improvements, and Manchester's hotels would pay ground rent and participation to the port. Construction started on the first Intercontinental Hotel tower in 1982, and the hotel opened in 1984. In 1980 the port also set aside a six-acre parcel south of Navy Field for a new public park for the working-class Latino Barrio Logan neighborhood that surrounds the Tenth Avenue Marine Terminal.

In spring 1983, newly elected mayor Roger Hedgecock was also trying to find a way to finance a new downtown convention center, but after considering Wilson's failures with ballot measures, he turned instead to the port, which had amassed a surplus of more than $80 million that was expected to continue growing at a rate of about $25 million per year. At that time there were rumblings that legislators in Sacramento were considering tapping the surpluses of California's largest and wealthiest ports and redistributing them throughout the state. So, in 1983, Hedgecock and his chief of staff, Michael McDade, approached Don Nay with a deal: "We need a convention center, and you need to get rid of your surpluses before the state takes them, so why not spend them in the region?" Nay agreed, and the new mayor kept his campaign organization in place, using it to promote a new port-financed, city-operated convention center that was approved by voters in November 1983. The city considered several inland sites, but then Doug Manchester approached the port and offered to reconfigure the Navy Field site to allow for the convention center while still leaving room for the second Intercontinental Hotel tower. The port paid cash for the construction of the new convention center and leased the facility and the land it sits on to the San Diego Convention Center Corporation. By the time the convention center had been completed in 1989 the cost had risen from an original estimate of $95 million to nearly $200 million.[6]

By the mid-1990s, the vitality created by the completion of Horton Plaza and its required two-thousand housing units, the convention center, and the new waterfront hotels had successfully stimulated urban redevelopment in downtown San Diego. The revitalization of the historic Gaslamp Quarter as a dining and clubbing nightspot created increased interest in downtown living, fueling the development of both low- and high-rise condominium and apartment buildings. But more important, in 1989 the port began to undergo an amazing transformation in the eyes of local politicians and the public. After operating as a quiet giant for more than twenty-five years, one day it wrote a check for $200 million to pay for the convention center, unintentionally attracting everyone's attention and ensuring its own new future as a visible, powerful, and potentially controversial redevelopment force in San Diego for years to come.

"Don Nay ruled the port staff with an iron fist," recalls former port commissioner and mayoral candidate Peter Q. Davis, who echoed many others. "He controlled a weak, fragmented, and disengaged commission by dividing commissioners and sending them on trade missions and other junkets so that there was never an unfavorable majority in town at any one time." Port staffers acknowledged that Nay was very politically savvy and that, indeed, "every day for twenty-nine years he woke up with four (out of seven) votes." But the Port Commission began to change as it became more diverse, more political, more youthful, and less willing to submit to Don Nay's yoke. After serving for nearly thirty years, Nay retired in 1995, and as former commission chair Frank Urtasun recalled, "The commission quickly took on a different character as a new generation of younger and more opinionated appointees with their own ideas began to take much greater interest in the business of the Port."[7]

Former port commissioner Mike McDade remembered that, "soon after he left, the Commission realized that Don Nay had been at the center of a hub-and-spoke organization and that all communications had flowed through the port director. Because Nay had never promoted or trained a second-in-command and there was no backbench of executive staff, the Commission chose to go outside of the region for its next director." The port's new director, Larry Killeen, brought container cargo and real estate development experience from leadership positions at the ports of Seattle and Tacoma and the Shell Oil Company. But when he arrived, Killeen recalled being

faced with an organization that was a creature of Don Nay and that was stuck in the 1960s in terms of management style, technological sophistication, and pub-

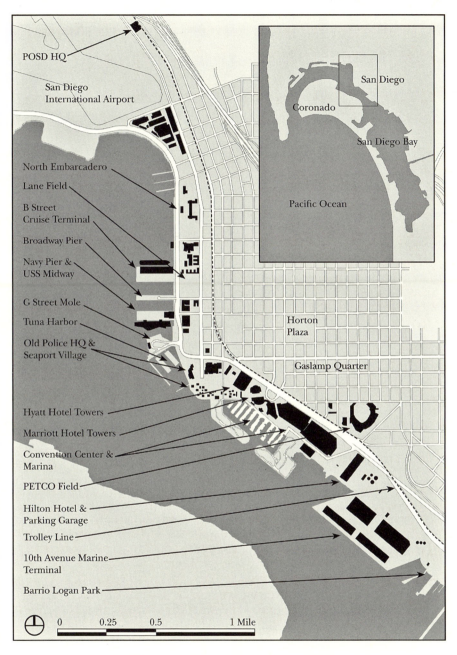

POSD HQ

San Diego
International Airport

San Diego

Coronado

San Diego Bay

Pacific Ocean

North Embarcadero

Lane Field

B Street
Cruise Terminal

Broadway Pier

Navy Pier &
USS Midway

G Street Mole

Tuna Harbor

Old Police HQ &
Seaport Village

Horton
Plaza

Gaslamp Quarter

Hyatt Hotel Towers

Marriott Hotel Towers

Convention Center &
Marina

PETCO Field

Hilton Hotel &
Parking Garage

Trolley Line

10th Avenue Marine
Terminal

Barrio Logan Park

0   0.25   0.5   1 Mile

Figure 4.1. The San Diego waterfront. Map by Whitney Parks.

Figure 4.2. Looking south along the Embarcadero toward the B Street Cruise Terminal. Photo by author.

lic relations. Nay had ruled in command-and-control fashion, gathering data from his staff and making all decisions and presentations to the commission himself. The port had no computers in 1995, and all communications went through a telephone switchboard that shut down every day between noon and 1:00 PM, when its operator went to lunch. There was no internal phone directory, and staff exchanged business cards to obtain one another's phone numbers. Nay sought to keep the port's profile low by omitting signage identifying the Port's nondescript headquarters building and by limiting the number of visitor parking spaces and therefore the number of visitors. And the port simply didn't return calls to the press if Nay didn't feel like it. Finally, in terms of planning, the port had no public workshop process, and the Port's master plan existed only in Don Nay's head.[8]

Killeen changed the culture of the port by integrating modern technology and emphasizing open communications and teamwork, both internally and with the public. During the second half of the 1990s, the port initiated its first-ever comprehensive land use plan for the entire bay, and the planning department grew, adding planners and architects as the port began to hold its first public workshops. During this period public interest in port planning and land use decisions grew, and the

San Diego Historical Society

Figure 4.3. Aerial view of the San Diego waterfront in 1979. San Diego Historical Society.

port found that development projects were becoming more difficult, taking longer, and requiring more staff to complete.

The port continued to use public processes for a variety of projects including the privatization of public marinas and moorings and the redevelopment of an old police station property that it obtained from the city in a land swap. One interesting variation was the participation model that evolved for the purpose of revitalizing the North Embarcadero. The Broadway Complex Coordinating Group first proposed a plan for the redevelopment of a stretch of rotting piers and substandard buildings on the waterfront north of Broadway Pier and the cruise terminal, but the port vetoed these plans in the early 1990s. So, in the mid-1990s, the North Embarcadero Alliance formed for the purpose of creating a "North Embarcadero visionary plan." The first ever of its type, this public-public alliance was originally comprised of representatives from

Figure 4.4. Aerial view of the San Diego waterfront in the first decade of the twenty-first century. Courtesy of the San Diego Convention Center Corporation.

five agencies: the city of San Diego, San Diego County, the United States Navy, the Centre City Development Corporation, and the Port of San Diego.

Turbulence

Despite some success in changing the culture at the port, Killeen was unable to build enough personal support among individual commissioners, so when his three-year contract was up in 1999 he chose to retire, and the Port Commission hired Dennis Bouey to replace him. In addition to his experience as director of the Port of San Francisco, Bouey had most recently served as director of Philadelphia International Airport and had previously been a deputy director at San Francisco International Airport.

Since 1962, the port had been operating San Diego's Lindbergh Field.

But the airport was landlocked, and over the years, as the region's population continued to grow along with tourism and convention business, local leaders became increasingly concerned with finding a solution to the limited capacity of Lindbergh Field. The port hired Bouey largely for his aviation experience, and within a few months of arriving he personally took charge of creating a plan that would solve Lindbergh Field's congestion problem. However, the new director soon locked horns with David Malcolm, a powerful port commissioner who was also a very close friend of California state senator Steve Peace. After only three months at the port, Bouey unveiled his new plan in a large public meeting that was held at the Holiday Inn on the waterfront in order to accommodate a full house of more than three hundred. But Bouey and his plan faced an orchestrated attack by a number of politicians and local leaders that culminated in Senator Peace's thinly veiled threat to Bouey that "those who oppose me will not remain standing."[9]

Peace was facing term limits, and he soon became a proponent of regional governance, lobbying for the creation of a new unit of government called the Regional Infrastructure Transportation Agency (RITA), which one county supervisor described as a "full-time employment act for termed-out legislators." Peace led the regional governance initiative, which sought ideas from a number of committees. One transportation committee recommended the creation of a new organization for the purpose of siting and developing a new airport. According to Larry Killeen, who sat on the committee, "Implicit in the recommendation was that such an organization would not take over airport operations until the new airport had been constructed." But Peace seized upon the idea as a way to embarrass and weaken Bouey and the port and to create a new opportunity for himself. In summer 2001 he pushed legislation through the California Assembly that created a new San Diego County Regional Airport Authority and laid the groundwork for the separation of the airport from the port in three to five years. A year later, Peace pushed through legislation that accelerated the transfer, requiring the new airport authority to take over operations at Lindbergh Field effective 1 January 2003.[10]

Peace also designed a novel governance structure for the new airport authority. The board would be composed of nine members, with six being paid $100 per meeting. The remaining three board members would serve as the executive committee and be paid a salary equivalent to that of a Superior County Court judge in San Diego, or approximately $140,000 per year. An ally of then-governor Gray Davis, Peace expected to be appointed to one of the three well-paid board slots when he had served out his last term and to serve as chair and influence the appointment of the other two directors. But things did not play out as Peace had hoped. As author of the energy deregulation legislation that led to California's energy crisis in the summer of 2002, Peace gained public notoriety and became a political liability for Davis. So, instead, the governor appointed Peace to the less prominent but nonetheless influential position of director of finance for the state in December 2002. Peace lost this job when Arnold Schwarzenegger defeated Davis in the 2003 recall election.

The Brown Act, California's sunshine law, requires that public agencies conduct their business in public. The act makes exceptions for specific business items such as real estate transactions and lease negotiations, personnel matters, and matters involving litigation, which may be addressed in closed, or executive, session. The port chose for many years to interpret this last item broadly, assuming that virtually any item of business could lead to litigation and therefore conducting all business that was potentially controversial in executive session. But this operating style alienated the public while increasing the potential for conflicts of interest and inside dealing.

The port's image reached its nadir in 2001 when two commissioners resigned over apparent conflicts of interest. In April 2003, David Malcolm, a friend of Senator Peace's and of one of the commissioners who had resigned, pleaded guilty to felony charges of violating the state's conflict-of-interest law. The state sentenced Malcolm to 120 days in a work-release program, three years of probation, and the payment of more than $260,000 in restitution, fines, and fees to the San Diego district attorney's office. Malcolm's crime was failing to disclose that Duke Energy had paid him more than $210,000 in consulting fees during a period when he was negotiating as commission chair on behalf of the port a lease for a port-owned power plant that was very favorable to the power company.

Port director Bouey was not able to earn the support of what had become a divided and activist commission, nor was he able to recover from his initial clashes with Malcolm that, in retrospect, stemmed from Malcolm's attempts to play a greater role in directly controlling the port himself. Bouey chose not to renew his contract and left the port in the fall of 2001. But this time, rather than searching outside of the region for a replacement, the Port Commission promoted the port's finance director, Bruce Hollingsworth, to executive director. A career port staffer, Hollingsworth immediately initiated a strategic planning process while promoting the new idea of the "open port" in an attempt to begin dispelling the long-held image of the port as an insider's group that made its decisions behind closed doors. At the same time, the new commission chair, Stephen Cushman, publicly declared an end to the days of individual commissioners personally negotiating deals.

Challenges and Opportunities for the Future

The Port of San Diego had weathered a rough six years of political turmoil, culminating in the separation of the airport, but by June 2002, Hollingsworth and the Port Commission had charted a new course. The port completed its first-ever strategic plan, which identified objectives, guiding principles, challenges, and indicators of success for five activity areas: aviation, environmental, maritime, real estate, and recreation. It also embarked on its first-ever marketing campaign, emphasizing the open port with a new mission statement, logo, and promotional campaign for recreation on the "Big Bay." The port's messaging program even included a card that was carried and handed out by all port employees that explained its mission and goals.

In 2003 the port celebrated its fortieth year in operation, boasting in its Big Bay advertising campaign that it was "3 Islands, 5 Cities, 27 Miles of Waterfront, 16 Parks, 2 Shopping Centers, 69 Restaurants, 14 Hotels, 10 Playgrounds, 16 Marinas, 2 Museums, 125 Cruise Ship Visits." The bay was lined with port-owned and-operated parks that were enhanced by public art, part of a program that had celebrated its tenth anniversary in 2006. The spoils islands had been developed to a large extent and were ringed with parks and marinas, while their streets were lined with yacht brokers as well as hotels, bars, and restaurants. Downtown, the second phase of the convention center was completed in 2001, and a third phase was already being planned. The Embarcadero was landscaped from the southern end of the convention center to Broadway Pier and served by a new light-rail line that ran all the way to Lindbergh Field. Doug Manchester's fourth waterfront hotel tower and second Hyatt was completed in 2003, plans for three more hotels were in the works, and one of these, the 1,200-room Hilton San Diego Convention Center, located just south of the convention center, started construction in 2006 and was scheduled to open in 2008. In 2003 the port began to take steps to acquire Navy Pier from the United States Navy, in preparation for the arrival of San Diego's newest heritage ship, the USS Midway, the longest-serving aircraft carrier in U.S. history, which opened to the public as a museum in 2004. Petco Field, the new ballpark for the Padres, located off port land across the Embarcadero from the convention center, was completed in 2004, and plans for Ballpark Village, a dense, urban residential neighborhood surrounding it, were beginning to take shape as the national boom in urban condominiums came to San Diego.

And, finally, a handful of major port planning initiatives for areas around the bay were all moving forward. By 2003 the membership in the North Embarcadero Alliance had dropped from five to two, but in 2005 the port and the city of San Diego's Redevelopment Agency, acting through the Centre City Development Corporation, approved the North Embarcadero visionary plan, including the first phase of improvements along the stretch of the Embarcadero from Seaport Village to Lindbergh Field. Later in the year the two agencies agreed to enter into a new joint powers authority and to split the costs of implementing the plan. In 2004 the port was lauded for its management of the San Diego Downtown Harborfront Design Competition, won by Sasaki Associates and Rob Wellington Quigley. The $213 million plan envisioned rehabilitating the Old Police Headquarters building, reconnecting the old street grid to the water's edge, and extending a large circular pier out into the bay. But for reasons of cost and other constraints, the port could not foresee completing the plan prior to 2018, so it opted to proceed incrementally. In 2006 it entered into an agreement with the owner and operator of adjacent Seaport Village for the revitalization of the Old Police Headquarters building and its surrounding site as an expansion of the successful retail destination and a complementary first phase of the Sasaki plan. The port was also praised for listening better throughout the planning process of the Chula Vista Bayfront master plan. After narrowing the field to two plans, the port accepted open bids from three development teams before selecting the winning proposal in late 2005, after two and a half years of community outreach and consensus building. In 2006 it came to an agreement with Gaylord Entertainment for the development of a $700 million hotel and conference center as a part of the plan. Plans were also in various stages of design and implementation for the redevelopment of Shelter Island and America's Cup Harbor, for street improvements in Imperial Beach, and for two projects in National City: a marina and an aquatic center.

As an organization, the port's greatest challenge was making the transition from the Don Nay era to the era of open port in a short period of time. Yet in just a few years, state legislators, local politicians, the public, and dedicated staff forced it to make dramatic changes in culture, organization, and its approach to public relations and public process. Local residents also forced it to change by demanding an increased say in land-use decisions on port property. In order to preserve view corridors, for example, the city required Doug Manchester to submit more than twenty-five different versions of the master plan for his second Hyatt tower before the neighbors and the city approved the final location of the building. These pressures led to increases in port staff and the creation of entirely new departments, including land use planning, architectural mapping services, and public relations. Finally, and most

Figure 4.5. The revitalized Gaslamp Quarter. Photo by author.

important, the airport separation fundamentally changed the port's financial structure. Previously the finances of the two operations were partitioned as a requirement of the Federal Aviation Administration, but they shared both a powerful balance sheet that made borrowing money easier and a variety of overhead costs ranging from executive functions to the harbor police force. Beginning in 2003, both organizations had to begin bearing the cost of redundant functions, and tight finances forced the port to cut costs by reducing payroll. As part of the separation, the port was also required to transfer $75 million in cash and make a $50 million loan to the airport, which together reduced the port's $200 million capital program by $40 million over five years, resulting in the cancellation and deferment of scheduled projects. The leadership at the port, having little choice, began to view the new situation in a more positive light, as an opportunity to focus on a narrower mission, that of managing waterfront real estate and maritime businesses.

Despite limited expectations, maritime business—both cargo and cruise—also continued to grow at the Port of San Diego. In 2002 the port attracted Dole, which shipped forty thousand fruit containers

Figure 4.6. Model of the North Embarcadero Visionary Plan. Courtesy of Sasaki Associates, Inc.

Figure 4.7. A public planning meeting. Courtesy of Sasaki Associates, Inc.

through Tenth Avenue Marine Terminal, and Chiquita followed in 2003. Further south, National City Terminal had become a major carport for Honda, Volkswagen, and several other car manufacturers who had found that the ports of Los Angeles and Long Beach had become too congested. The dredging of the shipping channel and four berths at Tenth Avenue Marine Terminal to forty-two feet allowed deeper draft vessels, including larger container ships, to begin calling at the port in 2006. And although shallow by other standards, the thirty-five-foot berths at National City Marine Terminal easily accommodated shallow-draft car transports, and the extension of the pier in 2004 increased this capacity, allowing two seven-hundred-foot car carriers to dock simultaneously. The port continued to experience dramatic increases in car imports, which grew from thirty thousand in 1990 to five hundred thousand in 2006. Congestion at the ports of Los Angeles and Long Beach also caused break-bulk cargo volumes to grow. In addition to fruit, lumber, and cement, San Diego began to receive steel and project cargos such as wind turbines, further boosting maritime revenues. Between 2003 and 2006, cargo volume at the Port of San Diego nearly doubled, and it planned for significant road improvements that would finally get trucks off the streets in the Barrio Logan neighborhood surrounding the Tenth Avenue Marine Terminal.

And, as in the case of Tampa, congestion at other ports also led to growth in the cruise industry in San Diego, while the port's location in a major population center ensured a large and ready drive-to market. Indeed, by 2006, approximately 40 percent of cruisers were local residents. Furthermore, Mexican itineraries, which were among the oldest and stalest in the industry, began to become popular again as the cruise industry reawakened to the great variety that Mexico had to offer. In 2004, Carnival Cruise Lines added itineraries from San Diego, and in 2005, Holland America followed suit and Carnival announced that it was introducing a year-round cruise schedule from San Diego, a first in the port's history. In 1996, San Diego had only 21,000 cruise passengers, but by 2000 this number had grown nearly nine times to 186,000, and by 2006 it had nearly tripled again to 519,000. In response to increasing problems of capacity and quality of experience at its one existing terminal, in 2004 the port began to entertain development proposals for a complex at the Lane Field/B Street Pier site that included a new hotel and a second major cruise terminal.

Although the port as an institution was relatively stable until Don Nay left in 1995, six years of turbulence followed his departure, due in part to new commissioners with strikingly different styles from their predecessors' and to the port's multijurisdictional structure. The two port directors who came from outside the region had difficulty working with these activist commissions. Ethics scandals, state audits, and lawsuits seeking to force the commission to conduct its business in the sunshine further buffeted the port. In response to these forces, the port adopted its first-ever ethics code in 2002, and despite a couple of minor episodes, by 2006 there had been little further trouble. Indeed, in an uncommon example of transparency and an understanding of trusteeship and good governance, the commissioner who filled out the remainder of David Malcolm's term and restored confidence in Chula Vista's seat resigned well in advance of acquiring interest in a company that did business with the port, as he sought to avoid even the potential appearance of conflict.

Another unfortunate result of this turbulence stemmed from the way the port collected and distributed revenues among the five cities. Historically, approximately 90 percent of port revenues flowed from waterfront property in the city of San Diego, and a large share of the remaining 10 percent were derived from cargo and maritime operations in National City. Don Nay succeeded for many years in convincing the board that the port had a redistributive role to play in the region and in promoting a policy to divide revenues among the cities in different shares that often caused resentment, particularly in San Diego and National City. This resentment grew in times of economic hardship when the cities looked to the port for financial relief. In the 1980s San Diego mayor Maureen O'Connor attempted to make a claim against port revenues to finance a new public library and to plug a hole in the city's budget, and Mayor Susan Golding made similar attempts in the following decade. In 1990 the five cities banded together to demand a share of port surpluses, claiming that they were all undercompensated for the public services they provided to the port, such as police, fire, sanitation, and maintenance. And in 1991, National City councilman Ralph Inzunzu said, "I would like to see a way that we could get out of the Port District," claiming that "Port decisions are tilted in favor of other municipalities." Inzunzu's son Nick, who served as mayor of National City from 2002 to 2006, and other politicians continued to question the value of having a regional port district at all, some proposing that it be dismantled and the tidelands returned to the five cities. As former port commissioner J. Mike McDade explained, "The thing that is so interesting about the Port and that causes all the aggravation is that the district is comprised of one large city and four smaller cities."[11]

Finally, the airport separation caused a major change in the port's organizational and institutional character and also demonstrated that the port was no longer impervious to powerful external political forces. While the threat that Senator Steve Peace would legislate the complete dismantling of the port in 2003 passed, and similar dramatic events seemed unlikely in the future, this separation demonstrated that such things were indeed possible. By comparison, at the bistate Delaware River Port Authority of Pennsylvania and New Jersey, precipitous changes to the agency's enabling legislation that are motivated by raw power politics are virtually unimaginable.

Chapter 5

Philadelphia and Camden

Waterfront History and Geography

The ports of Philadelphia and Camden experienced all of the same forces as the other three, including the loss of cargo, competition and conflict between overlapping units of government and maritime interests, and increasing demands from the public for input into land-use decisions. But the region was home to the most complex and fragmented system of government of the four, and the Delaware River Port Authority was very different from the other ports for two reasons: It was originally created as a toll bridge operation, and it enjoyed a bistate jurisdiction and governance structure. Politicians on both sides of the river came to see this agency as an ideal vessel with which to connect the two state port authorities—the Philadelphia Regional Port Authority and the South Jersey Port Corporation—and create a single, unified, regional port. After a half-century's efforts, however, port unification failed, but it quickly gave way to a new bistate economic development mission: urban waterfront redevelopment.

The oldest of the ports discussed in this book, Philadelphia and Camden face one another across the Delaware River, which flows north to south into the Delaware Bay. The Delaware's shipping channel begins at its outlet in the bay and runs upstream for 135 miles, terminating in Trenton, New Jersey, north of Philadelphia. The center line of the river serves as the state border between New Jersey and Pennsylvania, and by the time it reaches Philadelphia and Camden, the Delaware is a half-mile wide. In 1682, William Penn sailed up the Delaware and disembarked at what is now called Penn's Landing, founding the city of Philadelphia and the state that bears his name, and the port began to grow rapidly on both sides of the river. By the early part of the twentieth century, the ports of Philadelphia and Camden had become a single, regional, maritime economy and commercial hub centered on the industrial waterfronts of the two cities and linked by more than twenty ferry lines.

The introduction of the automobile and the completion in 1926 of the first Delaware River Bridge, with its ramps touching down more than a half-mile from the waterfronts on both sides of the river, initiated a shift in development to the inland areas surrounding the bridge approaches. It also led to the demise of ferry service between the two cities and the rapid decline of the commercial waterfront. The last ferry ran in 1952, and the opening of the Walt Whitman Bridge in 1957 stimulated more car- and truck-based suburban development inland in southern New Jersey, further accelerating the decline and abandonment of the urban waterfront. Although Camden was known in its industrial heyday as the "biggest little city in the world," by the 1960s its government was a den of graft and corruption, and the city had been wracked by poverty and abandoned by white flight.

Technological trends that affected other port cities in the second half of the twentieth century also affected the ports of Philadelphia and Camden, as the shift to containerization and the ever-increasing size and draft of ships made many finger piers on the central waterfront obsolete. But the port also suffered from a centuries-long history of governmental fragmentation and competition between public and private port operators as well as chronic underfunding by both cities and both states in the post–World War II era. These forces together drove many steamship lines away to New York, Baltimore, and other more modern and business-friendly ports on the coasts. By the 1960s, what remained of maritime operations had moved to new container facilities that the two state port authorities had built to the north and south where larger parcels of land were available, while the Sun Oil Company had built its own private oil port in South Philadelphia. Philadelphia and Camden were both left with large expanses of abandoned industrial property on their central waterfronts.

Finally, the locations of the two north-south interstate highways that were planned and constructed between the 1950s and the 1980s played an important part in shaping the waterfronts of the two cities in very different ways. The Center City section of I-95 in Philadelphia, planned in the 1960s but completed in 1979, was routed along the water's edge, just one block from the waterfront. Residents of the nearby neighborhood of Society Hill, one of the most successful urban renewal projects in the country, forced planners to depress the highway along this stretch to preserve sight lines. But I-95 still created a barrier between a small sliver of land on the water's edge and the rest of the city that was made even more impassable by the adjacent arterial road, Christopher Columbus Boulevard. At Penn's Landing, fourteen lanes of traffic combined from these two roads ensured a complete separation of the city from its waterfront.

I-676 in New Jersey was planned and funded during the 1970s and was

Figure 5.1. Aerial view looking west over Camden toward Philadelphia in 1926. The Library of Company of Philadelphia.

completed in 1980. Unlike in Philadelphia, however, the United States Department of Transportation required that the new highway directly connect the ramps of the two Delaware River bridges so that it was routed nearly ten blocks and almost a mile inland from Camden's waterfront. While Philadelphia was cut off from its one-block-deep waterfront, Camden had both the depth from the river's edge and the land area needed to create a new district and connect the waterfront to the old downtown core.

The Delaware River Port Authority

Regional leaders began discussing the idea of building a bridge between Philadelphia and Camden in the early nineteenth century, but nothing happened for nearly a hundred years. Then, in 1912 and 1919, respec-

Figure 5.2. Aerial view looking northeast over the Camden waterfront in the first decade of the twenty-first century. Courtesy of the Cooper's Ferry Development Association.

tively, the state of New Jersey and the Commonwealth of Pennsylvania each approved reciprocal legislation that created a pair of commissions for the purpose of jointly building and operating a toll bridge across the Delaware River. In 1922 construction began, and in 1926 the new Delaware River Bridge, later renamed the Benjamin Franklin Bridge, was opened to traffic.

An agreement between the two states in 1931 formally created the Delaware River Joint Commission and tasked the new agency with several additional duties including the planning for and provision of future crossings and the provision of passenger rail service across the river. But for the first time, this agreement also made it a duty of the agency to promote increased passenger and freight commerce on the Delaware River, "a highway of commerce between Philadelphia and Camden and the sea." Specifically, the agreement required the agency to study and make recommendations for the improvement of terminal, lighterage, wharfage, warehouse, and other port facilities, but the powerful Pennsylvania Railroad, which operated a major lightering business in New York Harbor, saw port improvements in Philadelphia as a threat. So it successfully lobbied local politicians to restrict the port's powers, and the final

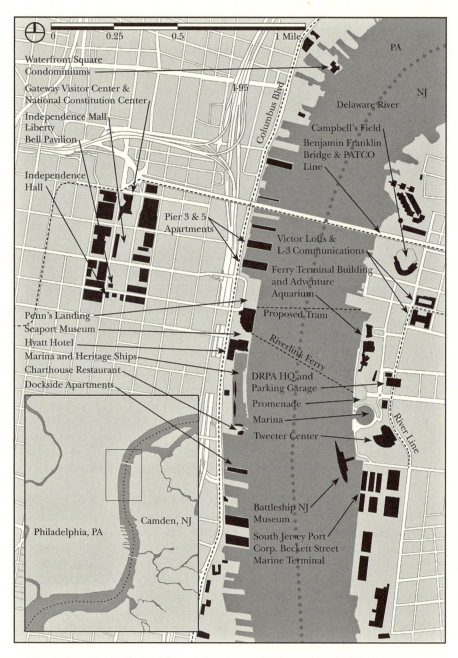

Figure 5.3. The Philadelphia and Camden waterfronts. Map by Whitney Parks.

agreement fell short of granting the agency the power to actually acquire, own, or operate port facilities.[1]

In 1935, through an act of the United States Congress, the agency was formally recognized at the federal level and continued as the Delaware River Joint Toll Bridge Commission. In 1947, Congress officially gave its consent to an agreement or "compact" between the two states, and the agency's duties and powers were expanded again to allow for the acquisition of a passenger ferry service. In both the 1935 and 1947 agreements, Pennsylvania legislators again attempted to grant the agency the powers it needed to operate as a port. But business interests in Philadelphia, led by the Pennsylvania Railroad, ensured that the subsequent legislation curtailed the agency's powers, specifically with respect to new bridge locations, the provision of freight rail service, and the acquisition of port facilities. In 1949 the Pennsylvania state legislature attempted once more to empower the agency as a port, hoping to improve upon the compromise agreement of 1947. The resulting compact amendment of 1952 continued the agency under a hopeful new name, the Delaware River Port Authority, and further expanded and defined its jurisdiction, powers, and duties. But once again, railroad interests succeeded in limiting the agency's powers to develop, acquire, and operate maritime cargo facilities, making it a port in name only. The 1952 compact amendment would be the last for forty years.

From its creation in 1919 the Delaware River Port Authority served primarily as a transportation agency, but in 1986 New Jersey governor Thomas Kean began to view the port as a potential major economic development engine for the region. Former port executive director Eugene McCaffrey recalled, "Governor Kean was looking for ways to finance infrastructure improvements in declining New Jersey cities and improve race relations within the state without raising taxes. He wanted to employ the port as a 'vessel' to unify the region's fragmented port and to use its toll revenues to improve port facilities, all with the goal of expanding the port and generating new high-wage-earning port jobs. Kean had cordial relations with Pennsylvania governor Robert Casey and, through a series of high-level meetings, was able to convince him of the merit of his plan." These meetings culminated in a 1988 "Port summit," where the two governors publicly agreed to unify the region's ports. In October 1992, after four years of effort and the approval of the two states' legislatures and governors and the United States Congress, President George H. W. Bush signed the Delaware River Port Authority's amended congressional compact into law.[2]

The compact granted the agency two important new powers. The first, and indeed the original purpose behind the compact amendment, was the power to acquire the Philadelphia Regional Port Authority and the

South Jersey Port Corporation and unify them under a single, new bi-state subsidiary called the Port of Philadelphia and Camden, which would be owned and operated by the Delaware River Port Authority. The second was the power to engage in economic development generally. Following the compact amendment, the Delaware River Port Authority hired Mercer Management Consultants, who in 1993 completed a strategic plan for the port that spelled out a two-year implementation plan for unification. In 1994 the governors of the two states met symbolically on a boat in the middle of the river to sign the unification agreement, and the Port of Philadelphia and Camden conducted a nationwide search before hiring a highly qualified new port director named Paul DeMariano. By the late 1990s, over a decade's worth of effort on the part of five governors, numerous legislators, a handful of port commission chairs and vice chairs, three executive directors, and one new port director had gone into the effort of port unification.

But by 1998 hopes for port unification and the transformation of the Delaware River Port Authority into a true port authority were dead. In 1993 and 1994 new Republican governors were elected to replace Democrats in both New Jersey and Pennsylvania, leading to a period of transition in both state governments. Slowness in commission appointments weakened governance at the port, stalled the implementation plan, and energized the two existing port authorities, both of which were operated as independent fiefdoms by powerful directors who were opposed to unification.

According to Peter Burke, a former port commission vice chair, Joe Balzano, the entrenched director of the South Jersey Port Corporation, saw in this transition period an opportunity to torpedo unification. Citing an obscure clause in his own port's bond indenture, he claimed that for the South Jersey Port Corporation to be acquired, the state first had to defease $88 million in port bonds, something the new administration was reluctant to do. Burke believed that Balzano's interpretation was conservative and flawed, and others concluded that a combination of poor work on the part of New Jersey governor Christine Todd Whitman's patronage lawyers, who failed to anticipate a number of legal challenges, and a lack of enthusiasm from Whitman herself, doomed reunification. Local officials on both sides of the river attributed responsibility to New Jersey politicians who felt that Pennsylvania would be the primary beneficiary of reunification and that the South Jersey Port Corporation was doing just fine without reunification. Some believed that reunification failed because local politicians and port executives felt threatened by the loss of two vessels for jobs through the elimination of the South Jersey Port Corporation and the Philadelphia Regional Port Authority. Still others thought that the real issue was the ultimate lack of willingness on the part of New Jersey to assume the South Jersey Port Corporation's debt. Pennsylvania contributed to the demise of reunification too, and despite numerous ceremonies with public officials from both states touting cross-river cooperation and a shared vision, conflict and competition raged as fiercely as ever on the waterfront. Finally, some wondered if DeMariano simply wasn't the right person for the Port of Philadelphia and Camden job, which required an apolitical executive who could share in leadership rather than someone who was attempting, as DeMariano seemed to be, to create a powerful, permanent position for himself.[3]

But perhaps the simplest explanation for the failure of port reunification came from former Philadelphia city controller Jonathan Saidel, who suggested that "the various port people and agencies fight amongst themselves until they as a group are threatened by potential change from the outside, at which point they band together to maintain the status quo." Whatever the cause, in 1998, after four years on the job, the Port of Philadelphia and Camden's new director moved on, unofficially spelling the end of a port unification effort that had fallen victim to patronage, turf wars, and a general lack of political will on the part of both governors. Yet by this time the port was already using its other new power—economic development—and was fast becoming a major force for revitalization on the urban waterfronts of Camden and Philadelphia.[4]

Redevelopment Begins

Waterfront property in Philadelphia and Camden was controlled and influenced by a confusing array of state, regional, and local governmental units and quasi-governmental agencies with overlapping powers and jurisdictions. First, both cities remained major owners of waterfront property, and each had its own separate waterfront redevelopment agency: In Philadelphia, the Penn's Landing Corporation was responsible for the planning, development, leasing, and operation of commercial, residential, recreational, and cultural facilities on city-owned land, while the Cooper's Ferry Development Association played a similar role in Camden.

Next, the two state-controlled public port authorities leased their land from the state governments. In 2006 the Philadelphia Regional Port Authority controlled approximately 377 acres of waterfront property on seven sites north and south of the central waterfront and acted as owner and landlord, leasing its facilities to private operators. The South Jersey Port Corporation controlled 353 acres on four sites, one of which was adjacent to the central waterfront, and it both owned and operated its facilities. In addition to competing with one another and with other private operators for shipping business, the two agencies were also often in competition with their adjoining waterfront redevelopment agencies and their city governments for the control of underutilized port land that abutted prime redevelopment sites.

Finally, overlaying the entire bistate waterfront was the Delaware River Port Authority. In 2006 the agency owned and operated four toll bridges, a commuter rail system, and a ferry line, and although it actually owned little waterfront property, it had jurisdiction over a port district that encompassed thirteen counties in the two states and nearly six thousand square miles. The port's most important power was its ability to sell revenue bonds backed by a dependable stream of bridge tolls, the proceeds of which could be used to finance not only improvements to its transportation facilities but also economic development projects.

The city of Philadelphia leased its waterfront property to the Philadelphia Redevelopment Authority, which in turn subleased the property to the Penn's Landing Corporation, a quasi-governmental waterfront redevelopment agency created by the city in 1970 to replace its Department of Docks and Wharves. Through these leases the Penn's Landing Corporation controlled a number of finger piers and other pieces of property on the urban waterfront, including Penn's Landing itself, the thirty-nine-acre site where William Penn first disembarked in 1682. The Philadelphia City Planning Commission first recommended the redevelopment of Penn's Landing in its 1960 comprehensive plan for Philadelphia, and the city drafted the first master plan for the site in 1963. This plan led to a series of public improvements that were built in the late 1960s and early 1970s to encourage private investment on the site. In 1982 the city commissioned another master plan and a set of design guidelines for Penn's Landing that were finalized in 1984 and that led to the construction of the Great Plaza, a large public amphitheater and event space, completed by the city and the Penn's Landing Corporation in 1986. Also in 1982, the planning commission prepared detailed district waterfront plans for seven areas in Philadelphia, including the Central Riverfront District. This plan was based on supporting the growth of the port, but it also recommended the development of residential and commercial uses at Penn's Landing, whose piers had become obsolete. The planning commission prepared new zoning maps for the waterfront based on this plan, and in 1983 it published planning and design standards for a continuous Philadelphia Riverwalk. By 2002 at least eight other plans had been created for the Penn's Landing site, six by private master developers. The first developer-proposed plan failed in 1968, and all those that followed failed as well, the last of which was a $300 million retail and entertainment center proposed by a mall developer, the Simon Property Group, that collapsed in August 2002. Despite these many attempts and for reasons of geographic isolation, poor planning strategy, and fragmented politics, by 2006, more than forty years after the completion of the first master plan, the site remained undeveloped.

Planning for waterfront redevelopment in Camden got off to a later start. In the early 1980s the Campbell Soup Company and RCA each contributed $100,000 and engaged the American City Corporation, a subsidiary of the Rouse Corporation, to draft a plan for Camden's waterfront. They also enlisted the help of the city of Camden, Cooper Hospital, and Rutgers University, forming a stakeholder group called the Greater Camden Movement to guide the planning process. The plan was completed in 1983, and the same group created the Cooper's Ferry Development Association in 1984 to implement it. The new agency would serve as master developer for an approximately 150-acre site that spanned the area between the Benjamin Franklin Bridge and Clinton Street and that was composed of undeveloped land owned by the Camden Redevelopment Authority, the Delaware River Port Authority, and the New Jersey Economic Development Authority.

By the early 1980s, the Penn's Landing Corporation and the Cooper's Ferry Development Association had each assumed responsibility for waterfront redevelopment in Philadelphia and Camden, respectively, but while they had similar duties, powers, and organizational structures, the two agencies took very different approaches to planning. The former focused primarily on the role of maintaining and operating Penn's Landing as a venue for public events, while its sibling in Camden emphasized a comprehensive, long-range planning approach to redevelopment. Further, because the ownership of waterfront property was more fragmented in Philadelphia, the Penn's Landing Corporation had greater difficulty assembling land. As a result, Philadelphia's urban waterfront was still a patchwork, with its largest developable parcel, the Penn's Landing site, spanning only one-quarter-mile of waterfront. By comparison, the Cooper's Ferry Development Association, in concert with the city of Camden and the Camden Redevelopment Authority, aggressively acquired real estate and assembled a large, contiguous, rectangular parcel of developable land with nearly a mile of continuous frontage on the river.

From its inception, the Penn's Landing Corporation pursued a fixed, prescriptive approach toward waterfront redevelopment. It considered only high-density commercial and residential projects on the Penn's Landing site that promised substantial contracts, rents, and tax revenues. But this approach failed repeatedly, and former Philadelphia commerce director and former Penn's Landing Corporation vice president

James J. Cuorato believed that "it also became a distraction, hurting the city by focusing too much attention and energy on Penn's Landing at the expense of planning comprehensively for the entire waterfront." On the other side of the river, the Cooper's Ferry Development Association abandoned a similar strategy early on, considering it unrealistic and unworkable. Instead, Executive Director Tom Corcoran recalled that his agency "transitioned from a prescriptive approach to a more flexible and 'opportunistic' approach through four major iterations of a master plan since 1983. While Philadelphia continued to have difficulty developing its one, high-density project, Camden moved towards providing lower-density entertainment, sports, and tourism attractions that couldn't be found elsewhere in the suburbs." By 2006 these projects, in concert with major infrastructure improvements planned by the Cooper's Ferry Development Association and funded largely by the state of New Jersey and the port, had combined to form a new urban core on the Camden waterfront. Perhaps more important, Camden's first new residential project, the Victor Building, the renovation of an old RCA industrial building into loft apartments, was completed in 2004, and for the first time in nearly fifty years new residents began to move back into the city.[5]

Funding Waterfront Redevelopment

For more than four decades a mix of city, state, and Delaware River Port Authority dollars financed waterfront redevelopment in Philadelphia and Camden. The city of Philadelphia made the first investment in waterfront redevelopment with the construction of the seawall, hardscape, and marina at Penn's Landing in the late 1960s and early 1970s based on the assumption that public improvements would stimulate private investment in major projects on the site. In the 1970s and in preparation for the bicentennial, the state financed the port of History Museum and turned it over to the city to operate. This publicly funded attraction was a financial failure, but private capital, conversely, built the very successful Chart House Restaurant. In the 1980s the city financed the Great Plaza, an outdoor public amphitheater, which was designed to further increase private interest in the site. In Camden, the New Jersey State Aquarium was funded by that state and completed in 1992. But in the same year, the Delaware River Port Authority became the primary source of funds for waterfront redevelopment on both sides of the river.

Not long after taking office in 1992, Philadelphia mayor Ed Rendell recognized that industry had left the region, so he began to envision a new economic development strategy for the city that was based on con-

Figure 5.4. Model of one development proposal for Penn's Landing. Courtesy of Cope Linder Architects.

Figure 5.5. Public concert at the Great Plaza at Penn's Landing. Courtesy of Cope Linder Architects.

vention business, historic tourism, arts, culture, and entertainment. Rendell's plan was focused on three loosely connected areas: the new Pennsylvania Convention Center that opened in 1993; Broad Street, which he christened the "Avenue of the Arts"; and Independence Mall, just five blocks from the waterfront. As Rendell's plan began to take shape in the form of proposals for tourism and entertainment projects in these areas, politicians in Harrisburg, and then in Camden and Trenton, began to envision the potential for a regional economic development strategy based on tourism.

At the same time, the drive for port unification was losing momentum. The staff and commissioners at the port were looking for other ways to use their new economic development powers along with their bistate jurisdiction and dependable stream of toll revenues for the purpose of transforming their agency into a powerful regional economic development engine. Former port commissioner and Pennsylvania state senator Joseph Loeper recalled how "the original intent of the compact amendment language was to give the port the power to engage in economic development projects that related specifically to the port and port businesses, thereby helping to create port jobs with head-of-household wages. But as interest in port reunification began to flag in the mid-1990s, the idea of a port-related economic development program began to lose its viability as well." Upon reflection, former Philadelphia Industrial Development Corporation president Bill Hankowsky saw the compact amendment example as "a lesson in drafting legislation that illustrates how important language is and how others in the future can reinterpret language in ways that were not originally intended by the drafters. For while economic development powers were added to the compact amendment at the last minute, almost as an afterthought, by the mid-1990s these powers had given the port a whole new raison d'être."[6]

In the beginning, however, the port's process for selecting economic development projects and allocating funds to them was virtually nonexistent, as demonstrated by an event that followed the New Jersey gubernatorial election in 1993. At the time, both states had Democratic governors, and Jim Florio was up for reelection in New Jersey, while in Pennsylvania Governor Casey had another year to go in office before the end of his two-term limit. But in November Florio lost unexpectedly to Republican Christine Todd Whitman. At this point, according to Bill Hankowsky, "interests on both sides of the river who had expected to have at least another year of relatively smooth relations between the states were confronted with the possibility of a Republican entering and either modifying or stalling the plans that both delegations had worked so hard to create." So in November and December of that year, the Delaware River Port Authority Commission undertook a frantic attempt to authorize $50 million worth of projects backed by accumulated surplus toll revenues and surplus proceeds from a bond issue that had been originally intended for bridge repairs. The process was simple, according to Jack Shannon, formerly with the Cooper's Ferry Development Association. "First, the New Jersey delegation identified a list of projects and values totaling something like $12 million. In response, the Pennsylvania delegation drafted its own list, except this list was for $15 million. Each delegation responded back and forth, the price rising in each round in a bizarre auction for public dollars, until the limit of $50 million was reached, split fifty-fifty, when the board voted to approve all of the projects." Hankowsky recalled how throughout this process "the Delaware River Port Authority staff, who had little economic development experience, simply stood to the side as the commissioners 'parked' funds designated for specific projects for which, in some cases, little planning, design, or due diligence work had yet been completed."[7]

As the port's spending increased, the political landscape between the states and on the port Commission began to change too. Governor Casey "did not care much about exercising the historical authority of the executive branch," according to Fred Voigt, the former executive director of the Committee of Seventy, a political watchdog organization in Philadelphia, "an attitude that was apparent in his appointments to the Port Commission." Casey did not take an active role in the port's governance and agenda; rather, in exchange for favorable budget votes from the Pennsylvania Senate, Casey appointed Democratic senator Vincent Fumo, head of the Senate Appropriations Committee, and Republican senator Joseph Loeper, Senate majority leader, as port commissioners. According to Voigt, "The DRPA had historically been a plaything of the southern New Jersey Republicans, but Fumo and Loeper set about evening up the division of funds and patronage."[8]

In a raw exercise of political power, Fumo soon used his influence to create a $40 million economic development fund fueled with toll revenues and directed generally toward projects in Philadelphia. Fumo's argument for establishing the fund was that it was required to offset disparities in spending between the states resulting from the low cost to New Jersey residents of commuter rail fares into Philadelphia. However, according to a March 2004 article in the *Philadelphia Inquirer*, accountability in the distribution of these funds was virtually nonexistent. Almost all of the funds were quietly allocated and spent during a nine-month period in 1999 by a committee shaped by Fumo and comprised of his supporters and associates. A large share of these funds was allocated to projects of direct interest to the senator, including grants for improvements at two schools attended by his children and a large contribution to a nonprofit organization that he had established in his district. The interests of most of the other committee members were also addressed and several of them received substantial low interest business loans. In short, the senator succeeded in capturing a share of commuter tolls and spending them to support his own, nonport agenda. Another article in the *Philadelphia Inquirer* from February 2007 detailed how these and other acts had caught up with Fumo, who faced a 267-page, 139-count indictment carrying a potential ten-year prison sentence for a variety of charges related to the allegedly illicit spending of public funds.[9]

The port's spending practices began to change again with Governor Tom Ridge's appointment of Manny Stamatakis to the position of Port Commission chair in 1996. Stamatakis was a Republican, a major Ridge contributor, and a wealthy, highly successful owner of a financial benefits corporation who also had a recent history of successful nonprofit governance to his credit. According to Charlie Bohnenberger, the director of Ridge's regional office in southeastern Pennsylvania and Ridge's liaison to the Pennsylvania delegation of the Port Commission, "The Ridge administration's specific mission for Stamatakis was to professionalize the port and make it an effective organization for the purpose of creating jobs." Stamatakis used his corporate, private-sector attitude, deal-making style, and general approach to doing business to improve

Figure 5.6. "We're Investing in the River." Courtesy Tony Auth, *Philadelphia Inquirer.*

the port's operations and project-selection decision-making process. Bill Hankowsky recalled, "Stamatakis took the position that previous grant-making practices had been 'crazy' and that the agency wasn't a foundation and couldn't behave like one." Stamatakis decided that the Delaware River Port Authority had to become more businesslike, making loans and loan guarantees with more standards attached for performance and making grants in exchange for an "equity stake" in the project and, in some cases, naming rights. As a result of Stamatakis's more aggressive corporate style, the port played a major role in the Penn's Landing Corporation's negotiations for the Simon entertainment center project; it acquired the patents to FastShip, a new shipping technology in which it invested $7 million; and concertgoers at the new Kimmel Center for the Performing Arts on Broad Street soon began to buy their tickets at the DRPA box office.[10]

Between 1992, when its compact was amended, and 2001, the outstanding debt of the Delaware River Port Authority grew more than five times, from $250 million to $1.44 billion. About $1.2 billion was invested between 1995 and 2000 alone, and while approximately 70 percent of this debt was committed to necessary improvements to the four bridges and the Port Authority Transit Corporation (PATCO) Speedline, the remaining 30 percent, or $443 million, was invested in more than forty regional economic development projects worth a total of more than $4.4 billion. Approximately 60 percent of this amount, or $212 million, was invested in waterfront redevelopment and tourism-related projects, most of which were located on or near the waterfront.

During this period the port began to help fund a broad array of projects throughout Philadelphia including two new stadiums in south Philadelphia, the Kimmel Center for the Performing Arts on the Avenue of the Arts, improvements to the Franklin Institute science museum and the Philadelphia Zoo, and the planned expansion of the Pennsylvania Convention Center. On Independence Mall the port helped to stimulate historic tourism near the waterfront by providing partial funding for the new Independence Visitors Center and the National Constitution Center, a museum dedicated to the U.S. Constitution designed by Henry Cobb of Pei, Cobb, Freed, and Associates. Port-funded projects on the central waterfront included a new apartment building, a tram that would cross the river and link the two waterfronts, and a major future attraction at Penn's Landing. On the southern waterfront, the port converted an old navy building at the former Philadelphia Naval Shipyard into a cruise terminal operated by its maritime subsidiary, the port of Philadelphia and Camden. And following the complete closure of the shipyard in 1995, it made its single largest investment with a $50 million grant to help finance the construction of new shipbuilding facilities and the improvement of an existing dry dock in order to lure shipbuilder Kvaerner to Philadelphia.

Conversely, the port's investments in New Jersey were all clustered around the Camden waterfront and included a new minor league ballpark, an apartment building, an aquarium, a children's garden, a new port headquarters building, an adjacent parking garage, an outdoor concert venue, and the Battleship *New Jersey* Museum. Just inland from the waterfront the port helped to fund a new cultural center, a charter school, several job-creation and facility-expansion projects for private manufacturing companies, and improvements to streets in Camden's central business district and to Admiral Wilson Boulevard, the major approach to the Benjamin Franklin Bridge.

In 1999 the port hired an entertainment-consulting firm to create a strategic plan for the development and marketing of a "two-sided waterfront destination." This plan was revised in 2001, when it became known as the "two cities, one waterfront" strategy. In 2002 the port announced that it was planning to create a new nonprofit organization called Independence Harbor, whose purpose would be to market and promote the "one" waterfront as a tourist destination. The new agency never actually came into being, however, and the two waterfronts remained separate and quite different in character.

According to Tom Corcoran, "tourism-based waterfront redevelopment was more focused in Camden because the Cooper's Ferry Development Association controls a larger site and because the New Jersey delegation of the port, particularly during the tenure of Vice Chair Glenn Paulsen throughout the second half of the 1990's, made a policy decision to concentrate its share of resources into the city of Camden, split evenly between waterfront redevelopment and neighborhood revitalization." Funds in Pennsylvania were spent in a more diffuse pattern, "because there were already major preexisting tourism areas such as Independence Mall that could be improved in support of the tourism agenda but that were not actually on the waterfront. Individual politicians who were members of the more fractious Pennsylvania delegation to the port were also able to push projects through that did not fit the waterfront redevelopment mission as closely and that were further from the waterfront."[11]

Challenges and Opportunities for the Future

The period of 1992–2006 saw the most rapid period of waterfront redevelopment in Camden and Philadelphia in more than a half-century. This was a result of the port's substantial program of investment in waterfront projects and the emergence of a tourism-based, regional economic development strategy that was shared by the two states, the two cities, and the port. Yet by 2006, while Camden's plans were coming to fruition in a consistent and coherent manner, Philadelphia still faced major challenges. Geography remained an important factor, as the Penn's Landing site, still considered the linchpin in the development of the Philadelphia waterfront if not the entire combined waterfront, remained hopelessly isolated from Center City because of its limited size and the location of I-95 and Christopher Columbus Boulevard. Two projects, a Hyatt hotel and the Dockside apartment building, were completed to the south of Penn's Landing, but while a public esplanade fronted the former, the latter completely blocked public access to the waterfront. So while the planning commission's idea of a continuous riverwalk remained a good concept, this and other individual projects over the years have made its realization increasingly difficult.

Transit connections between the two cities and their waterfronts and between each waterfront directly also remained incomplete, and the failure of the Simon project on Penn's Landing cast a long shadow over the

Figure 5.7. Wiggins Park Marina in Camden, with the Michael Graves–designed Delaware River Port Authority Headquarters in the background. Photo by Daniel Campo.

future of the aerial tram that was to have landed on its roof. Specifically designed to increase traffic between the two waterfronts, by 2006 the tram was still expected to go ahead, but it had few if any real supporters, and most local leaders considered it an unsightly $33 million boondoggle that would serve few riders, interfere with views of the majestic Benjamin Franklin Bridge, and was unlikely to actually be completed. Worse, the port had already sunk more than $10 million into piles and foundations on the New Jersey side before stopping construction, perhaps permanently. And finally, while the port considered investment in tourism on the waterfront good for its own business because it was expected to lead to an increase in toll revenues, there had been no studies done to demonstrate that this was true. It also remained to be seen whether there was sufficient demand for a self-sustaining waterfront destination comprised primarily of tourist attractions.

During this period the Delaware River Port Authority changed dramatically as an organization, beginning with Governor Kean's appoint-

Figure 5.8. The Camden Riversharks baseball team playing at Campbell's Field, in Camden. In the background is the Benjamin Franklin Bridge, the tolls of which helped to fund many projects in both cities. Courtesy of the Cooper's Ferry Development Association.

ment of Eugene McCaffrey as executive director in 1987. During his four-year tenure, McCaffrey led the charge to amend the compact, educating the staff and politicians on both sides of the river as to the port's potential power. McCaffrey also recalled how he began to transform the port "by integrating a new layer of executive staff, who possessed both technical expertise and entrepreneurial business skills, above the existing layer of technically qualified and experienced bridge and train engineers." Beginning with McCaffrey, the qualifications of executive directors also changed from insiders and technical professionals to entrepreneurial businessmen and leaders with political skills. The commission also changed in character, as Kean, Casey, and the four governors who followed them took a strategic approach to their appointments, and the two delegations became more cooperative both among themselves and with one another. While there was often friction within and between the two delegations, according to former executive director Paul Drayton, "For a critical period there was also agreement between the chair and the vice chair on an overall strategic approach to planning and project decisions."[12]

Figure 5.9. Downtown Camden, looking toward the Victor Lofts. Photo by
Daniel Campo.

The port was teetering on the brink of bankruptcy in the early 1990s,
but improved management, the use of tools such as strategic plans and
management audits, necessary cost cutting, and permanent staff reductions dramatically improved the agency's financial picture. During Paul
Drayton's tenure the port moved from two-way to one-way toll collections and later introduced the automatic E-Z Pass, which together led to
a reduction in patronage toll collectors from 215 in 1994 to 78 in 2002.
The port also created new units such as the Regional Economic Development department to manage its new waterfront redevelopment role.
Finally, the Port of Philadelphia and Camden, the agency's maritime
subsidiary that was originally created as a shell for the unification of the
port, became the operator of Philadelphia's cruise terminal and a new
intermodal yard. Public relations and image became more important as
the port became more involved in public-oriented projects, and the
agency developed new promotional materials, built a new and prominent Michael Graves–designed headquarters building on the Camden
waterfront, and rebranded itself as an enterprise. Toll increases in 1992

and 2000 boosted the port's bonding capacity, allowing many of these projects, but by 2002 these funds had all been allocated.

In 2004 the port quietly disbanded its Regional Economic Development department as its decade as a waterfront redevelopment agency began to draw to a close. By 2007 the port's finances were growing shaky once again because tolls had not been raised in seven years. Matters were made worse by a major conflict that erupted between the two states over a proposed project to dredge the Delaware's 103-mile-long shipping channel from forty-feet to forty-five-feet deep. Pennsylvania politicians and maritime interests argued that the project was required to maintain a competitive port, but south New Jersey politicians objected on the grounds of high costs (estimated at about a half-billion dollars), potential damage to the marine environment, and the question of which state would accept the contaminated dredge spoils. In December 2005, Pennsylvania governor Ed Rendell forced the Pennsylvania delegation to boycott commission meetings, effectively shutting down the agency until June 2007. The board didn't meet once over those eighteen months, so it was unable to approve annual capital and operating budgets as well as a crucial bond refinancing deal that would have saved the port $750,000 a month in interest costs.

More important, particularly on the New Jersey side of the river, was the rise again of the state as a major source of funds for waterfront redevelopment. Camden's long history of poverty, graft, and corruption forced New Jersey governor James McGreevey to take over the administration of Camden city government in 2003 after three successive mayors were indicted in one decade. As a part of the takeover, McGreevy also announced that the state would invest $175 million into Camden in three years to demolish old houses, rehabilitate others, build new business space, improve public safety, and generally attempt to resurrect Camden's economy. In 2005 the newly created Camden Economic Recovery Board contributed $25 million to finance the $57 million expansion and privatization of the New Jersey State Aquarium, renamed the Adventure Aquarium. The port contributed another $18.3 million, and Ohio-based developer Steiner and Associates invested $5 million for the right to take over operations at the aquarium and to act as master developer for a 30-acre site directly to the north—the only developable site remaining of the original 150 acres. Steiner proposed a "new urbanism" style residential development and town center for these 30 acres, and the master plan won a 2007 Congress of New Urbanism award. The role of private developers continued to expand, and in 2003 Carl Dranoff, the successful developer of the Victor Building, dropped out of the Penn's Landing competition in Philadelphia to concentrate on developing more new housing in Camden. By 2006 his newest project, Radio

Lofts, the conversion of another old RCA building into ninety condominiums, was in development. And in 2006 construction started on the Ferry Terminal Building, a new, four-story office building on the waterfront and the first privately funded new office building in Camden in more than forty years.

As in Camden, private developers and the state started playing a bigger role in Philadelphia too, and despite the lack of progress at Penn's Landing, development was beginning elsewhere on the waterfront. In 2005 a city council committee approved nine zoning bills, clearing the way for three major housing projects on the Delaware totaling 2,900 units. In 2006 residents began moving into the first two buildings of one of the projects, a five-building, 966-unit, gated, high-rise condominium complex with a separate amenity building and a marina, called Waterfront Square, located on a site just a few blocks north of the Benjamin Franklin Bridge. And in 2006 the Pennsylvania Gaming Control Board issued licenses to five private gaming companies for the development of five new casinos, the first ever in the state, two of which would be located in Philadelphia on waterfront sites north and south of Center City. The projects were expected to cost about $550 million each and bring six thousand slots to the city's waterfront.

Finally, as in Tampa, San Francisco, and San Diego, Philadelphia began to feel increasing pressure from citizens and residents who wanted a say in the planning process for the next attempt to develop a major attraction at Penn's Landing. In 2003 the *Philadelphia Inquirer* and the University of Pennsylvania's School of Design hosted a series of public meetings, guiding citizens in the development of a set of principles for waterfront redevelopment. The citizens then participated in a workshop to develop three different schemes for the Penn's Landing site and then voted to pick the most appropriate scheme. The Penn's Landing Corporation and the mayor's office asked the four development teams competing for development rights to incorporate these ideas into their proposals, but while the mayor short-listed two teams, both of their projects would have required significant public subsidy—as much as $50 million for one scheme—and development on the site stalled once again for lack of funds. So in 2006, with one year left in his administration, Mayor John Street made an attempt at a legacy project by embracing the idea of comprehensive waterfront planning through broad public participation. In 2006 he signed an executive order creating the Central Delaware Advisory Group, a forty-five-member committee representing a broad array of interests, and charged it with the responsibility of creating a new master plan for the central waterfront. This group's efforts were led by a division of the University of Pennsylvania's School of Design called Penn Praxis, which was specifically created to bring aca-

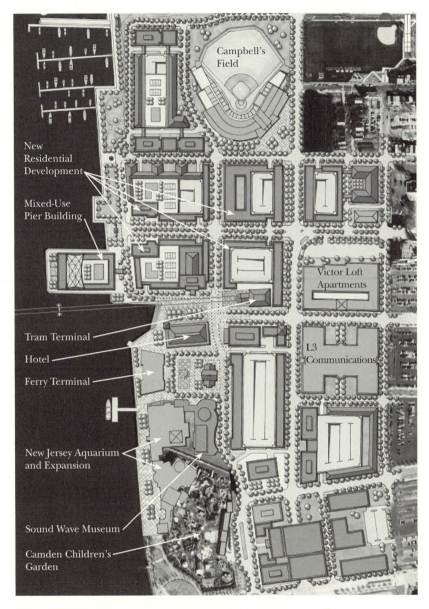

Campbell's
Field

New
Residential
Development

Mixed-Use
Pier Building

Victor Loft
Apartments

Tram Terminal

Hotel

L3
Communications

Ferry Terminal

New Jersey Aquarium
and Expansion

Sound Wave Museum

Camden Children's
Garden

Figure 5.10. Steiner's mixed-use plan for the Camden waterfront. Courtesy of
Torti Gallas.

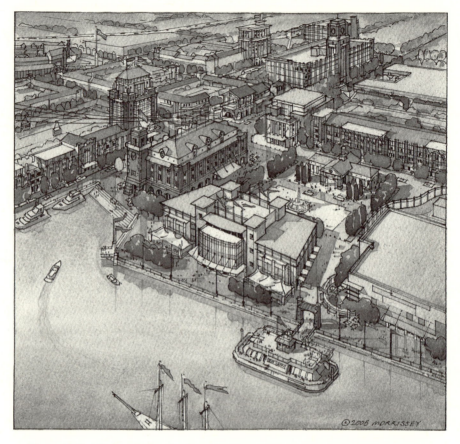

Figure 5.11. View of Steiner's plan. Design and watercolor © 2005 Michael B. Morrissey. All rights reserved. Used with permission.

demics and practitioners together to provide public outreach services to the community. In spring 2007 the new group began to meet to walk the riverfront and hold planning workshops, but it remained unclear whether or not the city's next mayor would feel bound to continue the process or accept its results.

But by this time the role of the Delaware River Port Authority in waterfront redevelopment had receded. The port served as a major source of funds for projects on both sides of the river for a decade, helping to prime the urban redevelopment pump while searching for a viable regional economic development strategy that suited its mission, jurisdiction, and revenue sources. Over more than twenty years the agency shifted its emphasis from port reunification to economic development to tourism before settling on the two-sided waterfront strategy and then fading into the background, at least for the time being, as the states and private developers began to reassert themselves. In 2007 there were murmurs on both sides of the river about a possible toll increase in 2008, suggesting that the port may soon be back in business, invoking once again the policy question of whether or not toll revenues should be spent on seemingly unrelated waterfront redevelopment projects.

But unlike any of the other four agencies, and despite similar swings in mission and purpose, the Delaware River Port Authority remained relatively insulated and stable for more than twenty years of major change. Even uncertain revenue cycles related to the politics of toll increases and Pennsylvania governor Rendell's virtual shutdown of the commission for a year and a half failed to destabilize the agency. Indeed, for reasons that will be further explored in Chapter 8, of the four ports studied in this book, the bistate Delaware River Port Authority was least affected by political incursions, the press, and public demands for participation in planning and funding decisions.

The next chapter will look more closely at the countervailing forces that affected these ports as they began to search for new missions and diversify into new lines of business.

Chapter 6

The Changing Waterfront

Global Forces, Local Politics, and the Challenges of Implementation

Between the 1960s and the 2000s, Tampa, San Francisco, San Diego, Philadelphia, and Camden—and many other port cities throughout the United States and the world—were buffeted by a powerful combination of external forces including the globalization of trade and capital, technological innovation, federal and state policies, location, geography, and coastal form. At the same time, local politics, changing economic factors, distressed maritime interests, and an activist citizenry began to play an increasingly influential role in land-use and development decisions on urban waterfronts. But how exactly do global and national forces combine with location, geography, and coastal form to establish the preconditions for waterfront redevelopment? Furthermore, how do local politics and economic factors influence land use on the waterfront? And finally, how do all of these forces come together to help or hinder a port authority in its attempts to implement waterfront redevelopment?

This chapter explores how this combination of forces led to the decline of the industrial port and the rise of a new diversified waterfront, a place where traditional maritime uses competed for space and resources with a whole new mix of nontraditional maritime and nonmaritime uses that was unique to each city. The local port authority attempted to play the lead role in planning for and developing this diversified waterfront, branching out beyond cargo operations and seeking to attract private capital and residential, commercial, and entertainment projects to its waterfront property. But as it moved away from its traditional industrial purposes, politicians, other governments, maritime businesses, labor unions, and private interests, who all feared that the port was overreaching, began to challenge its jurisdiction and powers. In this murky and rapidly shifting context, a form of intralocal competition for control of the waterfront and waterfront projects began to escalate. Formerly stable and sheltered port regimes faced pressures they had never experienced before as a variety of diverse interests made conflicting demands on the port. Together, these countervailing forces hindered the four ports in their efforts to diversify into new lines of business and ensured a form of development on the waterfront that was often unplanned, inconsistent, and piecemeal. As we will see in Chapters 7 and 8, these forces also fundamentally changed the ports as business organizations and as governmental institutions.[1]

This chapter begins with a review of important ideas about waterfront transformation, urban political economy, and the challenges of implementing waterfront redevelopment. When considered together, these ideas form an analytical lens through which to better view the experiences of the individual ports in the sections that follow.

Forces on the Waterfront

In a study of urban waterfronts based primarily in the United Kingdom, Riley and Shurmer-Smith found that the typical "structuralist, top-down approach" to analyzing waterfront revitalization overemphasized the role of forces at the global and national scales. This approach suggested that policies and events that lacked an overtly local and spatial element were nonetheless powerful determinants of spatial change at the local level.[2]

Global forces played a major role in waterfront revitalization, effectively setting the process in motion. Major economic shocks such as the OPEC oil shortage of the early 1970s caused oil companies to shift oil drilling operations and write off abandoned port facilities and berths. Technological innovations including containerization and roll-on/roll-off, or "ro-ro," technology made many cargo berths and finger piers obsolete, and the explosive growth in air travel had the same effect on ocean liner berths and piers. The fall in the price of oil and the relative cost of cars, relative increases in wealth, and the resulting growth of the tourism industry contributed to these effects. And the increased mobility of capital and the globalization of services impacted waterfronts as shipping companies found it easier to relocate to avoid restrictive unions and other irritations, as they rarely owned extensive shore facilities and their capital was invested primarily in their ships. Finally, the virtual abandonment of the urban industrial port in combination with the increased caché of waterfront living and working attracted global real estate development companies that saw the potential profitability of redevelopment projects on large sites at the water's edge in the urban core.[3]

National forces included transportation and infrastructure development policies that impacted individual ports, for example, decisions related to the development of new highways and railways and the improvement of existing ones that affected access to ports. Other influential national policies included the growing reliance on private capital for redevelopment, the use of empowerment zones, free port zones and other tax advantages, and the degree to which governments chose to sponsor or privatize particular industries. Finally, the shift in thinking in the 1980s that led to the view of waterfront redevelopment as being not a national industry problem but rather a local, inner-city redevelopment problem led to reduced national spending on waterfronts in general.[4]

But Riley and Shurmer-Smith argued that the top-down view based on these global and national forces was inadequate for explaining spatial change on individual waterfronts at the local level. They proposed instead an integrated approach that overlaid top-down and bottom-up forces on the actual spatial situation of the individual port. Unlike top-down forces, bottom-up forces vary greatly across individual local situations and include the activities of local port-related businesses, unions, and governments, many of which have become increasingly involved in public-private ventures with private sector firms for waterfront redevelopment. The sum of the forces acting on an individual port cannot be understood until the top-down forces are combined with these bottom-up pressures and considered in the context of geography, coastal form, road and rail networks, centrality of location, and existing trading links. Riley and Shurmer-Smith concluded that while top-down forces did not vary much across different ports, the strength of bottom-up forces varied greatly. As a result, top-down forces predominantly influenced ports with weak bottom-up forces. Where strong bottom-up forces dominated, however, top-down forces were less influential and the top-down approach therefore could not adequately explain outcomes. By highlighting the important role played by bottom-up forces, Riley and Shurmer-Smith's model began to address the tremendous heterogeneity that exists among different ports and waterfronts and the increased complexity of analyzing waterfront redevelopment from the bottom up.[5]

This model was based primarily on cases in the United Kingdom, where a strong, centralized national government played an important role, but it did not address the federalist system in the United States, where the national government is less powerful and additional layers of states' rights and historically strong local governments dominate policy at the local level. Therefore, at the four U.S. ports considered in this book, bottom-up forces should be even more powerful, and an understanding of the role played by urban political economy in urban redevelopment at the local level becomes even more important.

URBAN POLITICAL ECONOMY

In his 1981 book on urban politics, *City Limits*, Peterson observed that local governments actively pursue development for the purpose of economic growth as their single most important policy objective. He also found that developmental policies are the product of highly centralized decision-making processes involving political officials and businessmen, ensuring that conflict is limited, the public is generally broadly supportive, and opposition groups rarely gain the strength necessary to impede development. Peterson broke new ground with his observation that, by concentrating on development policies, fiscally constrained governments engage in a zero-sum game of interlocal competition with one another at the expense of redistributional policies such as affordable housing. But Peterson's most controversial assertion was that development that enhances the local economy benefits all citizens. In their 1987 book *Urban Fortunes*, Logan and Molotch challenged Peterson's conclusions that economic development is a pure public good. Instead, they argued that property in urban areas has both "exchange value" and "use value" and that economic development is not necessarily good for the entire city, as it can result in rising rents, pollution, and displacement.[6]

Elkin expanded on the theories of both Peterson and Logan and Molotch with his 1987 book *City and Regime in the American Republic*, in which he describes a structure comprised of three axes around which city politics revolve: the mutual attraction between elected politicians and businessmen, city officials' need for coalitions and a flow of benefits to keep coalitions intact, and the individual functional bureaucracies of city government that seek to maintain and expand autonomy. Following on Elkin, in 1989, Stone demonstrated in *Regime Politics* how limited formal authority in American government, particularly at the local level, increases the importance of informal relationships between government and business in urban politics. In Stone's model, governing elites cannot provide more than the most basic levels of service without the support of a larger governing coalition. This coalition provides the institutional capacity that government alone lacks in exchange for business opportunities and control of the downtown growth agenda by the business elites.[7]

And in *Mega-Projects*, Altshuler and Luberoff sought to reconcile these various theories of urban political economy with outcomes from actual case studies of major urban "mega-projects" over the past half-century. Altshuler and Luberoff first described how mega-projects are different from regular urban redevelopment projects because they are nonroutine, much larger, and more costly; take a long time to complete; are influenced by multiple levels of government; and require a stable political base throughout multiple political regimes and market cycles. The authors stopped short of offering a single urban political theory of their own or a critique of the existing theories, but they did conclude that several theories are useful in understanding the politics of mega-projects.[8]

Although Peterson claimed that local officials and civic leaders pursue development not only for personal reasons but also in the interests of their own jurisdictions, Altshuler and Luberoff saw the pursuit of development as simple rent seeking. They did, however, credit Peterson with refocusing urban theory on the idea of localities as economic competitors that have negligible market power. They also agreed that in this context local interests recognize that the prime objective of local policy must be to attract capital, so they seek to create a stable investment climate by insulating projects from the type of day-to-day politics that discourages investors.[9]

Altshuler and Luberoff found that regime theory offers a distinctive contribution by exploring the dynamics of local business-government collaboration. Regime theory emphasizes that private business owners and political officials can better expect to accomplish their objectives when working together, a point also made by Logan and Molotch. Altshuler and Luberoff also found that regimes are most stable with respect to business dominance of economic development issues. However, they warned that, even in this arena, today's growth coalitions must accommodate the interests of a large number of diverse local interests if they hope to succeed. They concluded that regime theory helps in forming an understanding of the politics of mega-project authorization and financing because mega-projects require exactly the type of public-private cooperation that regime theory explains.[10]

Finally, Altshuler and Luberoff found that Logan and Molotch contributed in two important ways to an understanding of mega-project politics. First, they correctly identified the main fault line in urban development politics as being between the pure financial value of urban land versus its value to residents and the community as a nonfinancial resource and asset. Second, they explained how institutions, including units of government and individual businesses, vary widely in the degree to which they are politically active based on both the strength of local political ties and the extent to which strategies require favorable government action for positive outcomes. Altshuler and Luberoff concluded that developer and land-owner-driven mega-project coalitions base their claims on exchange values while their opponents emphasize use values including neighborhood preservation and the environment.[11]

Waterfronts are at the center of all of these ideas, as ports continue to play an important role as regional economic development engines while maritime operations continue to provide high-wage union jobs and revenues to private companies. Government officials and developers collaborate on real estate projects that will lead to contracts, private profits, and public tax revenues while citizens pressure the same politicians and the port to limit development and provide more public space. Multiple units of government at different levels often influence waterfront redevelopment, but unlike mega-projects, these governments are more likely to be competing with one another rather than collaborating. And finally, all of these groups battle over the exchange and use value of public land in their cities. Together, these ideas help to move beyond theory and policy by shedding light on the most difficult aspect of waterfront redevelopment, its actual implementation.

IMPLEMENTING WATERFRONT REDEVELOPMENT

In a case-based study of waterfront redevelopment politics, Gordon identified two different political periods, beginning with the brief start-up period when a broad, cohesive coalition assembles around the two basic arguments of stimulating economic development and revitalizing the city's urban waterfront. Once the project appears viable and a redevelopment agency has been created and put into operation, interest groups within the city begin to compete for larger shares of the benefits, and the cohesiveness of the original coalition gives way to divisive internal debates centered on the themes of housing, public access, and jobs and economic development. For a waterfront redevelopment authority to withstand the forces of this second phase it must maintain a positive relationship with the sponsoring government that appoints the agency's board and has ultimate financial responsibility for its actions. But the agency must also build consensus, cooperation, and trust at the local level in order to ensure smooth relations with a municipality that has power over services, infrastructure, and bureaucratic processes that can be used to hinder redevelopment efforts.[12]

Gordon also found that political success in waterfront redevelopment is measured in terms of development progress. While it typically took fifteen to twenty years to build the consensus required to initiate development and to begin showing measurable progress, once development was underway politicians considered success to be built results within only two to three years. More important, when development had occurred within this time frame, agencies were able to withstand changes in regime. Unproductive agencies, however, were more exposed to politically motivated incursions as new political leaders sought to influence agency policy and development direction when they did not see built results.[13]

In a different study of waterfront planning and design based on the same four cases, Gordon found that incremental plans were more successful than master plans for mega-projects, particularly as waterfront redevelopment projects usually entail the development of huge sites over many decades. More important, incremental plans that provide a mix of uses that are politically acceptable in combination with well-designed streets, parks, and public spaces that are accessible to the public will be applauded by politicians, the press, and architectural critics.[14]

And in another study of waterfront redevelopment finance, Gordon identified a critical relationship between the ability of individual authorities to act quickly and independently and their subsequent ability to take advantage of market cycles and realize development income earlier. The window of opportunity, or the period during which an agency can initiate development projects in order to take advantage of peaks in the market, is typically open for only one to two years. Those agencies that had greater freedom of action were able to move more quickly and take advantage of market cycles. As a result, these same agencies were also able to realize revenues years earlier than their slower moving peers.[15]

Gordon observed from all of these studies that "waterfront redevelopment projects must be measured in terms of political, design, and financial success." Accordingly, he concluded, "the successful waterfront redevelopment agency relies on an incremental approach to design, a high degree of political autonomy, and the related ability to move quickly and flexibly to time individual development projects with market cycles."[16]

These conclusions about the implementation challenges faced by waterfront redevelopment agencies are sobering, but port authorities that take on these duties are likely to face even greater hurdles. Because they were not originally created to implement waterfront redevelopment, they often do not have the clear power and authority to do so, they often have not been granted the necessary powers and tools, and they find it increasingly difficult to obtain either when they continue to technically operate as a port. These weaknesses are exacerbated by local officials and the public, who remain skeptical of the port's motives and are unwilling to increase the powers of an agency that has a historical reputation for being too powerful, arrogant, and aloof. Such a port clearly lacks the type of autonomy that Gordon found was required for the successful implementation of waterfront redevelopment. But how did these ports find themselves in such a predicament, and how did they discover a way back out?

Forces of Port Decline and the Rise of the Diversified Waterfront

TOP-DOWN FORCES

By the 1980s many of the global forces outlined by Riley and Shurmer-Smith had begun to affect all four waterfronts, as had important top-down policies at the national level, although not evenly. First, American military policy had a great impact on the health of a number of the country's ports. Military force reductions in the post–Vietnam era affected many military bases, and the Base Closure and Realignment Act of 1988 began shuttering large sections of ports and eliminating a major source of unionized ship repair, ship services, and cargo handling jobs. These two forces combined to reduce the navy's presence in San Diego and to completely close the Philadelphia Naval Shipyard in 1995. Following the events of 11 September 2001, the Homeland Security Act of 2002 and, specifically, the Maritime Transportation Security Act of 2002 together had the effect of an unfunded mandate, requiring ports to finance capital and operating security improvements from their own sources. At the same time, the war in Iraq led to a boost in cargo business in some cities as the military designated San Diego, Philadelphia, and twelve other of the approximately 130 ports in the United States as "strategic military seaports" for the shipment of military cargoes destined for the war zone.

The federal government, through the Army Corps of Engineers, also funded and administered most of the dredging and harbor improvement projects in the country. Many ports required regular dredging to maintain minimum depths in channels and at berths for cargo, cruise, and other maritime operations. Requests for dredging projects, however, far exceeded the availability of funds, so many projects remained on waiting lists for decades. Those ports with shallower waters and longer channels faced a greater risk of becoming obsolete as channels and berths silted up while the drafts of ships continued to deepen.

In addition, an anachronistic federal law—the Passenger Services Act of 1886—restricted the growth of the cruise business in some cities. Originally written to protect unionized American service jobs on passenger ships, the act prohibited foreign-flagged passenger vessels from calling at two American ports consecutively. Because virtually all cruise ships were foreign-flagged, this law served only to restrict cruise itineraries, placing many ports at a disadvantage because of their geographic locations. Ports located in the middle of the coasts faced the greatest challenges because, for example, a cruise ship was not permitted by law to call at New York and then Boston or, similarly, at San Francisco then Seattle.

Federal, state, and local politics also influenced national policies, and as a result, federal programs were rarely implemented evenly or fairly. During the 1950s, for example, United States senator and presidential hopeful William Knowland of the East Bay area used his power to funnel federal grants to Oakland for the development of a modern container port. Because it lacked its own patron, San Francisco was forced to sit idly by and watch its cargo business evaporate in a zero-sum game of interlocal competition. Similarly, in 1988, congressional politics began to play a very influential role in base closure decisions throughout the country.

Finally, variations in how waterfront land was owned and controlled at the federal, state, and local levels also influenced flexibility at several ports. For example, as trustees of the state, the ports of San Francisco and San Diego controlled large, contiguous stretches of waterfront property, while at the same time they were constrained by the State Lands Commission, which had the power to review and approve—or reject—their plans and projects. Conversely, on the East Coast, the Delaware River Port Authority and the Tampa Port Authority both had more flexibility and independence when it came to land-use decisions, but they operated on waterfronts where the land was a patchwork controlled by a number of public and private sector interests of which they were but one. So while California ports lacked the independence from state oversight that their East Coast counterparts enjoyed, they were better positioned to comprehensively plan for and consistently develop large, contiguous sections of their waterfronts.

LOCATION, INFRASTRUCTURE, AND GEOGRAPHY

Geographic location remained the most important determinant of past and future success for the four ports. Centrally located ports in the United States attracted steamship lines because they offered both the shortest sailing routes and direct access to the hinterlands via major highway and rail infrastructure systems that had linkages to the east and west as well as the north and south. Further, ports that were not limited in their ability to grow by natural or manmade barriers and lack of land were best positioned for the development of modern cargo facilities.

Despite their long histories as major ports, none of the four cities was well located for modern cargo operations. Philadelphia and San Francisco were both centrally located on the coasts, but Philadelphia was at the end of a 135-mile shipping channel, and San Francisco occupied a location on a densely developed peninsula. Philadelphia was well located for certain niche cargoes destined for the region, but cargoes destined for other parts of the country could avoid an extra day of steaming time by calling at New York, Norfolk, or Savannah. Cargoes shipped to San Francisco took two days to travel south through the peninsula's congested rail corridor before arriving in Oakland when they could have been shipped directly there in the first place.

Located at the southern end of the west coast, San Diego no longer had any rail or highway connections to the East. Rather, like San Francisco, all cargo had to travel north to Los Angeles before heading inland. Finally, because it was located on the Gulf coast at the end of a forty-two-mile-long channel, Tampa had limited potential as a major international shipping hub, although it remained viable because it exported bulk cargoes that were mined within the region and imported petroleum and chemical products.

San Francisco and San Diego both suffered from a lack of infrastructure and a lack of available land adjacent to cargo facilities, which together limited their ability to grow as ports. Rail and highway congestion through the peninsula and a tunnel that was too low for double-stack container cars further limited cargo throughput from San Francisco. The lack of highway infrastructure at the Tenth Avenue Marine Terminal had the same effect in San Diego, although in 2006 the port began to consider roadway improvements that would get trucks off the street in the Barrio Logan neighborhood. But because both ports were surrounded by mature residential neighborhoods, future expansion in the urban cores of the two cities was out of the question.

Located on the mainland and in the heart of the northeast corridor, Philadelphia was served by the best infrastructure network of the four ports. The port had access to I-95, the major north-south interstate highway on the East Coast, and multiple rail lines on either side of the river that also served points north and south. The urban ports of Philadelphia and Camden, however, lacked access to large land areas. This issue was further complicated by competition between the ports and among other private and public sector uses for control of waterfront property.

Tampa had the best land situation of the four ports. In the past the port used its dredge-fill program to expand the industrial port on Hooker's Point, and in the mid-1980s it began to engage in an aggressive program of land acquisition, buying property on the urban waterfront and in several other industrial port areas. Over time, this strategy allowed it to redeploy existing downtown maritime operations to Hooker's Point, creating a separate industrial port largely out of sight of the public, while at the same time creating space for the development of a new urban cruise port and waterfront. Road and rail access to Tampa's port were also adequate, so its primary constraint remained its long and congested shipping channel.

While upland geography is important, the character of the land below the water's surface also influences a port's future prospects. Changing tides and currents are constantly at work reshaping submerged lands, and ports in areas with relatively shallow water must regularly dredge if they are to maintain shipping channels of adequate depth. In addition, to stay competitive many ports are required to deepen their channels and berths to accommodate larger ships with deeper drafts. The costs of dredging, however, have risen dramatically over time in response to increased environmental concerns, as dredging disturbs polychlorinated biphenyls (PCBs) and other settled pollutants, and contaminated dredge spoils are more costly and difficult to dispose of.

Dredging programs are more important than ever to all four ports. The constantly increasing size of cruise and cargo ships forced the Tampa Port Authority to expand its turning basin at Ybor Channel, and the port sought the federal funds needed to create 3.5-mile-long passing lane along a straight stretch of its 42-mile channel to relieve congestion caused by increased cruise ship traffic. The Army Corps of Engineers scheduled the funding of this project for 2030, although the port hoped to have it moved up on the list to 2010 as there was already enough demand to justify its need in 2003. By 2005 the port had convinced the state of Florida that the project was a top priority and was poised to receive $12.4 million in state funds to cover the costs of the work.

Similarly, in the 1980s, the Delaware River Port Authority began seeking federal funds needed to deepen a 103-mile-long stretch of its shipping channel from forty feet to forty-five feet. Critics considered the project a waste of money, but local boosters argued that it was not a major improvement at all but merely what was required to stay competitive with other ports as ships continued to grow in size and draft. Opponents in New Jersey feared being forced to accept the potentially contaminated dredge spoils, and as political observers described it, the real fight was over "who eats the mud." By December 2005, Pennsylvania governor Ed Rendell was so frustrated and angry at the impasse that he had his state's delegation boycott Port Commission meetings for a year and a half, finally forcing a compromise solution with New Jersey politicians in 2007 that would allow the project to go ahead.

The Port of San Diego always considered cargo a core business, but it also recognized as early as the 1960s that its location on a large shallow bay was sure to limit its long-term potential as a major cargo port. The navy maintained a fifty-foot-deep channel for aircraft carriers that extended as far south as the Tenth Avenue Marine Terminal, but the port bore the responsibility for maintaining the channel that continued from there all the way to the National City Terminal to the south, which it deepened from thirty-six feet to forty-two feet in 2006. Because of the shallowness of this channel, for many years National City was limited to niche cargos such as automobiles because auto transports have shal-

Figure 6.1. Break-bulk cargo handling on San Francisco finger piers in 1936. San Francisco History Center, San Francisco Public Library. Reprinted with permission from Corbis.

lower drafts than container ships. Finally, San Francisco Bay was shallow throughout, and some even believe that by 2030 it will lose all of its shipping, including Oakland's, to the two major deepwater coastal container hubs to the south and north, Los Angeles/Long Beach and Seattle/Tacoma.

THE RISE OF THE DIVERSIFIED WATERFRONT

While the combination of federal and state policies, location, geography, and infrastructure all limited the futures of these four cities as cargo ports, many of these same factors combined with other advantages to create the preconditions for urban redevelopment on the waterfront.

San Francisco and Philadelphia benefited from their locations in the center of major population centers—the Silicon Valley and the north-

Figure 6.2. Modern container facilities at the Port of Oakland, circa 1980s.
Courtesy of the Port of Oakland Archives.

east corridor—that offered large and diverse work forces, a variety of
lifestyle types for residents and workers, and plentiful attractions downtown for residents and tourists with expendable incomes. While the
other two cities were located in smaller population centers, San Diego
drew from its proximity to Los Angeles while Tampa was close to major
tourist attractions, including Disney World, only an hour's drive away.
Finally, all four cities benefited from good airlift capacities at local airports and good highways and commuter rail systems.

San Francisco and San Diego possessed the highest quality waterfront
real estate of the four ports, with long, uninterrupted panoramic views
of big blue bays and the rugged beauty of the Pacific coast at Point Loma
in San Diego and the Marin Headlands in San Francisco. Because they
controlled contiguous stretches of public land, both ports also had the
ability to plan and develop their waterfronts more comprehensively and
consistently. By comparison, the waterfronts of Philadelphia and Cam-

den faced one another across a half-mile-wide, mud-colored tidal river. The city of Philadelphia codified plans for a continuous public riverwalk in 1983; however, a combination of fragmented land ownership, weak code enforcement, and slow, patchy, uncoordinated development left Philadelphia's waterfront incomplete and discontinuous. On the other side of the river, the Cooper's Ferry Development Association, which controlled a larger contiguous waterfront site in Camden, more rapidly and consistently developed a series of public attractions and new housing linked by a riverwalk that was more than a mile long. Tampa's urban waterfront was at the end of a shipping channel, surrounded by islands and peninsulas, and its views across the narrow Ybor and Garrison channels included a shipbuilding facility and bulk cargo silos. The gated community of Harbour Island overlooked Hooker's Point and petroleum tanks that their owners painted with murals of flamingos and manatees in response to the complaints of residents. Views of the larger bay from downtown were limited, and as a result the residents of the region were slow to discover their waterfront.

Finally, federal laws restricting itineraries in combination with northern climates and locations in the centers of the coasts limited the growth of the cruise industry in San Francisco, San Diego, and Philadelphia, while Tampa was perfectly positioned for expansion. Because San Francisco and Philadelphia are such large population centers, they benefited in a way from the events of 11 September 2001, as the drive-to cruise market grew in popularity because cruisers were frightened to fly, at least for a period. However, this market continued to grow long after 11 September as cruise companies realized the enormous potential of the drive-to market even after the fear of flying had receded.

But top-down forces such as base closures, the funding of dredging projects, and maritime laws, in combination with local geography and transport links, reflect only a partial view of how the preconditions for urban waterfront redevelopment evolved in these four cities. And while each port was clearly different along these dimensions, the uniqueness of local governing regimes and political cultures in each city amplified these differences while also playing a major role in development outcomes.

Changing Political Contexts

INTERGOVERNMENTAL COMPETITION AND CONFLICT

The four ports owned or controlled large swaths of coastal land and had broad jurisdiction over their waterfronts, but because they were originally created as industrial port authorities, each ran into conflict as it assumed the mantle of its city's new waterfront redevelopment agency. The city governments and other agencies challenged the ports' legal and moral authority on the waterfront and, in some cases, entered the waterfront redevelopment business alongside the port. This created several additional layers of complexity on the waterfront that led to more rapid, if uncoordinated, development in some instances and the stalling of development in others.

Redevelopment was first complicated by competition between agencies that were each trying to develop similar projects on or near the waterfront. The new arena that the city of Tampa decided to locate on Garrison Channel was in direct competition with the MusicDome concert venue that the port was attempting to develop on an adjacent parcel. Whether or not there was enough demand in the region to support two such similar facilities, the city's decision to go forward with the arena was the primary cause for the collapse of the port's project. Ironically, the design of the MusicDome incorporated huge hanger doors that could be opened to give concertgoers views over the stage, across the channels, and toward the bay, whereas the arena was a large windowless box that took little advantage of its a prime waterfront location. Nevertheless, the completion of the arena, called the Saint Pete Times Forum, helped to increase activity and stimulate further growth on the waterfront. In another example from Tampa, Mayor Greco prioritized the redevelopment of nearby Ybor City, leading to competition between the Centro Ybor project and the port's Channelside Shops project when there did not appear to be enough demand to support both.

Similarly, two and a half years into the development of his retail and entertainment project at Penn's Landing, legendary mall developer Mel Simon brought in Disney as a potential partner and introduced them to Philadelphia mayor Ed Rendell. But to Simon's horror, Rendell encouraged Disney to partner with the city's Redevelopment Authority and independently develop another site just eight blocks away from the Simon project. Ultimately, both entertainment projects failed. In San Francisco, both the Redevelopment Authority and the port were attempting to develop waterfront hotels in the late 1980s, and the Redevelopment Authority later played a major role in developing AT&T Park and the South Beach neighborhood. In general, however, there was less competition for development between agencies on the two California waterfronts because the ports controlled large stretches of property while land control on the two east coast waterfronts was more fragmented.

A second form of complexity stemmed from competition between different agencies for the control of one project or site. In Philadelphia, interest in the redevelopment of the Penn's Landing site rotated between the city of Philadelphia, which expected contracts and tax revenues; the Penn's Landing Corporation, which legally controlled the site; and the Delaware River Port Authority, which had an interest as a major investor. Control over the disbursement of contracts was also an important factor, and in the fall of 2003, Philadelphia mayor John Street attempted to accelerate the selection process to ensure that a contract with the next developer of Penn's Landing would be in place prior to the November election. That strategy failed, so in 2007, the last year of his mayoralty, the termed-out Street finally embraced planning, encouraging a big public process as a legacy project. Similarly, in San Francisco, Mayor Willie Brown used his influence over the Port Commission to ensure that it awarded contracts to several developers who had supported him in the past. And in an intergovernmental competition that led to public-public collaboration, five agencies, including the city, the county, the navy, the port, and the Centre City Development Corporation, banded together to create the North Embarcadero Alliance to stimulate development north of the urban waterfront in San Diego, in part because the port was not perceived to be acting fast enough on its own.

More important, the lack of clear authority on the waterfront in combination with intralocal competition and conflict between agencies significantly reduced the autonomy of the port, thereby increasing the degree of difficulty for developers who had to clear multiple hurdles. Maurice Cococcia of Lend Lease concluded, "San Francisco is unusual in that the regulatory process makes things harder. Usually when a city takes on a project of the magnitude of the cruise terminal it establishes a single, special-purpose entity just to do the one job. In this case the project is being run by the port, but because it doesn't have complete control and jurisdiction, Lend Lease has been required to manage numerous regulatory agencies and constituencies when it would normally assume it could run them all through one coordinating agency." But Jesse Blout, director of the Mayor's Office of Economic and Job Development added that, "because the port must work with other departments, there are always conflicts that require the mayor's coordinating influence and clout to resolve." According to Blout, "The port and other enterprises benefit from having the mayor's office involved in the negotiations with the developer because, for example, Lend-Lease is more likely to take things seriously when they are coming from the mayor than when they are coming from the port." Former port planning director Paul Osmundson agreed, recalling that while the mayor was criticized for exerting too much influence in development decisions, "without leadership from Mayor Brown there would have been endless and constant bickering and questioning about the wisdom of any of these projects—even the Ferry Building, which everyone now sees as a huge success."[17]

MARITIME TENSIONS

Maritime interests created another form of competition and conflict that influenced the ability of the port agencies to implement new, non-traditional maritime and nonmaritime plans and projects on waterfront land. During the second half of the twentieth century, cargo volume declined and became an increasingly smaller share of overall revenues at all four ports as waterfront property was abandoned and slid into decay. But the shipping companies, labor unions, and liberal politicians in these cities fought to preserve underutilized waterfront land for potential future maritime uses, buttressing their claims with romantic notions of the return of cargo and previous, happier times as a "working waterfront." Maritime businesses were long accustomed to paying below market rents on public port property, but their interests ran even deeper. They argued that once waterfront property with deepwater berths and direct access to road and rail networks was committed to other uses, the result could only be further declines in the cargo business. Redevelopment would reduce both flexibility and the potential for growth while at the same time signaling to shipping companies that the city was no longer seriously interested in cargo. More important, once one nonmaritime development was allowed, the precedent would be set and more nonmaritime development would surely follow, ensuring the demise of the greater industrial port.

In the 1980s the Tampa Port Authority saw these pressures building and so began to acquire land and plan for the relocation of industrial uses from the urban waterfront to the industrial port to make more room for the cruise industry and real estate development downtown without displacing existing maritime tenants. Even then, maritime interests sought to block nonmaritime development projects on Ybor Channel, which would have required the relocation of two ship-repair companies to parcels that the port already owned. Maritime interests in Philadelphia attempted to block the spot zoning for one parcel of private property zoned for port use that ultimately became an Ikea furniture store and another in the navy yard that the governor hoped to use for a new food distribution center. And in San Francisco, maritime interests were so intransigent and unwilling to engage in any give-and-take with respect to land use that some believe the port could see no other way to clear the path for a real and viable future as a real estate development agency than to put a virtual end to shipping.

If the major fault line in urban development politics is between

Figure 6.3. The diversified waterfront on Tampa's Ybor Channel. Courtesy of the Tampa Port Authority.

exchange value and use value, then maritime interests made an argument for port land's having both. In all four cities maritime interests argued that waterfront property with deepwater berths and convenient road and rail access was irreplaceable, that once gone it would never be returned to port use, and that it therefore could not be judged purely based on its current exchange value. Rather, underutilized port land had exchange and use values that would be realized in the future, when maritime business increased once again.

Whose Waterfront?

In all four cities a similar debate simmered over whether waterfront property should be valued for its highest and best use or as an important natural resource to be enjoyed by the broader public. The amount of conflict was directly related to the proximity, size, and age of nearby neighborhoods as well as the maturity and strength of nonprofit citizens and special interest groups. The natural beauty of the waterfront was also important, as were citizen's attitudes toward the waterfront as a public asset. Finally, conflicts over the value of land were influenced by local political culture and the demand for development, from both private developers and public officials.

Residents of Philadelphia's long-settled Society Hill neighborhood and the more recently settled Old City neighborhood to the north only periodically voiced their opinions on waterfront redevelopment. Society Hill residents objected to a new high-rise hotel on the waterfront that they argued blocked views, but neither the city nor the developer heeded their protests, and the hotel was completed and opened in 2000. Both neighborhood groups objected to the Simon project and the more recent proposals for the Penn's Landing site, and by 2007 the new Central Delaware Advisory Group was promoting public space over private development and maritime interests.

In San Diego the residents of the working-class Latino Barrio Logan neighborhood that surrounded the Tenth Avenue Marine Terminal relied in part on race and class issues when they successfully pressured the port into developing a waterfront public park for their neighborhood in 1980. However, the area was torn by continuing conflicts between the aspirations of the port and maritime interests for future cargo growth, neighborhood demands for more high-wage port jobs, and the residents' frustrations with cargo-related truck congestion and pollution from exhaust on the neighborhood's streets. Later, in the 1990s, downtown San Diego's new and more affluent residents began to influence port decisions affecting waterfront views, the adaptive reuse of an old historic police station, and an undeveloped parcel called "Dead Man's Point."

The Channel District in Tampa was the newest, smallest, and least influential of the neighborhood groups affecting the four ports. Only a few hundred residents lived in the nine-square-block neighborhood in 2003, but by 2006 developers had announced plans for as many as three thousand new condo units within the district and along the water's edge. As growth accelerated, Channel District residents voiced their opposition to several proposed projects, including a high-rise hotel and conference center and several condominium towers on the grounds that they would block views and had no reason to be located on the waterfront anyway.

The greatest amount of sustained conflict took place in San Francisco, where residents of the dense neighborhoods adjacent to the waterfront first organized in 1969 to stop the development of a proposed high-rise office tower complex next to the Ferry Building on the waterfront. The group succeeded in blocking this project, and ever since a wide variety of actors has taken interest in both individual projects and overall plans for the waterfront. San Francisco Tomorrow, the Telegraph Hill Dwellers, and other neighborhood groups continued to apply constant pressure on the city and the port, as did a variety of other groups representing more specific interests. For example, the swimmers who use Aquatic Park took a keen interest in Fisherman's Wharf, just to the south, as both existing conditions and proposed developments would affect the quality of the water they swam in. The environmental group Blue Water Networks opposed the development of Lend Lease's cruise terminal project because pollution from foreign-flagged cruise ships went unregulated. According to Jennifer Clary, president of San Francisco Tomorrow and also a staff member at Clean Water Action, "When a cruise ship pulls in, it is like thousands of SUVs running their engines in the city."[18]

The conflict between those interested in developing land to its highest and best use and those interested in its nonfinancial value to the public can also lead to unusual alliances and strange bedfellows. In an example of "the enemy of my enemy is my friend" theory, the most important force on the San Francisco waterfront for several decades was a product of the unlikely alliance between antigrowth and promaritime interests. The historically powerful longshoreman's union led liberal politicians and the owners of cargo and shipbuilding companies in insisting that two-thirds of the waterfront continue to be reserved for maritime uses despite the fact that much of the property was underutilized and decaying. At the same time, the antigrowth groups saw that by aligning themselves with these powerful interests they could, together, stall redevelopment on the waterfront. This alliance remained powerful from 1969 until 1996, when Andy Nash, the former president of San Francisco Tomorrow who had coauthored Prop H, reversed his stance and supported the development of the new ballpark after accepting that less than one-third of the waterfront was still being used for maritime purposes. Similarly, by hitting on the strategy of historic preservation and adaptive reuse as a way to redeploy their pier buildings for revenue-generating commercial uses, the Port of San Francisco converted antigrowth interests—who were also typically pro–historic preservation—into an unsure ally. But despite differences in strength and degree of cooperation, promaritime and antigrowth forces in all four cities played important roles in opposing the development aspirations of their ports, influencing implementation in the process.

Implementing Waterfront Redevelopment

THE PORT AS REDEVELOPMENT AGENCY

Former San Francisco city planning director Dean Macris recalled, "State legislators under pressure from local officials transferred the San

Francisco port to the city because, among other reasons, it was perceived to be too independent and disconnected." According to Macris, "Back then it was difficult to talk with port people—they were entirely resistant to broader city interests." The port tried to maintain its autonomy, but over the years it slowly became more like a city department. San Francisco's former city planning commission chair, Toby Rosenblatt, believed that "history drove the attitudes of the port's management through the 1970s and 1980s. The port's view back then was that 'there are other barriers to development in the way so we'll deal with waterfront redevelopment when we have to, but not happily.' Planning coordination between the port and the planning commission was begrudging at best, and the plan for the northeast waterfront area sat on a shelf for ten years after it was completed because the port lacked any real interest in implementing it." According to Rosenblatt, "The port really didn't start to change until the Agnos administration of the late 1980s." Macris concluded, "The port finally realized only in the late 1990s that it wasn't going to be much of a port anymore and that because it sat on such valuable land its future was as a de facto redevelopment agency."[19]

Maurice Cococcia of Lend Lease, the developer of the new cruise terminal project, concluded that the port remained "stuck halfway in between its past as a port authority and its hoped-for future as a redevelopment agency." According to Cococcia, the port "hasn't gotten there yet and is not able to act as fast as the typical redevelopment authority." Jesse Blout, director of the Mayor's Office of Economic and Job Development, added, "One of the biggest barriers for the cruise terminal project was the Port's inability to transform itself from a maritime entity into a redevelopment entity."[20]

Yet the port is a creature of its makers, who specifically designed it to be less autonomous and "stuck halfway in between." A lack of political and financial autonomy combined with unreasonable expectations doomed the port to a twilight existence where it remained neither an independent agency nor a part of the city.

The Port of San Diego remained considerably more independent than its northern cousin. According to Gail Goldberg, former planning director for the city of San Diego, "There is an understanding within the city that the port can basically do what it wants. For many years there was virtually no interaction between the port and other city agencies. However, beginning in the 1990s, when residential growth in downtown led to criticism of the port for not including the public in its planning decisions, public and political scrutiny increased dramatically."[21]

Of the four ports, San Diego's is the most mature and sophisticated as a waterfront redevelopment agency, in part because it was originally granted the powers and authority to operate as one. The port completed a number of complex hotel deals, and former port director Larry Killeen believed that "the port's real estate staff are as technically skilled as those at the [highly regarded] Port Authority of New York and New Jersey." But some developers who built projects on the waterfront saw the port as overstaffed and spoiled because it earned its own revenues from the gross and did not care whether private sector developers and businesses were successful. And because the port controlled such valuable waterfront real estate, it also had the potential to act with the inefficiency of a monopoly, a point underscored by a 2002 state audit that found a lack of competitiveness in developer selections and contracting decisions at the port and that questioned whether it was fulfilling its public trust duties.[22]

The Delaware River Port Authority offered the most confusing example because it remained everything but a port authority, despite its name and its more than seventy years' worth of effort to become one. The port's transformation from a bridge authority into a regional economic development agency in 1992 and the failure of port reunification in the late 1990s only added to the public's sense of confusion. Further, a high degree of fragmentation existed, as five different waterfront-related agencies, two cities, and their respective redevelopment authorities all operated within overlapping jurisdictions.

This fragmentation led to both inefficiency and political incursions into redevelopment efforts while it further limited the public's ability to understand which agency was responsible for what on the Philadelphia and Camden waterfronts. The port also didn't own any waterfront real estate, and although it provided a large share of project funding, it could not technically be considered a waterfront redevelopment agency. And the two agencies that were responsible for waterfront redevelopment couldn't have been more different in terms of operating style. Tom Corcoran at the Cooper's Ferry Development Association took a long-range strategic approach to planning and development while Dominic Sabatini emphasized the Penn's Landing Corporation's purpose as an operating entity that managed a venue for public events on the waterfront. As a result, the Cooper's Ferry Development Association became an effective, independent, single-purpose waterfront redevelopment agency while the Penn's Landing Corporation remained a day-to-day public events operation that viewed its waterfront redevelopment role as secondary. Indeed, because of its overemphasis on operations, the city of Philadelphia's Commerce Department and the mayor's office both continued to play major roles in redevelopment attempts over the years.

The Tampa Port Authority made the best case for its role in waterfront redevelopment by treating the creation of a downtown cruise port and entertainment district as integral, yet secondary to the larger strategy of expanding the port's cruise business. Because Tampa remained an active bulk and general cargo port and because the cruise business was also a maritime use, it was better able to justify the relevance of its own direct role in waterfront redevelopment as a maritime-related activity. Even then, as the cruise business grew and cruise revenues were used to finance other cargo-related activities, relations between maritime interests and the port remained uneasy.

But David Kitchens, an architect and urban designer whose firm created the *Garrison Seaport Plan* for the Tampa Port Authority and also designed the Channelside Shops, echoed Maurice Cococcia of Lend Lease, claiming that "the port just hasn't gotten there yet as a waterfront redevelopment agency. They don't understand the real estate business, they don't understand what needs to happen on an ongoing basis to be successful, they don't have the mentality of a developer, and because of all the executive staff turnover and the failure of the early anchor projects, a lowest-common-denominator type of thinking at the port replaced the original vision." Kitchens recalled, "By the mid-1990s the port's attitude was simply 'we are good at repositioning ship hulls, so we'll do that.' "[23]

In retrospect, Cococcia found from his experiences in San Francisco, Sydney, Melbourne, and elsewhere that "waterfront redevelopment projects are best run by agencies created specifically for the purpose." Kitchens agreed, suggesting that "Tampa would have been better off if it had created a separate and independent downtown entertainment district or authority for the purpose of redeveloping the waterfront and simply compensated the port for the use of its land."[24]

Finally, and perhaps most important, despite ongoing redevelopment activity, public officials and civic leaders in all four cities continued to question the prerogatives of their ports as independent waterfront redevelopment agencies. Former San Diego mayor Susan Golding asked, "Why does an independent agency have the power to make important land-use decisions in the city of San Diego?" Jim Chappell, a planner in San Francisco, echoed Golding, asking, "Why does the city stop one block from the waterfront," and perhaps more important, "Why does San Francisco continue to have a port at all?" And in Philadelphia, where the Delaware River Port Authority financed sports, culture, and entertainment projects miles from the waterfront, former city controller Jonathan Saidel simply asked, "Exactly where does the port stop and the city start?"[25]

Although all four ports attempted at different times to create and implement comprehensive plans, none succeeded in realizing these grand visions. The *Garrison Seaport Plan* for Tampa's waterfront focused on the development of mixed-use functions, and three major anchor projects all surrounding new cruise terminals that were to be buried within the development and partially financed by it. Conceptually, the port could have implemented this master plan in phases, but to be successful it depended on the anchors' going ahead roughly in parallel. But a combination of forces killed the first two anchor projects and forced the developer of the third to repeatedly modify his project until it emerged as a smaller entertainment, retail, and movie complex that finally opened in 2001. During this period, a lack of demand for waterfront development, a declining real estate market, and several changes of executive leadership at the port led to the loss of the grand vision described in the plan. More recent projects occurred in an incremental and piecemeal fashion without the benefit of either a comprehensive plan or design guidelines. "The loss of vision had permanent effects," recalled David Kitchens, "as the port brought an industrialist attitude into a different kind of community." For example, "The port's decision to site a new parking garage right on Channelside Drive eliminated forever any possibility of retaining the original concept of pedestrian-scale retail along the street while maritime and industrial attitudes led to bulkhead designs and other decisions that were not as pedestrian friendly as they could have been." Kitchens concluded, "It was a killer that the port director, senior staff, and board turned over so much at the port in such a short amount of time, as the vision went away."[26]

The case in Philadelphia was somewhat different, for while demand for waterfront redevelopment was higher, the severe constraints of the Penn's Landing site, primarily the barrier between the waterfront and the city caused by I-95, required a form of development that could be entirely self-sustaining. Long known for having a bad case of "Inner Harbor envy"—the desire to replicate the type of development at Baltimore's Inner Harbor despite very different site and waterfront conditions—Philadelphia continued to seek master developers who would build huge, dense commercial projects that would generate significant tax revenues and big contracts for local developers and builders. But according to Arthur Jones, a principal at Bower Lewis Thrower Architects, a firm that over the years worked on six of the past projects designed for the site, each project charted the same trajectory, "becoming larger and larger in program, size, and cost, spiraling upward as developers struggled to include enough uses and attractions to keep visitors in the complex long enough to ensure that rents were paid, while at the same time providing enough parking to support every visitor."[27]

On the other side of the river, the Cooper's Ferry Development Association began in 1983 with a similarly dense, commercially driven plan that dictated uses. But once it became clear that there was little demand for such uses on Camden's waterfront, the organization quickly shifted to a more incremental and opportunistic form of planning. Under this strategy, Camden's waterfront experienced constant and consistent development progress over several decades. San Francisco never had a comprehensive plan, and while the new waterfront land-use plan dictated uses generally, it also allowed for incremental development. Finally, the plan for the most developed of the four waterfronts—San Diego—existed only in Don Nay's head until 1995. So despite these grand visions, virtually all development on the four waterfronts was piecemeal.

Yet perhaps more important, development did happen in all four cities despite the failure or simple lack of master plans. Indeed, incremental development led to more authentic and vibrant mixed-use communities in Tampa and Camden, where grand visions were replaced by opportunistic development and a mix of entertainment attractions, sports facilities, retail, commercial office space, low- and high-rise housing, and cultural institutions.

Unfortunately, while a piecemeal rather than a planned approach to development may have led to better diversity of uses in some cities, it also left the door open to questionable project selection, location, and design decisions. In particular, because the costs of assembling large parcels elsewhere in the developed urban core were prohibitive, cities, redevelopment agencies, ports, and private developers followed the path of least resistance when they settled on large, available, and comparatively cheap waterfront sites. As a result, all four cities developed or attempted to develop large windowless boxes on their waterfronts, including aquariums, convention centers, malls, arenas, and casinos, and they all considered many more. They also considered mixed-use and office projects that may not have been the best use but that were the only way to earn rents from waterfront land. Even so, these projects were later credited with jump-starting development, increasing activity, and stimulating more and higher quality development on the waterfront.

The proposed uses and designs of individual projects also mattered. Citizens generally opposed developments that they felt would squander local assets to cater exclusively to out-of-town tourists or wealthy homeowners. Downtown residents in all four cities protested hotel towers that would have blocked views from their condominiums and taken up valuable waterfront property. They also balked at themed entertainment projects and inauthentic developments that lacked a local or maritime character. While these projects sometimes made more financial sense than others from the port's perspective, they rarely held up to public scrutiny and more often went unrealized. The plan for a museum in Tampa based around the old pirate ship *Whydah* was originally viewed as being viable because there was a history and legacy of piracy in Florida, but once it collapsed, the projects that followed, such as the "Dinosaureum," received only fleeting support. Conversely, San Francisco considered a sailing center, a fishing center, and a bay center, but while all three aligned better with maritime interests and received public support, none made any financial sense. San Francisco had its greatest success when it hit on the strategy of combining historic preservation and adaptive reuse as a way to redeploy maritime pier and bulkhead buildings for revenue-generating commercial uses that were the most authentic possible solution. Another developer proposed a San Francisco–themed entertainment center on the waterfront that featured a fog machine and a simulated earthquake, but port tenants and residents vehemently rejected the project, calling it the "Disneyfication" of the waterfront. An even more dubious proposal was for the "Titanic II," a full-scale replica of the ship that was proposed as a floating hotel on the waterfront. Following in the wake of the popular movie and called simply "unbelievable" by the head of the Fisherman's Wharf Association, the project was also an attempted dodge around the waterfront hotel ban, as it would have technically been a boat rather than a building. And going from the sublime to the ridiculous, in 2003 a New York developer treated Philadelphia to a $3 billion proposal for a huge, themed, mixed-use waterfront project called "Atlantis" that the architectural critic of the *Philadelphia Inquirer* characterized as a "glossy collage." When asked what the connection was between Atlantis and Philadelphia, the developer responded, "There's nothing Philadelphia-specific about the Atlantis plan. It's a one-size-fits-all development. If it doesn't work here, there's always San Diego."[28]

Finances

Waterfront redevelopment schemes based on comprehensive master plans were generally unsuccessful but so were schemes based on comprehensive financial plans. For example, Tampa's comprehensive master plan relied on three different privately funded anchor projects. These projects were to provide both the planning and architectural framework and the financial critical mass necessary to stimulate development on the waterfront, in part by subsidizing the costs of new infrastructure and cruise terminals. Yet after two of the three projects failed to get off the ground, little remained of the master plan. The projects could have been implemented in phases from a design-and-construction standpoint, but the failure of the anchors spelled both the plan's financial doom and the general loss of a comprehensive vision for the waterfront. Similarly, San Francisco was banking on a future stream of rents from a single major cruise terminal project to be built on one of its piers. These revenues would increase the port's bonding capacity and, in turn, allow it to sell more bonds and revitalize its capital program, improving other piers and generating even more rents from other new projects. But when the cruise terminal project fell apart, so did the port's entire financial plan.

Similarly, the Penn's Landing Corporation put all of its eggs in one basket more than a half-dozen times, repeatedly relying on a single master developer to provide both the vision and the funding for a mega-project at Penn's Landing. By 2006, and despite more than forty years of effort, development still had not occurred. At all four ports, major, comprehensive financial structures turned out to be as fragile and ephemeral as their physical plan counterparts.

A more fine-grained and incremental approach to planning and finance would have allowed for more, smaller developers to win contracts, but in practice these four ports competed for investment primarily from only a handful of large, nationally known developers who could bankroll big, risky waterfront projects. When the pirate museum folded in Tampa, New York developer Roland Betts took his capital to San Francisco, where he then failed again politically in his attempt to develop a west coast version of Chelsea Piers. Similarly, after a group of Danish investors interested in developing a cruise terminal were driven away by Prop H, a team comprised of the Simon Group and Disney considered the project, and then in 2000 international developer Lend Lease stepped up to the plate. In addition, over the years, major developers who made proposals for projects at Penn's Landing in Philadelphia included Rose Associates and the Rouse Company.

The large national developers are better capitalized than their smaller, local competitors, who are less likely to take on large public-private urban redevelopment projects. Mike Hogan, the local developer of the Channelside Shops in Tampa, concluded, "Only the largest developers, like the Simon Group, have the capital and the capacity to engage in these types of projects." According to Hogan, "The extraordinary amount of time and effort it takes to complete a project through a public agency reduces redevelopment to a form of pro-bono work that only the largest firms can afford to engage in for their own altruistic reasons."[29]

Finally, the relationship between autonomy and an agency's ability to time projects with market cycles played a major role in the failure of many projects to get off the ground. For example, the Port of San Francisco tried to remodel the Ferry Building six times starting in the 1970s, issuing requests for proposals and hiring developers each time, but failing largely because of the port's historical operating style, manifested as a basic lack of urgency. The fifth attempt teamed Continental Development, from southern California, with world famous architect I. M. Pei, yet while the project seemed viable, the city was slow to uphold the port's attempts to condemn and terminate leases in order to vacate the building. In the interim the market turned down, the project stalled, the developer sued, and the city and the port paid $3 million to settle and regain control of the building. After this bruising experience the port began to let all of its leases run down so that the same situation would not occur again. But the project was more complicated because it required the relocation of the port's offices from the building, so the port decided to redevelop the adjacent Pier 1 into a new commercial office building that would house its own permanent new headquarters and several other rent-paying tenants. The port ran an expedited process for this project, and the mayor stepped in and formed a three-member panel to review development proposals and choose a winner. There was little public interest in the project despite San Francisco's usual emphasis on process, so the mayor picked the developer AMB, and Pier 1 was completed, went to market at the high point in the real estate cycle, and was very profitable.

The port ran a quite different and much more public process for the sixth and final attempt at redevelopment of the Ferry Building. Former finance director Ben Kutnick credited Planning Director Paul Osmundson and Staff Planner Alec Bash, "who both had a lot of respect and credibility in the community and together ran a very good process. Bash wrote the best RFQ/RFP book that I have ever seen and was instrumental in achieving public consensus." But by the time this project was completed in 2003, the market had turned down again following the bursting of the tech bubble. During the four years the project was in development, rents went from $60 per square foot to a high of $100 before dropping to $30 when the building opened in 2003. Mayor Willie Brown didn't help with this timing by pushing a number of port projects in 2001 and 2002 as he approached the end of his administration. This stretched the capacity of the port's development staff too thin, slowing down all projects, including the Ferry Building, and inadvertently ensuring that it would hit the market at the bottom of the cycle.[30]

Whereas Camden continued to complete projects, the last two attempts to complete projects at Penn's Landing in Philadelphia also hit the low points in the market and failed. The Tampa Port Authority's comprehensively planned, three-anchor project also fell apart during a recession, although the port succeeded in completing several projects including the Channelside Shops, a new cruise terminal, and a new parking garage. Only the Port of San Diego had a consistent track record of timing its projects well with market cycles. Between 1980 and 2006, the port successfully developed the Seaport Village retail project, four hotel towers, a convention center, and numerous other projects on the waterfront, largely because it benefited from a high degree of autonomy from local politics. In general, political autonomy was directly related to financial success, as port authorities with less independence and unclear prerogatives faced greater challenges when they attempted to time their projects with real estate cycles.

Politics, design, and finance are connected in important ways, but these cases illuminate several new and important interconnections that influenced outcomes on all four waterfronts. First, the ports' lack of a clear prerogative and the related lack of power, ability, or willingness to make the transformation to a redevelopment agency created a gap on the waterfront between the ports, their cities, other redevelopment agencies, and private developers. Other political entrepreneurs and redevelopment actors rushed to fill this gap, and the ports lost autonomy, fell subject to greater scrutiny, and remained exposed to political incursions as the competition for control of the waterfront heated up.

Rather than incrementalism, this competition for control led to a less attractive form of piecemeal development, where public and private entities fought for the right to develop waterfront sites and the many different entrepreneurs on the waterfront viewed comprehensive plans and design guidelines only as constraints. In short, fragmentation on the waterfront led to inconsistent planning and development and poor project choices. It also often resulted in a messy, more complicated, and therefore more time-consuming development process, which increased the likelihood that the window would shut before most projects could make it through development and get to market. As a result, only those ports with true autonomy and the power to act quickly, flexibly, and independently were able to more consistently manage the development process and hit the market cycle at the peak rather than at the trough. Perhaps the greatest irony, which appeared in all four cities but most starkly in San Francisco and Philadelphia, was that just the right combination of these forces could create a real estate version of the perfect storm, as projects were condemned to a development and approval process that would always take just long enough to ensure that they hit the market at the trough every time. Worse, in cases like Penn's Landing and the Ferry Building, this cycle of failed development was repeated over and over again with only the actors changing.

The Diversified Waterfront

Over the past half-century the physical character of the waterfront in all four cities changed dramatically as break-bulk cargo handling virtually disappeared, modern container cargo facilities were developed away from the downtown core, and other uses took the traditional place of cargo on the urban waterfront. Global forces and federal and state policies, particularly those related to military base closures, the cruise industry, and the funding of dredging projects, influenced all four ports. However, geography and local forces, including politics, economics, and the increased reliance on private capital, were at least as important to outcomes on the waterfront, particularly when it came to nonmaritime real estate development.

The four ports stepped into these turbulent waters when they began to pick up the mantle of waterfront redevelopment agency for each of their cities in the 1980s. The ambivalence and conflict created by the ports' entry into waterfront redevelopment stimulated competition for control of the waterfront as elected officials, other units of government, maritime interests, private developers, and the public attempted to fill what was perceived to be a gap in jurisdiction, expertise, and moral and legal authority on the waterfront. These various actors competed with the ports for the control of waterfront land and projects, and this intra-local competition often led to poor planning, inappropriate land-use choices, failed projects, and inconsistent development—a zero-sum game played out at a very localized level, on the waterfront. The resulting fragmentation ensured that no single agency or entity could claim clear authority as primary waterfront redevelopment agency.

This competition for control of the waterfront also influenced the planning, design, and implementation of waterfront redevelopment. Ports quickly learned that their comprehensive plans could not survive changing political regimes and market cycles. Plans and guidelines that were not codified into law stood little chance of being implemented, and indeed, the main reason that the Port of San Francisco completed a land use plan was because it was legally required to do so by the voters through Prop H in order to end a development moratorium.

Preexisting port agencies also brought with them images and reputations based on old operating styles. In the past the ports served industrial economic development purposes out of the public's eye and ran like powerful, independent fiefdoms, seeking little consensus from politicians and the citizenry. But while this style worked for industrial cargo operations until the 1970s, it was ill suited to the new and rapidly evolving conditions on the diversified waterfront. All four port agencies suffered from increased public scrutiny and reduced political autonomy. And because they started as ports they had more difficulty making the transition to waterfront redevelopment agencies, in part because they often didn't have the right powers to begin with.

This chapter offers an external, high-level view of how a variety of forces over nearly a half-century fundamentally changed these four waterfronts spatially, politically, and economically. Yet this view offers only part of the picture. The next chapter takes the view from the ports, looking from the inside out and seeing how they were affected by these forces as they entered into new lines of business, struggled to work with an increasingly diverse set of interests, and changed fundamentally as business organizations through their attempts to develop diversified waterfronts in their cities.

Chapter 7

The Rise of the Diversified Port

Innovation, Leadership, and Operating Style

The forces described in Chapter 6 changed not only the waterfronts politically, economically, and as physical places but also the ports that once dominated them. In response to these forces the four ports diversified into new lines of business, but in the process of doing so they began to transform themselves as organizations. Each began to distance itself from its past as a single-purpose, governmental port agency and began moving down a winding and unfamiliar path toward a more entrepreneurial and private-sector-style approach to doing business.

The behaviors of general-purpose governments and private sector companies as they grow and change are fairly well understood, but less is known about how hybrid, public-private entities like port authorities innovate and evolve as organizations, particularly when they diversify into new lines of business. Specifically, how important to success are the roles played by appointing officials, commissioners, executive directors, and senior staff? How do changes in governance and leadership style influence changes in operating style and image? Finally, are ports capable of innovating and making the changes in leadership and operating style that are necessary if they are to succeed as diversified waterfront redevelopment agencies?

This chapter considers how each of the four ports moved beyond a governmental mentality as it diversified, learning how to act more like an innovative and entrepreneurial private corporation while at the same time struggling to balance increasing demands from politicians and the public for a voice in port land-use decisions. A new breed of port directors and senior staff was required to initiate and manage these changes, but a combination of external and internal divisions over priorities and increased public scrutiny created a politically unstable environment for these leaders and the durations of their tenures waned. While all four agencies had many successes, these forces combined to hinder each one in its attempts to fully transform itself from a distressed cargo operation into a financially viable and vital new business organization as a diversified port. A closer look at ideas about innovation, the qualities of leaders, and operating styles in public and private organizations will shed light on how, paradoxically, these ports became more like general-purpose governments even as they attempted to act more like private sector companies.

INNOVATION IN ORGANIZATIONS

In *Built to Last*, Collins and Porras found that "visionary" Fortune 500 companies succeed over long time frames because they are imbued with a clear sense of mission and focus and because they continually build upon the company as a permanent institution. Other companies focus on developing individual products and technologies that are not long lasting. Collins and Porras also found that successful companies rely on experimentation, trial and error, opportunism, and accident rather than brilliant and complex strategic planning. These organizations try a variety of different approaches, keep what works, discard what does not, and "cluster" their various efforts around a specific goal or idea rather than taking a completely random or scattershot approach.[1]

But in the book *Bureaucracy*, Wilson identified a quite different situation in the public sector, where bureaucratic organizations are created specifically to resist internal innovation. Wilson found that bureaucratic organizations establish rules to prevent the arbitrary use of discretion by bureaucrats and that rules therefore serve as the foundation of an agency, where stability and routine are the highest priority. As a result, one of the major problems in bureaucratic agencies is that, because they are so rule oriented, bureaucrats are more strongly influenced by constraints than they are by goals. Wilson also emphasized the importance in bureaucratic organizations of the related roles played by turf and autonomy, often over that of budget. Autonomy is the level of independence required to allow a group to develop and maintain an identity, and the turf, or "monopoly jurisdiction" within which other bureaucratic rivals, cannot compete. One result of the preoccupation with turf and autonomy is that it is extraordinarily difficult to coordinate the work of different agencies because they spend much of their effort negotiating the terms of how each will maintain its own preexisting autonomy rather than deciding how to accomplish the new task. Wilson concluded that innovation within bureaucratic organizations is rare, as it requires an unusual exercise of judgment, personal skill, and misdirection, a combination of skills not typically found in government executives. So how important is the role of the leader in public and private organizations?[2]

THE ROLE OF THE LEADER

Collins and Porras found that CEOs of visionary companies typically spent much of their careers with their companies and were promoted through the ranks. They also enjoyed longer tenures, averaging more than seventeen years, while their peers at nonvisionary companies averaged only eleven. The authors speculated that there might be a negative correlation between charismatic leaders, who are often hired from outside, and profitability and the building of a visionary company. Their findings suggest that by training and promoting leaders from within, companies benefit over the long term from greater continuity in management style. Collins and Porras further speculated that rather than bending companies to fit their personalities, successful CEOs are products and reflections of the companies within which they grew and developed as professionals. They offered the example of Jack Welch, CEO of General Electric (GE), who was successful exactly because he was a product of GE's culture, a fact that is often glossed over in the management literature on the charismatic leader. Collins and Porras concluded that despite the trend of bringing in outside talent to change and reinvigorate the cultures of companies, long-term, stable leadership by executives who "grew up" within their organizations offered greater value.[3]

In a study of thirteen entrepreneurial leaders in government, Doig and Hargrove considered both the qualities required of successful entrepreneurial leaders and the limited powers such leaders have over their organizations. The theory that best captured their view of organizational behavior was one advanced by March that held that, while leaders do have some impact, the crucial variable is the "density of administrative competence" within the organization. Doig and Hargrove found that successful leaders use two distinct styles, one based on rhetorical skills and the other on coalition-building skills, and that while coalition-building skills are particularly important, most leaders rely on some combination of both. Wilson also distinguished between two types of executive, the politician and the career bureaucrat, but he went one step farther in finding that the key strategy employed by all successful executives is that of "finding a constituency." Wilson concluded that while the thirteen executives explored in Doig and Hargrove's study differed across all other dimensions, the one trait they shared was that they had found or maintained the support of key external constituencies. Doig and Hargrove concluded more generally that success is often the result of a match between the individual's personal skills, the specific organizational task that is being attempted, and favorable historical conditions.[4]

Allison compared public and private sector managers and found that public managers work on a shorter time horizon that is based on political necessities and electoral cycles. Unencumbered by such constraints, private sector managers often serve much longer tenures than their public sector peers and therefore have the luxury of taking a longer perspective. Because public managers operate in the public realm, they face greater scrutiny and influence from politicians, the press, and the public for their actions, whereas private sector managers can operate in relative secrecy. As a result, public managers are subject to persuasion from a variety of actors and therefore claim to have many superiors, whereas their private sector peers typically report to only one boss. Public managers are also subject to a form of close scrutiny by legislators and sometimes the courts that is rare in the private sector. Finally, while public sector managers rarely have a clear bottom line, private sector managers do, in profitability, market performance, and survival.[5]

Finally, in *The Public's Business*, Walsh compared a number of public authorities and found that their leaders conform more to a private sector executive model, similar to that of Collins and Porras, than to Allison's public manager model. According to Walsh, the ideal leader of a public authority combines both perspectives and has a commercial viewpoint and initiative, is decisive, cares about public interest, and is politically skilled. Walsh found that authority executives usually display some combination of administrative and political skills. But unlike Allison, Walsh found that sponsoring governments have little control over authorities and that their boards pay only intermittent attention to the activities of the director and staff. As a result, their executives enjoy as much discretion as the presidents of private firms, but they are even more autonomous, as they receive little if any oversight from investors and can operate largely in secrecy. Autonomy is further enhanced by the job security that results from the difficulty of measuring an authority executive's performance. Walsh concluded that, unlike Wilson's bureaucratic organizations, public authorities attract highly motivated and skillful builders, administrators, and power seekers. These executives, however, soon begin to confront a new set of social forces that affects both their agency's operations and their own fortunes as leaders.[6]

OPERATING STYLE AND IMAGE

In *New York: The Politics of Urban Regional Development*, Danielson and Doig identified an important shift in constituency demands that began in the 1960s, which affected the operations of government agencies. In the past, public agencies relied on the values of expertise and professionalism, both in their organizational cultures and in their justifications for projects and programs, but events throughout the 1960s and 1970s caused the public to lose faith in these two values, leading to increased mistrust of government. In the New York City metropolitan region alone, scientific approaches to problem solving failed as large projects such as the World's Fair and the World Trade Center in New York City lost money despite projections by "experts." After being stymied by the public in its attempt to build a fourth jetport that was justified by projections of increasing air travel, the Port Authority of New York and New Jersey invested heavily in improvements at Newark Airport, but the expert's projections again missed the mark, resulting in substantial losses. According to Danielson and Doig, these types of failures by public agencies not only left the idea of expert studies in tatters but also opened the door for the increasing role of participation, which has since had a major effect on government and authority activities in the three areas of environmentalism, neighborhood effects, and social equity. The emergence of participation as a new influence required agency directors to dramatically modify their operating styles to address new and increasing numbers of constituencies, and those who failed to do so—most famously New York's Robert Moses—risked losing control of their agencies and their jobs.[7]

A port hoping to engage successfully in long-range programs such as waterfront redevelopment would seem to benefit most from the approach to innovation used by visionary private sector companies, relying on institution building over individual programs and on long tenures from leaders who have come up through the organization. But while authority managers, including port directors, enjoyed the same tenures as their private-sector peers for many years, increasing demands for public participation began to push them more toward Allison's politicized, short-term model of public sector leadership. Operationally, a port would also find itself increasingly torn between a real financial need to act entrepreneurially and autonomously and the public's growing demand for influence in port decisions. But together, these shifts pose a potential dilemma, as ports attempting to diversify by implementing new major, long-range programs stand to lose the very type of leadership and operational autonomy required to do so successfully. A look at how the four ports weathered these countervailing winds will help to identify the opportunities and constraints a port faces when it attempts to reorganize and diversify into new lines of business.

The New Port

The Changing Meaning of "Maritime"

The new combination of forces acting on the waterfront forced all four ports to do something they had never been required to do before:

accept the decline of their core purpose—maritime cargo operations—and begin to radically reenvision their futures as diversified business organizations. At stake was each port's survival.

Visionary commissioners and staff at both the Tampa Port Authority and the Port of San Diego perceived the limits of cargo as a revenue base and saw that their future survival lay in exploiting other unique assets. Tampa sought to take advantage of its ideal geographic location, actively marketing itself to cruise lines as a unique waterfront destination anchored by a secondary cruise port that would relieve congestion at the fast-growing ports of Miami and Everglades. San Diego sought to put its beautiful waterfront real estate to higher and better use by seeking proposals from developers for innovative new retail-, tourism-, and hospitality-based projects like Seaport Village.

Like San Diego, the Port of San Francisco controlled valuable real estate, but while it sought new sources of revenues from rents, politicians and the public sought at the same time to limit and control its development activities on the city's beautiful waterfront. The port began considering proposals by developers for mixed-use commercial projects during the mid-1980s, and in 1990 a new strategic business plan specifically identified waterfront redevelopment as a primary strategic goal.

Finally, New Jersey governor Kean envisioned transforming the Delaware River Port Authority from a bridge and transportation operation into a powerful regional economic development engine by using toll revenues to recapitalize the port financially while unifying it as an institution. Kean built a bistate political constituency around the port, and he and Governor Casey of Pennsylvania appointed activist commissioners and staff and held them responsible for ensuring that necessary organizational changes would occur, culminating in the 1992 compact amendment.

By the 1990s all four ports had laid the groundwork for diversification and urban waterfront redevelopment as major new purposes, but they soon faced one major obstacle. Traditional maritime interests were unwilling to recognize that the urban waterfront was undergoing major, irreversible changes as a result of containerization and the globalization of the shipping industry. For decades, shipping companies, labor unions, politicians, and other local leaders refused to accept the decline of labor-intensive, break-bulk cargo-handling processes and the permanent loss of so many stevedoring jobs that offered high wages and good benefits. These same leaders also resisted the ports' attempts to redevelop obsolete finger piers and other underutilized port property to accommodate new uses. And some simply could not accept the end of their city's era as a historically important port. In vain, they chose instead to develop and promote new strategies designed to attract cargo and stevedoring jobs and to block the reuse of waterfront property. Maritime interests argued that once port property adjacent to deep water and road and rail facilities was converted, it would never revert back to maritime use, sending a signal to the shipping industry that the city was no longer committed to a future as a port. And while new uses would create additional revenues for the city and port authority, the larger port, as a regional economic engine, would be pushed into decline, and good, blue-collar jobs would be lost. Port authorities countered that in many cases cargo had already left for good and that it was time to move on. Nonetheless, the political pressures stemming from this misplaced maritime pride caused all four ports to implement policies, business practices, and investment and land-use decisions that were at best questionable and, in many cases, had disastrous consequences.

All four ports engaged in unsustainable financial practices by oversubsidizing loss-making maritime operations with the revenues from other, more profitable businesses. By 1986 the Port of San Francisco, for example, was almost entirely subsidizing declining maritime operations with rents from seafood restaurants on Fisherman's Wharf. Yet when the port sold bonds to finance improvements at its container facilities it invested none of the proceeds in the infrastructure improvements needed by these more profitable, rent-paying tenants.

Poor capital investment decisions are another product of maritime pride. In 1969, San Francisco gambled and lost on lighter-aboard-ship (LASH) technology, an alternative to containerization and then, in 1971, when it was too late, invested in container facilities and cranes without any prospects for leases, on nothing more than the "build it and they will come" theory. In 1984, Port Director Gene Gartland hoped to spend an additional $60 million to improve container facilities, but the port's finance staff and bond counsel determined that it did not earn enough net operating revenues to pay the debt service on such a large issue. So Gartland had bond counsel size an issue—$42.5 million—to exactly match forecasted net revenues, yet despite this investment, by 1987 the port's two container terminals were still operating at only a fraction of their capacity. Tampa, San Diego, and Philadelphia and Camden all made similar investments in terminal facilities and cranes, but none of these facilities ever operated at anything near capacity.

Finally, maritime pride led to conflicts in land-use policies and decisions. At all four ports maritime interests strenuously fought the redeployment of underutilized and abandoned port property for non-maritime purposes. They sought to preserve flexibility for the future, when cargo would return or expand, yet when successful they denied the port the revenues it needed to operate and to recapitalize its deteriorating infrastructure and facilities while depriving the public of a vibrant waterfront. A conflict erupted in Philadelphia, for example, when the city sought to rezone a piece of long-vacant port property so that a major Ikea furniture store could be built on the site, leading to claims that such a change would eliminate future flexibility for the port. Similarly, representatives of maritime businesses in Tampa claimed that the port placed too much emphasis on the cruise business and related waterfront redevelopment. For, although these businesses helped to financially revive the Tampa Port Authority proper, they also diverted the agency from its core purpose of supporting less profitable private cargo and shipbuilding companies and promoting the health of the greater port as a regional economic engine. The port countered that a substantial share of the revenues derived from the cruise business and from real estate had been used to recapitalize cargo facilities in the industrial port. The Port of San Diego was caught between demands for union port jobs from the residents of the Latino neighborhood that surrounds the Tenth Avenue Marine Terminal and complaints by those same residents of cargo-related truck traffic, noise, and exhaust on their streets.

The enabling legislation that created these ports limited them to traditional industrial maritime operations including container, break-bulk, and bulk cargo shipping; ship services; ship repair; and in some cases commercial fishing. The legislation also listed the types of infrastructure projects that ports were allowed to finance and build in support of these activities, including, for example, "wharves, docks, piers, quays, slips, bulkheads, public landings, terminals, storage and sheddage facilities, warehouse, refrigeration, cold storage and quick-freezing plants, stockyards, elevators, shipyards, marine railways, drydocks," and so on.[8]

When ports began to engage in new activities, they often reinterpreted the meaning of "maritime," a strategy that served two purposes. First, they sought to buffer themselves against the claims of maritime interests, politicians, and labor leaders who challenged the port's commitment to its traditional cargo purpose. Second, they hoped to initiate new projects while avoiding the costs in time, money, political capital, and increased public scrutiny of seeking the necessary amendments to their enabling legislation that would allow them to engage in these new activities.

Thus port leaders, politicians, private developers, and residents all sought through reinterpretation, and sometimes through legislation, to reshape the meaning of these uses and facilities, often expanding the definition of "maritime" to include a much broader range of water-based activities. Cruising, recreational boating, sport fishing, marinas, yacht repair, and even "mega-yacht" services have grown as maritime businesses, particularly in Tampa, San Francisco, and San Diego, as have harbor tours, dinner cruises, and commercial seafood restaurants on all four waterfronts. The ferry systems that were driven out of business by new bridges in San Francisco, San Diego, and Philadelphia during the first half of the twentieth century also returned.

All four ports struggled with this reinterpretation, but San Francisco engaged in the most exhaustive process, as the port, the city, the Bay Conservation and Development Commission, the State Lands Commission, and the Citizen Advisory Board all worked together throughout the land-use planning process required by Prop H. The final waterfront land-use plan incorporated an inventory of existing land uses and a new plan that listed in great detail future allowable land uses. But it was after a long and arduous process that these many and varied interests came to understand how little land was still in use for active cargo operations and to agree on the new meaning of "maritime" for the San Francisco waterfront.

New Businesses on the Old Waterfront

The single most important new global trend in nontraditional maritime business is the rise of the cruise industry. In 1958, Pan American Airlines offered its first nonstop Atlantic crossing on a Boeing 707, and soon the proliferation of the commercial jet airplane spelled the demise of the ocean liner as a form of point-to-point transportation. In desperation, enterprising steamship companies began to redeploy their passenger ships, offering cruises as a new vacation alternative. The cruise industry took off, growing at an average rate of 8.5 percent per year from 1980 through 2005, and the number of passengers and cruise ships both swelled. As with cargo ships, improved designs and shipbuilding technologies allowed passenger ships to continually increase in size. Between the 1960s and the 2000s, ships grew in length from 400 to 1,100 feet, and passenger capacities increased from 400 to 5,600. Technological innovation led to shallower drafts, although height above the waterline, or "air-draft," grew to nearly 200 feet on the largest ships, limiting access to some ports constrained by lower bridges.[9]

All four ports were attracted to the cruise business because it promised to preserve some traditional stevedoring jobs while adding a host of new service jobs within a region, ranging from food service and catering companies to cab and limo drivers, florists, and piano tuners. Environmentalists expressed concern over unregulated emissions from ships, but the cruise business was otherwise perceived by most as relatively clean and visually attractive when compared with other traditional waterfront industries. More important, the cruise business promised to be lucrative for the port agencies, as cruise ships helped to replace lost cargo-ship dockage and wharfage fees while revenues were further boosted by substantial passenger charges. In 2005 the Tampa Port Authority earned $10.28 per passenger, which included fees, parking, dockage, and wharfage, equating to $7.9 million in revenue based on 772,000 passengers, or 23 percent of the port's total operating revenues of $34.6 million for the year. But cruising also offered larger benefits, as cruisers spent their dollars on transportation to and from the cruise terminal, lodging, entertainment, shopping, and tourist attractions, injecting more cash into the regional economy.

But not all ports were created equal, and a port's ability to enter the cruise business was influenced by several important factors related to geographic location. First, ports located in the middle of the coast could not offer short, round-trip itineraries to exotic foreign destinations such as Mexico, Canada, and the Caribbean because sailing times were too long. The U.S. Passenger Services Act of 1886, an arcane federal law that prohibited foreign-flagged passenger vessels from calling at two U.S. ports consecutively, further limited itineraries from these ports. Finally, climate determines a port's potential as a homeport, a seasonal home-port, or merely a port of call. For these reasons, southern ports, and particularly those on the South Atlantic and Gulf coasts, were best positioned to make cruising a major year-round business and a dependable source of revenues.

These constraints affected the four ports in different ways. First, while San Diego was only a day's sail from Mexico, Mexican itineraries were some of the oldest and least popular, so the potential for growth in San Diego's cruise business remained limited, although in 2003 these itineraries began to regain their popularity as cruising was on the rise. San Francisco was a two-day sail from either Mexico or Canada, and its only viable itineraries were longer, two-week return trips or one-week, one-way sails to or from Alaska via Canada. Like San Francisco, Philadelphia was too far away for short southern itineraries, although it developed a heritage trail itinerary that traveled up the east coast to call on ports in Canada. Following the events of 11 September 2001, San Francisco and Philadelphia both benefited from their locations at the centers of huge population areas as the "drive-to" market picked up dramatically while cruisers became fearful of "fly-to" cruise packages. But the drive-to market continued to prove lucrative well after 2001, and all four ports saw their passenger numbers grow as cruise lines created new itineraries and repositioned their boats to these and other large population centers. Finally, southern ports could serve as year-round homeports, whereas ports in the north, such as San Francisco and Philadelphia, could offer only seasonal cruising.

Cruise consultant Richard Gehring concluded that to be competitive a port must have a combination of "a great port and city, great airport

TABLE 2. PORT ACTIVITIES ON THE DIVERSIFIED WATERFRONT

Activity	Examples
Traditional maritime	Cargo (bulk, break-bulk, niche, container, etc.), ship building/ship repair, ship services, commercial fishing
Traditional non-maritime	Toll crossings, airports, commuter rail lines, other transportation services, related public safety functions
Nontraditional maritime	Cruise ships, harbor tours and dinner cruises, marinas and recreational boating, yacht and mega-yacht repair and services, water quality and habitat restoration
New nonmaritime	Commercial real estate development (new and adaptive reuse) including residential, office, retail, and mixed-use projects; tourism attractions including convention centers, ballparks, arenas, stadiums, hotels, aquariums, museums, entertainment complexes, heritage ships, and waterfront light-rail lines; public access including parks and public art

Source: Peter H. Brown and Peter V. Hall, "Ports and Waterfronts," in *Infrastructure Planning and Finance: A Guide for Local Officials,* ed. Vicki Elmer and Adam Liegland (Point Arena, Calif.: Solano Press, forthcoming).

and airlift capabilities, great tourist destinations and cruise itineraries, and a strong population center that will provide a drive-to market." All four ports succeeded in expanding their cruise businesses, but Tampa was best positioned geographically to take advantage of this growing market. Within a day's sail of both the western Caribbean and Mexico, Tampa was able to offer dozens of itineraries from four days and up, and it hoped to offer Cuban itineraries when relations were restored between Cuba and the United States. Tampa also benefited from its early strategy of becoming not only a cruise port but also a waterfront destination. By developing its own attractions and marketing others in the region, including Busch Gardens and Disney World, Tampa established itself as both a homeport and a minor destination city for cruiser-tourists.[10]

Real estate development proved to be the most lucrative business line that the four ports engaged in, although its nonmaritime character often led to controversy. Each port attempted to aggressively redeploy underutilized waterfront property in support of economic development projects that promised new revenues. They sought to stimulate waterfront redevelopment by inviting private developers to submit proposals for projects conceived at the schematic level by the port. Tampa and San Francisco actively solicited proposals for projects that would serve as component pieces of comprehensive plans, but all four ports were also open to unsolicited proposals and all considered a wide variety of projects that represented incremental additions to very general plans. By 2006 each city was able to boast a unique array of waterfront attractions including hotels, convention centers, restaurants, aquariums, museums, retail and entertainment centers, ballparks, arenas, stadiums, commercial office buildings, housing, and supporting parking garages.

With the single exception of the San Diego Convention Center, none of the ports acted directly as developer on a major project, and all assumed only minimal risk by playing the role of landlord. They asked developers to assemble teams, make detailed proposals, and invest their capital, assuming the lion's share of the risk in return for a potentially significant reward. The ports stimulated this investment by financing the infrastructure improvements necessary to create developable parcels. In return, they received rents from ground leases as well as "participation," or percentages from the sales of food, beverages, other retail concessions and hotel rooms. The ports then used these revenues to pay off the debt incurred to finance its infrastructure improvements, develop new projects, and subsidize other loss-making programs and projects.

Public agencies are risk-averse by nature, and, indeed, the four ports kept their investments in these projects to a minimum, declining the opportunity to share in potentially big returns. Some developers thought that the ports missed out more than they should have, but the Port of San Francisco's former finance director, Ben Kutnick, echoed other port officials, citing a combination of public purpose and the port's role as trustee as the primary reasons behind a port's aversion to risk. "Although the port had an important role to play in managing the public process, it was inappropriate for it to fill the role of developer. The port had a large and very tight operating budget, and it could not afford the financial risk and potential negative cash flows that would come with the inevitable down market cycles. Developers are paid to assume this risk and are better able to survive the lean years." This stance served the port's and the public's interest, but risk aversion in combination with a lack of in-house real estate expertise increased the risk to private developers, as ports had difficulty delivering approved parcels on schedule for projects for which there was current market demand. Thus developers faced not only the usual market risk but also approval risk and therefore an increased risk of missing market cycles, all of which created enormous uncertainty.[11]

Yet even when they assumed only a small share of the risk, the new rents generated from formerly idle land resulted in an immediate, substantial, and permanent net increase in revenues for the port. More important, early projects created a snowball effect, stimulating increased private interest and leading to yet more projects and more revenues. The Tampa Port Authority, for example, took a substantial risk and then lost a prime waterfront parcel and had to pay down its loan guaranty following the failure of the Florida Aquarium. But in the bargain it gained a new ship berth that became central to its growing cruise business, and the completion of the aquarium stimulated the private development of a new entertainment complex directly to the south of and adjacent to an existing cruise terminal. The port then promoted these waterfront attractions, luring a major cruise line into adding ships and departures from Tampa. In 2002 it completed a new terminal to the north of the aquarium, and in 2004 it began to consider proposals for a hotel/conference center and new condo towers on sites farther to the north. The port's parking garage, which served the cruise terminals from across Channelside Drive, continued to realize substantial and ever-increasing revenues. By 2004 all 750 spaces in this garage were full on busy days, and the port was drafting plans for the area that included two more garages. In 2005 the Trammell Crow Company, a real estate development firm, signed the United States Post Office to a lease for the first building at Port Ybor, and another private developer was moving ahead on Downtown Channelside, a major condo tower and grocery store project on the 3.5-acre site south of the Channelside Shops. By 2005 the port's greatest challenge had become relocating a handful of healthy maritime businesses from the remaining parcels along Ybor Channel to other sites in the industrial port.

In addition to real estate development, the four ports also engaged in a number of other new non-revenue-generating functions, either in response to pressures from politicians and the public or as required by amendments to their enabling acts. They all financed, developed, operated, and maintained public access spaces, parks, and public art. Tampa and San Diego engaged in environmental activities including the improvement of water quality, environmental preservation, and the restoration of habitats. Finally, local general-purpose governments successfully coerced all four ports into contributing financially to projects such as waterfront light-rail lines, aquariums, and convention centers. Port leaders often supported these risky projects only under pressure because they believed that the cost in lost political capital of not contributing would be more difficult to bear than the actual financial costs.

In just a few years these ports began to innovate, trying to move beyond their original, single-purpose functions of serving the maritime industry with slips, piers, cargo facilities, labor, and maritime services.

Yet the skills required to develop and manage cruise operations, real estate development, and other nonmaritime lines of business are different from those required to manage a cargo operation. So how did the leaders and staff at each port change to engage in these new functions?

New Businesses, New Skills, New Staff

THE NEW DIRECTOR

For many years licensed professionals with maritime experience served as directors at the four ports. Maritime lawyers and civil engineers with harbor engineering experience were most common. Eugene Gartland had been a maritime lawyer in San Francisco, although his personal friendship with Mayor Dianne Feinstein helped him secure the job of port director. Don Nay was a maritime lawyer and an insider at the San Diego Harbor Department, the Port of San Diego's predecessor agency. Nay stayed on with the new organization, and the commission appointed him director when his superior retired. The commission at the Delaware River Port Authority promoted James Kelly from his position as director of the World Trade Division. Ports usually promoted senior port staff to the position of director, although in some cases they appointed a local member of the community who had relevant expertise or a close former association with the port. A typical example is Emmett Lee, a West Point graduate, army officer, and civil engineer who had retired from the Army Corps of Engineers. The Tampa Port Authority hired Lee as deputy director because he had become known by the port Commission and staff and in the region through his harbor improvement work for the Corps. Within two years the commission had promoted Lee to executive director.

In the 1980s, however, ports began to replace directors who had professional and maritime backgrounds with directors who offered a combination of public and private sector experience and a more diverse range of experiences and skills. These new directors had experience working as civil servants for port, transportation, and aviation agencies, but they had also gathered private sector business experience in container sales, cargo marketing, and real estate development. They also had better financial, analytical, and public relations skills than their predecessors.

Larry Killeen is a good example. The Port of San Diego hired Killeen both for his prior experience as port director in Tacoma, where he had expanded that port's container operation, and for his private sector real estate background with Shell Oil Company. The Port of San Francisco hired Michael Huerta for his very relevant experience as the commissioner of the New York City Department of Ports, where one of his primary responsibilities had been to fold his own agency, which owned New York's obsolete maritime facilities, into the city's Economic Development Corporation.

And at the Delaware River Port Authority a different trend emerged, as appointing officials began to choose directors primarily for their political pedigrees and connections, which were more important than technical skills on the politically complicated bistate waterfront. In 1987, New Jersey governor Kean appointed Eugene McCaffrey, an insurance man and former campaign manager, as director. According to McCaffrey, "I had previously succeeded in implementing major changes at another state agency that had been having difficulties, so Kean entrusted me with the task of transforming the port." After spearheading the effort to amend the port's compact, McCaffrey was followed briefly by a highly regarded professional transportation engineer named George Warrington, who later went on to successfully run Amtrak and New Jersey Transit. Warrington, however, lacked the enthusiasm and political skill required to handle the port's bistate commission politics and was soon followed by Paul Drayton. An attorney with experience in transportation policy at the federal level, Drayton had also been chief counsel and head of New Jersey's Authorities Unit under Governor Florio, where he oversaw the activities of thirty-eight public authorities including the port. Drayton had political connections on the Pennsylvania side of the river too, and he used his personal skills to increase esprit de corps among the rank and file. He played touch football with employees, organized meetings with different groups over their coffee breaks, and asked them what kinds of obstacles they faced in getting their jobs done, all in an effort to get the staff to begin seeing themselves as part of a single, larger, and more strategically oriented operation. The trend toward political appointees reached its nadir in 2003 when the New Jersey governor named that state's senate majority leader, John J. Matheussen, as CEO in what became a successful attempt to shift the majority in Trenton by forcing the senator's resignation. Notwithstanding the manner of his appointment, Matheussen's political experience and skill served him well at the port, where he received high marks for his stabilizing leadership during a transitional period as economic development waned and the port began to focus again on its core mission of transportation.[12]

By the 1990s all four ports had replaced directors who had technical expertise in a single profession with directors who offered multiple types of expertise and more diverse backgrounds and skill sets. But to find these uniquely qualified directors, ports had to look beyond their own borders.

Outsiders and Tenure

In the 1980s all four ports began to hire outside directors for two different but interrelated reasons. First, they were seeking leaders with broader experience and specialized skills that their predecessors lacked, and second, they were attempting to shed their parochial images by reaching beyond the usual circles in their search for the very best talent. The first reason is a product of the monopoly characteristic of port authorities. When a port chooses to diversify into new lines of business, the necessary talent often does not exist within the organization or even the region. As a result, all four ports hired new directors from other places who had different combinations of experience in cargo, real estate development, public relations, transportation, and aviation that could not be found locally.

The second reason is in response to external pressure for more accountability. Politicians, the press, and the public began to demand that agencies with responsibilities and duties to the public should be run by the best talent available, not just by an agency bureaucrat who had succeeded only in rising through the ranks. By the late 1980s, the Tampa Port Authority and the Port of San Francisco had responded to these pressures by mounting nationwide searches for new directors. The Delaware River Port Authority and the Port of San Diego followed in 1991 and 1995, respectively. Finally, a powerful private sector trend also may have influenced appointment decisions at port authorities. For, during this same period, many private corporations replaced their CEOs with new, often charismatic leaders from other companies who were expected to transform cultures and bring fresh, new insights and operating styles to staid, stale organizations.

Yet the outsiders faced a different set of challenges. After mixed experiences with two outsiders, the Port of San Diego promoted its newest CEO from within, in part because he had a better understanding of both the organization and the local political context through his long career with the port. In retrospect, his two predecessors had suffered from a lack of both local knowledge and political support, and the port had suffered along with them. Similarly, although the Delaware River Port Authority hired a well-regarded port director from outside the region to run its new port subsidiary, he was unable to master the waterfront's fragmented, bistate political environment. In response to mounting criticism following two nationwide searches that nonetheless ended in the promotion of insiders, the Tampa Port Authority achieved the best of both worlds. In 1998 the Port Commission hired an experienced and skilled outsider—the former deputy director of the port of Houston— who was also a former insider. George Williamson had previously served as the Tampa Port Authority's marketing director and was familiar with both the organization and the local political context. He also had private sector experience in container sales, public sector experience in cruise and cargo marketing, and strong public relations and personal skills. Fluency in five languages including Spanish further enhanced Williamson's value when he represented the port not only within the Gulf region but worldwide. With this diverse background and executive-level administrative experience at two of the largest Gulf ports, Williamson epitomized the new, multitalented port director.

Finally, in the 1980s, all four ports began to experience another new and important trend related to length of tenure for port directors. The four directors who were in place in 1986 served tenures averaging more than thirteen years; however, the eighteen directors who succeeded them served for an average of only three and a half years each. As the ports diversified, their directors had to become ever more skillful, yet their tenures still became shorter as the job changed fundamentally from one that was more akin to a low-visibility, private sector CEO to that of a highly visible leader of a public-serving agency. These new directors served a broader array of competing interests, and as a result, their jobs were now more political and more difficult than ever before. Gone were the days when the port director position was filled by a trained professional with a maritime background who rose up through the ranks, was assured of job security, and quietly led a huge, single-purpose agency while making the vast majority of hiring and contracting decisions with little or no external influence.

A New, "Second Layer" of Staff

Gene McCaffrey found that when he became executive director at the Delaware River Port Authority in 1987 the members of his senior staff "were among the most qualified and skilled technical experts in their professions—rail and bridge engineering—but they were too narrowly focused. The staff was also comprised largely of twenty- to forty-year veterans with a 'this is what we do' attitude, and there were no interconnections between the bridge, train, and economic development groups." McCaffrey realized that in order to successfully transform the port into a regional economic development agency he had to hire a new kind of senior staff with multiple skill sets and broader and more diversified backgrounds. By the time he had left, McCaffrey had "inserted a 'second layer' of staff over the technical experts that was comprised of people with technical expertise as well as entrepreneurial vision and drive; business, financial, and marketing skills; and interpersonal and management skills." Leaders at the Tampa Port Authority described a similar type of change, claiming that the type of senior staff that were working at the port in the 2000s would be marketable in any industry, whereas the people they had ten to fifteen years before were civil servants who could survive in a bureaucratic setting but would fail in the private sector and other industries. Similar transformations at the senior staff level took place at the ports of San Francisco and San Diego.[13]

The balance of the work force changed more slowly, though. Some port executives claimed that their work forces were less bureaucratic than they used to be and less bureaucratic than other units of government. In Tampa, port leaders argued that their employees had become more self-selecting and knew that they were working for a more entrepreneurial type of organization, that expectations were higher, and that nonperformers did not last. Similarly, Paul Drayton tried to convince workers at the Delaware River Port Authority that they should see themselves as part of a larger enterprise. But there were limits: when Drayton attempted to improve customer service by requiring unionized toll takers to say "thank you," the union filed suit and the courts ruled against him. Similarly, unionized maintenance staff at the Port of San Francisco nursed a long-held distrust of the administrators, who they referred to as "those people at Pier 1." Despite the hiring of more senior staff with broader professional backgrounds, the large share of the work force at all four ports remained unionized police officers, construction tradesmen, maintenance staff, and at the Delaware River Port Authority, train engineers and toll collectors.

Changing Operating Styles and New Images

PAPER ORGANIZATIONS

As the four ports developed new strategies and diversified into new lines of business, they also began to transform their organizational structures and corporate appearances. Until the mid-1980s the four port agencies were still government-like and structured around functional departments that served maritime users and industries. Hence, a director led the port with the assistance of key senior staff including the deputy port director in charge of maritime operations and a chief harbor engineer.

But in the late 1980s, each of the ports began to make changes that were both function-driven and symbolic, starting with position titles. First, each port changed the title of its head staff position from *port director* to *executive director,* suggesting a more diversified yet still public-serving organization. The *executive director* soon became the *chief executive officer,* and by 2003, CEOs led the Delaware River Port Authority and the Port of San Diego, and a port director and CEO led the Tampa Port

Authority. Through three reorganizations between 2000 and 2002, the Port of San Diego made the most complete transformation in appearance from public agency to private sector corporation. While terms such as *maritime, facilities and maintenance,* and *real estate* remained in titles at middle-management levels, by 2002 the agency was being led by a senior staff comprising chief executive officer, chief operating officer, and chief financial officer.

As titles changed so did internal structures, as new directors at all four ports regularly redrew organizational charts in an effort to emphasize new and different priorities and put their own individual stamps on their agencies. Following the advice of management consultants, Michael Huerta flipped the Port of San Francisco's organizational structure on its side, abolishing function-based departments and replacing them with two major client-serving departments that were comprised of pieces of the former functional departments. Under this structure, the cargo services department served cargo, shipbuilding, and other maritime companies, while the tenant services department served restaurants at Fisherman's Wharf and other nonindustrial tenants. This structure was designed to provide a complete range of tailored services to each user group, including sales, marketing, leasing, inspections, permitting, engineering, and maintenance. Symbolically, Huerta's structure was the first to recognize the importance to the port of its long-neglected nonmaritime tenants.

When Dennis Bouey became port director in San Francisco, he undid Huerta's organization, changing it back to a functional department structure and eliminating the maritime department completely. Contrary to popular opinion at the time, Bouey believed that maritime was essentially dead and that the future of the port was as a real estate operation. Bouey's change angered maritime interests, and when Doug Wong took over as director in 1996 he reinstated the maritime department. The other three ports had very similar experiences, as new directors regularly changed organizational charts and added, combined, and eliminated departments.

Over time the ports allowed their maritime departments to decline in number of employees and in relative importance, although they remained influential for historical and political reasons. At the same time, real estate departments that were previously staffed by "one guy with a filing cabinet full of old leases," as Richard Gehring in Tampa recalled, grew as new and different types of land uses created a need for both greater expertise and more staff. Planning did not even exist as a discipline at any of the ports until the mid-1980s, but as the role of public participation in projects grew, so did the amount of time and effort required to manage the process. In response, all four ports created new planning departments, but they also came to rely increasingly on a range of consultants to provide specialized expertise and additional capacity. These departments continued to grow, and while there was only one planner and two property managers on staff at the Port of San Francisco in 1987, for example, by 2001 the staff of the real estate and planning and development departments numbered thirty-five.[14]

All four ports also added public-, media-, and governmental-relations departments and positions, as well as communications, publications, and marketing functions. The growing role of public relations was the result of the port's increased profile as it became involved in projects that affected the public directly. New cranes on the industrial waterfront attracted little attention in the 1960s and 1970s, but beginning in the 1980s proposals for new high-rise hotels and condos that threatened to block the views of nearby residents did. All four ports began to buttress their CEOs by hiring dedicated spokespersons to better represent their agencies to the public and the media and by creating new marketing and publications departments. In the past, ports published dry annual reports that matched the appearance and quality of those of the steamship lines with which they did business. But by the 1990s all four agencies had started to reshape the public's image of the port with a wide variety of glossy, image-rich printed and electronic materials, banners, signage, events, and programs. These campaigns were targeted at a broad range of audiences in an effort to explain the services, programs, and facilities that the port provided to its users and to the public. Several ports also transformed governmental relations from an unofficial duty of the port director into an official department led by a senior staff person. At the local and state levels ports increasingly sought financial assistance and land grants while fending off the claims of municipalities to port revenues and surpluses. Ports also sought capital grants at the federal level through the Army Corps of Engineers for dredging projects that were necessary to maintain water depths in shipping channels and at cargo and cruise ship berths. And, after the events of 11 September 2001, all ports sought grants to cover the capital and operating costs of infrastructure improvements and increases in security personnel required by the unfunded mandates of the Homeland Security and Maritime Transportation acts of 2002.

Finally, all four ports increasingly relied on a wide variety of outside consultants to supplement their in-house capabilities. Like their private sector peers, in the beginning they hired management consultants to help draft initial performance audits, strategic business plans, and reorganization plans because the ports lacked the in-house expertise needed to envision future opportunities and implement the changes necessary to achieve them. As maritime operations the ports had little in-house experience in planning and real estate development, so they also hired outside planners, architects, and designers to create new land-use plans and new visions for the waterfront. In addition, ports hired public relations firms that used surveys and other methods to gather opinions and impressions of the port from tenants, users, and the public, while graphic designers helped to create new images of the port as an organization, a place to be, and an experience.

NEW BUSINESS PRACTICES

Along with changes to organization and image came financial restructuring. All four ports sought to improve business practices in an effort to increase revenues from existing and new operations, reduce costs, and earn a better return on their capital investments. The Port of San Francisco and the Tampa Port Authority both increased revenues by doing a better job of estimating the value of property and increasing historically low rents to market levels. After years of allowing many tenants to remain in arrears for months at a time, the Port of San Francisco overhauled its accounting system and collection methods, which in turn led to increased revenues and improved cash flow. And in the face of political and labor opposition both the Port of San Francisco and the Delaware River Port Authority reduced payroll by trimming their work forces to reflect the realities of financial pressures, reduced workloads, and new labor-saving technologies. Yet even when the financial advantages were obvious, such changes were difficult. The Delaware River Port Authority was the last major toll-crossing authority in the northeast corridor to switch from two-way to one-way tolls, a change that eliminated half of its patronage toll collectors. Soon after, even more toll collectors were eliminated when the agency implemented the E-Z Pass electronic toll system.

In response to scrutiny from politicians, the press, and the public, all four ports adopted more transparent consultant-, developer-, and contractor-selection processes. These new processes were designed to ensure that the port obtained the best prices for services and projects, and in some cases the best combination of price and quality. However, politicians, commissioners, and staff continued to influence selection processes for individual projects at all four ports, often resulting in poor decisions. The staff at the Port of San Francisco led a very transparent and thorough public selection process that used technical rankings to identify the best-qualified and best-capitalized developers for two major projects on the waterfront. But Mayor Willie Brown coerced the Port Commission into selecting different developers with whom he had personal connections but who were less qualified and less well capitalized.

After years of struggles, both projects failed, delaying needed rents to the port and the highest quality waterfront possible to the public.

By comparison, beginning in the early 1990s, the Tampa Port Authority took a more hard-nosed business approach to its projects, making it policy to engage only in ventures that offered a return on investment of at least 12 to 15 percent. The port also refused to build facilities without first negotiating long-term leases that guaranteed the rent needed to cover its debt service. The port's new Cruise Terminal 3 on Ybor Channel, for example, was only built after one of the major cruise lines signed a long-term lease guaranteeing not only rent on the facility but also a minimum annual passenger throughput. Finally, in the past, the port did not start charging rent until a facility was complete, but on this and subsequent projects it started charging rent the day the deal was struck. This policy provided an additional incentive for a tenant to get its facilities built and its operations up and running as soon as possible rather than dragging its heels, while the port was better able to assess how serious the prospective tenant really was.

In a different example of increased business acumen, when the city of Tampa attempted to coerce the Tampa Port Authority into taking over dilapidated municipal marinas, the port balked, anticipating a lose-lose situation and a costly public relations nightmare. The port would have been required to increase slip fees—raising the ire of recreational boaters—in order to cover the huge capital costs of improving the marinas after decades of deferred maintenance by the city. Worse, port leaders anticipated that once the marinas were off their hands, city politicians would side with boaters and publicly oppose the port when it did try to raise fees.

The Port of San Francisco had the most difficulty improving its financial situation, in part because its operations were closely monitored and controlled by the mayor and the city's Board of Supervisors, both of whom sought revenues and contracts while claiming to protect the public's interest from the port's ineptitude. So while Dennis Bouey succeeded in increasing revenues by boosting rents to market levels on a number of waterfront properties, he faced scathing criticism from local politicians when he reduced the port's work force in the face of a tide of red ink. He also came under attack from a grand jury investigation when he pulled the plug on a rail improvement project that would have been almost entirely funded by the federal government but that one study showed would not have increased cargo volume in San Francisco. And Bouey endured yet another barrage of criticism for shutting down one of the port's two container terminals and diverting its cargo to the other, despite the fact that once the switch was completed the terminal that remained open was still operating at only a fraction of its capacity.

The last but perhaps most important aspect of financial restructuring was the matching of unconnected sources and uses of revenues in order to justify a port's project decisions. Until the 1980s, port revenues and expenses were directly related, with revenues from cargo operations financing ongoing cargo operations and reinvestment in cargo facilities. However, legislators forced all four ports to subsidize parks, public art, environmental cleanup, habitat restoration, and other non-revenue-generating projects and programs. In response to these new pressures, some ports sought to justify one type of revenue-generating project as necessary for the support of another, more popular but non-revenue-generating project. A good example is the deal struck between the Port of San Francisco, the Bay Conservation and Development Commission, and the State Lands Commission, which allowed for use of surplus rents from commercial projects for the construction and maintenance of public parks in exchange for the regulatory agencies' loosening their permitting requirements.

Finally, while these ports each benefited from monopoly powers, they were not all created equal when it came to revenue-generating capacity. The Delaware River Port Authority and the Port of San Diego had long been cash cow agencies that amassed enormous reserves and enjoyed good credit ratings and high bonding capacities because they charged for price-inelastic monopolistic services such as air travel, bridge tolls, ground rents, and participation. Although they each faced periodic financial crises, they were slower to improve their business practices because they lacked the financial pressure and therefore the discipline. A 2002 audit found that the Port of San Diego was wasting public resources by using noncompetitive selection methods when choosing contractors and developers and by charging below-market ground rents to several developers. Because it had long benefited from a huge and dependable revenue stream driven by monopolistic rents and participation, the port never had a strong financial incentive to negotiate aggressively on contracts and rents, other than for abstract public purpose reasons. Similarly, from 1993 to 2004, the Delaware River Port Authority acted more like a grant-making foundation than a transportation operation, allocating funds derived from excess toll revenues to sometimes dubious projects on both sides of the river based on limited due diligence and minimal expectations for repayment of loans and return on investment.

Conversely, for a variety of reasons, including economic demand, geographic location, and restrictions in federal and state laws and enabling acts, the Tampa Port Authority and the Port of San Francisco faced very real limits to their ability to generate new revenues. As a result, they both became more businesslike and creative when it came to matching revenues with expenses and the funding of new initiatives, while the other two behaved more like monopolies and bureaucratic organizations.

THE IMAGE OF THE PORT

In the days of cargo-driven port authorities, the image of the port was of little importance to anyone other than the executives of the steamship companies that called at the port, who cared only about the quality of facilities; the rates for dockage, wharfage, and labor; and road and rail access to the hinterlands.

But as ports diversified into new lines of business, they changed fundamentally as they began to serve not one but many types of clients and users. As shipping declined, the image of the port as an industrial cargo facility became less important as there were fewer maritime clients, while at the same time other users began to demand recognition and attention. In just twenty years the port's users grew to include nearby residents and workers; tourists; hotel guests; restaurant patrons; visitors to aquariums, museums, and other attractions; park users; recreational boaters; sport fishermen; cruise and ferry passengers; airline passengers; automobile drivers; and rail commuters. And despite this range of new users, steamship lines and ship-service and -repair companies remained, although they were fewer in number. Not surprisingly, the growth in numbers and types of users created a more complex job for ports. According to Lori Musser, the Tampa Port Authority's former manager of public relations, "Because the port means different things to different people and covers such a large and discontinuous area geographically, our biggest challenge has become branding the port."[15]

All four ports sought to develop and project new images through logos, brochures, tourist maps, fact sheets, and more. They retired old corporate seals and graphics displaying industrial maritime imagery, replacing them with new logos that sought to reposition the ports—as agencies, places, and experiences—in subtle but important ways. The Tampa Port Authority replaced its former logo, a boxy line drawing of a cargo ship plowing through the waves, with a sketchy, freehand image of a shiny white cruise ship circling the globe in shades of violet and teal. The Port of San Diego abandoned its corporate seal and adopted a colorful new graphic displaying a series of brightly colored pennants designed to reinforce the port's emphasis on waterfront tourism and recreational boating. And since completing its strategic *Compass Plan* in 2002, the port's published materials have been filled with images of compasses, suggesting new courses and directions.

Ports also integrated slogans and mission or vision statements into marketing materials, public relations programs, and messaging cam-

Figure 7.1. The Tampa Port Authority's old logo. Courtesy Tampa Port Authority.

Figure 7.2. The Tampa Port Authority's new logo. Courtesy Tampa Port Authority.

paigns in order to reinforce both current activities and future aspirations to port users and employees. San Diego promoted itself as the "open port" in attempt to move beyond a long-standing historical reputation as an insider's club with a closed-door operating style. Paul Drayton's idea of "enterprise," conversely, was as much an attempt to convince staff in the previously disconnected bridge and train divisions at the Delaware River Port Authority that they were part of a single organization with goals and purposes that could only be achieved through cooperation.

First adopted by private sector companies, mission and vision state-ments promoted by management consultants and popular business liter-ature proliferated throughout the public sector as well. Port leaders used these tools to state and reinforce agency purposes, goals, and objec-tives. Like the organizations they represented, mission statements were fluid, evolving both subtly and dramatically as different strategies played out in different ways. By 1997 the Delaware River Port Authority had changed the emphasis in its mission statement from "port reunifica-tion" to "regional economic development," and by 2001 the agency had further sharpened the emphasis to "regional tourism."

As previously discussed, all four ports used new position titles as tools for internal reorganization, but they also used them to change their external corporate images as they sought to mirror the organizational structures and titles of the executives and companies with which they did business. So while the deputy port director in charge of maritime operations once met with the vice president of maritime operations from the China Ocean Shipping Company, it soon became more appro-priate for the port to have a chief executive officer who could meet with the CEOs of a variety of private sector firms including shipping compa-nies, cruise lines, real estate developers, hotel and retail operators, and financial institutions. Port leaders also hoped that new titles and struc-tures would convey a more professional and businesslike image of port operations, recasting the old, bureaucratic, government port in the image of a new and entrepreneurial private sector company. And on a more personal level, new titles served to stroke the egos of senior staff who sought to emulate their private sector counterparts.

Perhaps most important, the four ports successfully transformed the image of the waterfront as a place. In San Francisco, the pivotal event in this transformation was the city's removal of the Embarcadero Freeway following the Loma Prieta earthquake. This led to the city's renovation of the Embarcadero Plaza and the port's subsequent renovations to Pier 1 and the Ferry Building that together initiated the transformation of a separated, dark, industrial wasteland at the foot of Market Street in San Francisco into a bright and cheerful public place. Today the waterfront is integrated with the fabric of the city, and it has expanded to the north and south through the development of new parks and attractions, AT&T Park, and the Mission Bay neighborhood. The Tampa Port Authority's decision to build new cruise terminals on Ybor Channel initi-ated the redevelopment of Tampa's waterfront, and by 2004 it was com-mon to see three or more fifteen-story-high, gleaming white cruise ships tried up stem to stern alongside new public attractions, just a short trol-ley ride from the newly redeveloped Ybor City. From 1997 through 2005, the Delaware River Port Authority supported the remarkable transformation occurring on the Camden waterfront, contributing to the replacement of a mile-long strip of vacant industrial buildings with a string of attractions that includes a ballpark, aquarium, performing arts center, park, marina, new housing, and the battleship *New Jersey*. The Port of San Diego's transformation of the waterfront surrounding San Diego Bay was underway the longest, but the addition of public parks, hotels, a ballpark, and light-rail line along the Embarcadero contributed to the rapid rate of new residential construction in the urban core that began in the 1990s. Three of the ports sought to change both the image of the agency and the image of the waterfront by moving out of offices in old, dilapidated, and innocuous buildings virtually unknown to the public into brand new, custom-built, architecturally significant new headquarters buildings on prominent waterfront sites. The Delaware River Port Authority went so far as to hire world-renowned architect Michael Graves to design its new headquarters. Only the Port of San Diego bucked this trend, choosing instead to remain in a bombproof concrete building that once served as the corporate headquarters for Consolidated Aircraft during World War II.

Finally, the ports started taking credit for the financial contributions they made in support of projects, nonprofit organizations, events, and programs. The most remarkable example is the Delaware River Port Authority, which was virtually invisible in 1992 but by 2004 had become the public sector equivalent of a major corporate citizen in the region. It set a new standard among the four ports, seeking equity stakes and naming rights in exchange for its investment capital. Indeed, once the $250 million Kimmel Center for the Performing Arts was completed, patrons of the Philadelphia Orchestra began to buy their tickets at the Delaware River Port Authority box office.

The Diversified Port

All four ports were forced by geographic, political, and economic realities to adapt as organizations, breaking out of old operating styles that served in times past when the port was a thriving, single-purpose maritime operation and becoming more flexible as they diversified into new lines of business. Diversification caused each port to become more like a visionary company as port officials tried a variety of strategies and tactics, discarded those that didn't work, improved those that did, and at the same time clustered their efforts around their primary strategic aims of expanding into nontraditional maritime businesses and real estate development. As the ports diversified, they went outside of their own organizations and often their regions to hire a new type of executive director who combined new skills, a multidisciplinary background, an entrepreneurial bent, and stronger political instincts. The four ports also worked to shed their government images, striving to become ever more private-sector-like in their overall structures and appearances. They changed staff titles, organizational and financial structures, and operating styles while seeking new ways to finance non-revenue-generating programs and projects with the proceeds from other more profitable operations.

Paradoxically, however, as the ports diversified, they became subject to greater scrutiny from politicians and the general public and ever-increasing demands for participation in the areas of neighborhood effects, social equity, and the environment, which in turn reduced their autonomy and limited their ability to innovate and adapt to change. Diversification also led to sustained conflict and a struggle for control over land use, particularly where maritime operations remained a major component of the port's business. The port's lack of skill in real estate development and inability to deliver sites within a reasonable time frame was exacerbated by this struggle, as opportunistic politicians interfered with port projects, often delaying them enough to miss the open windows in the real estate market cycles and ensuring poor market timing and failure.

At the same time, while new executive directors from the outside helped these agencies through their transitions, they faced another set of challenges owing to lack of institutional knowledge and local political support. In the 1980s port directors began to face the worst of both worlds as they sought to implement new, controversial, long-range, capital-intensive waterfront redevelopment programs while facing ever-mounting, short-term political pressures. The shrinking tenures of executive directors also reflected an important shift from the public authority model, which is similar in many ways to the private sector model, where the CEO is in place for many years, toward a public administration model, where executive directors last only a few years. This heightened an existing conflict as the port attempted to engage in new, controversial, long-term programs such as real estate development that promised to take many years or even decades to implement, while its own leadership became increasingly short term and ever changing. As a result, unlike their private sector peers, the ports had greater difficulty implementing stable and long-lasting plans and strategies. These plans fell victim as short-range priorities and the differing skill sets of regularly changing directors dominated each port's shifting agenda. Comprehensive plans to rapidly redevelop the waterfront were implemented more slowly and incrementally.

But just as important, all of these trends—increased conflict stemming from diversification, reduced executive director tenures, and the modification of operating styles in response to constantly increasing public participation—point to another, more fundamental change that occurred during this twenty-year stretch from the early 1980s to the present: the slow move toward a more politically driven and representative type of government and the devolution of the port as an institution.

Chapter 8

Devolution and the End of Autonomy

Autonomy, Leadership, and the Bistate Archetype

The root of public authority, power is autonomy, and the Port Authority of New York and New Jersey has long been the most autonomous and powerful of them all. Academics have studied New York's famous port since its creation in 1921, and port authorities and other types of special purpose governments around the United States and the world have sought to emulate it ever since.

Public authorities benefit from a high degree of autonomy in theory, but how autonomous are they in practice, and how is their autonomy affected when they engage in new functions? How does the character of leadership change as an authority engages in new functions, and how does this in turn affect the overall character of the institution? Much of the knowledge of public authorities is based on the example of the Port Authority of New York and New Jersey, but is this agency representative of all authorities, and if not, how is the understanding of authorities limited by an emphasis on just this one, example? More generally, as authorities engage in new functions, does their institutional character change and if so, what does this mean for port authorities that attempt to implement waterfront redevelopment?

This chapter looks at how autonomy and the power to act diminished at all four ports as they engaged in waterfront redevelopment beginning in the 1980s. Reduced autonomy was the product of a number of forces; while diversification into new business lines opened the ports to increased scrutiny from a wider array of interests, other social and political trends that began to take root in the 1970s played a role, too, forcing them to take into account the demands of more diverse interest groups. With the loss of autonomy, all four ports became more representative and in several cases evolved—or rather devolved—from one type of governmental institution into another.

This trend calls into question the long-held view of the Port Authority of New York and New Jersey as the idealized and archetypal public authority. Comparing a similar bistate port authority—the Delaware

River Port Authority—with the other three ports demonstrates how the bistate authority is fundamentally different in important structural ways and thus more able to remain stable and autonomous through turbulent periods of change. The other three ports, however, remained much more exposed to countervailing political winds that caused them to change dramatically as institutions in only two decades. Indeed, for most authorities, and particularly for those in transition, significant autonomy has never been more than a fleeting and unrealizable ideal. An examination of the theoretical foundations of authority autonomy and the origins and characteristics of New York's famous port will help to illustrate why this is so as we begin to disentangle the authority ideal from the experiences of these four ports beginning in the 1980s.

THE PUBLIC AUTHORITY AND THE IDEAL OF AUTONOMY

Scholars who study public administration rely on two criteria to distinguish the public authority as a subtype of special district government. First, states grant public authorities the power to issue tax-exempt debt, but they do not grant them the power to tax, so authorities must rely solely on revenues from projects to pay down their bonds. Second, appointed boards typically govern public authorities while either elected or appointed boards may govern special district governments.

As public corporations chartered by one or more governments, authorities are permitted to sell tax-exempt debt, are exempted from property taxes, and have the power to establish rates and charges for the services and products that they provide. Authorities are also permitted to establish personnel systems that allow them to avoid the civil service regulations typically required of general-purpose governments. While most authority revenues come from user fees, charges, tolls, and rents, legislatures may also subsidize authorities with tax revenues, grant exemptions, and grant the power to levy property and sales taxes.

But it is the simple definition of a public authority—a special district government that lacks taxing power and is governed by an appointed board—that serves as shorthand for scholars, politicians, and public administrators, because these two characteristics distinguish agencies that are politically autonomous from those that are less so. First, the lack of taxing power provides a form of financial independence by insulating an authority from the voters. Because it is not allowed to sell general obligation bonds backed by tax revenues, it also is not required to go to the ballot box to seek approval from the voters to issue debt. Lack of taxing power further enhances political autonomy because agencies can avoid pressure and influence from politicians and the public that are based on claims of "taxation without representation." Because it does not receive revenues from taxes, an authority must run itself like any other financially self-sustaining business, earning enough revenues to cover operating costs and debt service.

Second, an appointed board is more insulated from short-term political influences and electoral cycles than an elected board. Because appointed directors cannot be easily removed and do not have to satisfy the electorate, they can make decisions that may be unpopular in the short run but that may be good for the residents of the city and the region in the long run. Further, because directors usually serve overlapping terms, an appointed board ensures continuity in governance and agenda over time that four-year electoral cycles do not provide. This quality is particularly important to authorities because they exist primarily to develop and operate major projects that can take many years to build and pay off.

Most important, financial independence and political insulation combine to create a high degree of autonomy for a public authority—a much higher degree than that enjoyed by general-purpose governments and other special districts. Indeed, Walsh observed that authority executives have created a "virtual theology" around corporate-style, revenue-self-sustaining business practices and autonomy from politics as the "twin foundations of their enviable power base."[1]

GOVERNANCE AND ADMINISTRATION

Mitchell describes the governance structure of a public authority as being fairly simple. Typically, "a governor, mayor, or legislative body appoints a governing board composed of three or more citizens to make policy, supervise administrative activities, oversee the issuance of bonds, safeguard the public interest, and keep the public informed through hearings and public notices." These board members usually serve overlapping terms, are not compensated for their work, and cannot be removed until their term expires except in cases of wrongdoing. Both Mitchell and Walsh suggested that citizens are willing to act as uncompensated board members because they are personally interested in the programs and activities of the authority and because of the opportunity to act in a high-level decision-making role on important civic issues without having to run for elected office.[2]

Walsh found that many authority boards throughout the United States were based on the businesslike precedent set by the Port Authority of New York and New Jersey. That port relied on strong leadership by professional businessmen, and from its creation in 1921 through the late 1970s, its board comprised bankers, brokers, insurance men, and other successful businessmen. A 1991 survey of authority boards by Mitchell found that board members still came primarily from business and professional fields, although a broader range of occupations was represented by this time, and the number of government officials in ex officio positions on boards had increased.[3]

But in a 1997 survey of authority directors, Mitchell noticed that ideas of trusteeship had changed and that some board members held multiple views of trusteeship, as they felt responsible not only to the authority but also to other constituencies and interests, such as underrepresented segments of the community and the environment. Mitchell's finding identifies the beginning of a shift away from the port authority precedent and the beginning of a radical change in board politics and behavior that all four port authorities experienced.[4]

Finally, looking at leadership, Walsh determined that the typical executive director of an authority enjoys many of the benefits of a private sector CEO. These include a prestigious position, high salary, substantial influence over the board, access to cheap capital without having to go to venture capitalists or shareholders, and the power to bestow favors such as jobs and contracts and to operate in relative secrecy. She also noticed that technically skilled managers are usually promoted to executive director from within but that, as authorities experience cycles, outsiders are sometimes recruited during periodic times of stress. Executive directors enjoy greater job security than their private sector counterparts because job performance is so difficult to measure and the board is therefore seldom in a position to fire or force an executive director to resign. Rather, a lack of competition combined with virtually assured revenue growth means that an executive director who avoids scandal has tremendous job security and is protected from everything but political upheaval. Mitchell concluded that, because their positions are relatively secure, most directors view authority management as a long-term career. The significant levels of autonomy and stability enjoyed by public authorities is in part a product of how they are structured, governed, and managed, and the first modern authority, the Port Authority of New York and New Jersey, served as the template for all authorities that have been created since.[5]

The Port Authority of New York and New Jersey as Archetypal Public Authority

The states of New York and New Jersey had been in conflict over port operations and state borders since the early nineteenth century as the constant and rapid development of rail networks in the New York City area resulted in incredible rail congestion in the port area surrounding New York Harbor. The lack of any bridges or tunnels to Manhattan complicated matters further, as rail transport stopped at the western edge of the Hudson River, where freight was broken down prior to being shipped across the river on lighters or small freighters.[6]

This conflict reached a boiling point in 1916 when the state of New Jersey filed a formal complaint with the Interstate Commerce Commission, charging that the railroad rates applicable to their territory, because they were equivalent to New York's, unfairly resulted in New Jersey's subsidizing New York's costly terminal operations. In what became known as the New York Harbor Case, the commission denied the New Jersey application in all of its aspects but left the door open for future claims, forcing New York to take the matter seriously. In their final ruling, the commission also offered an analysis that pointed the way toward a cooperative solution to the problem, so Julius Henry Cohen, the brilliant lawyer and counsel for the New York State Chamber of Commerce who had defended New York State in the harbor case, began a study of authorities.[7]

Although there were some examples in the United States, Cohen looked instead to England, where there were more than one thousand successful authorities in operation, including a number of port authorities. Cohen was particularly interested in the Port of London Authority, which became his model for the Port of New York Authority. Bard noted how, facing a unique legal problem as he contemplated a new authority for New York Harbor, Cohen elaborated upon the distinction between "sovereignty" and "jurisdiction" by conceiving of a port authority that was corporate in form, enjoying jurisdiction by compact under two sovereignties. Cohen's study led to the Compact of 1921, which gave the new authority, now the Port Authority of New York and New Jersey, broad powers in the port district, an area described as everything within an approximately twenty-mile radius of the Statue of Liberty.[8]

But Walsh points out that, while Cohen's compact was based on the Port of London Authority, because it was a product of the Progressive Era and reform politics, its attitude toward representation in governance was quite different. The Port of London Authority's commission was comprised of diverse interests including government officials, ship owners, and other private groups, but New York's port eschewed such representation in favor of the businesslike model promoted by the New York Chamber of Commerce. Thus the port's board specifically excluded local machine politicians based on a political strategy that promoted a nonrepresentational and allegedly nonpolitical governing body. Similarly, those industries that were most directly interested in the port were also not represented, specifically airlines, shipping firms, trucking companies, bus lines, and automobile associations. There were numerous bankers on the board, however, despite their interests in bond issues.

This model of governance relied on the proposition that the financial community's confidence in the agency depended on the dominance of corporate-style management and governance because the relationship between money and the board was direct. Over the years this argument was supported by the financial press, which claimed that the port's "A" credit rating from Moody's was due to business leadership on the board.[9]

Walsh found that integral to the effective functioning of the port board was the assumption that businessmen do not represent political viewpoints, that differing opinions have no place in the leadership of an enterprise, and that elected governors should not take a personal interest in authority business. The "socialization" of the new board member was also important as it ensured consensus in the boardroom. Through this process a newcomer became acquainted with rules and operations and accepted the values of the leadership required to sustain unity. These appointment methods served to ensure a stable and unified board and to prevent foes from redirecting the authority's agenda. Walsh concluded that at the Port Authority of New York and New Jersey, the progressive ideal of authority governance—an apolitical board of directors engaged in authority business—had been realized with just two exceptions. First, directors were often quite political, and second, the board had not taken as active a role in administration as was hoped for. Walsh suggested instead that the Port Authority of New York and New Jersey precedent was based on agreement rather than conflict in the boardroom, but she also asked if more debate wouldn't be better, as it would ensure that more diverse interests were represented. Finally, Walsh pointed out that while this type of board has not proven to be as apolitical and disinterested as was hoped for by progressives, its homogeneity created cohesiveness, as board members had many affinities and shared interests.[10]

Walsh also found that the port's executive director played an important leadership role over the years, perhaps more so than originally intended by the authors of the compact. Austin Tobin, in particular, was very skillful at managing the board and coddling individual members to ensure that he had their support and trust and therefore control over the agenda, which the board typically rubber-stamped. The maintenance of these values over a long and stable period depended on both the board's character and the personality and leadership skills of the executive director. Indeed, Tobin's departure after a nearly thirty-year tenure led to turmoil, instability, and a weaker board, as his successors were less skillful at building and maintaining both a strong board and a constituency among its members. Walsh suggested that in the post-Tobin era the agency was unable to withstand steadily mounting criticism that would have been manageable in previous times under more stable leadership.[11]

In a testimony to the strength of the port's governance model, Walsh found that "subsequent attempts by local groups to make port authority direction more dependent on local politics did not prevail against the founders and the principles they had expounded." She concluded that as the first twentieth-century authority, the port served as a precedent and that many authorities throughout the country copied its governance structure over the years. Finally, while there are slight variations to this precedent, by and large governing boards are both remarkably alike and remarkably like the Port Authority of New York and New Jersey.[12]

The Autonomy Myth

THE CREATION OF A PORT AUTHORITY

Despite theories of political insulation and financial independence and the example of the Port Authority of New York and New Jersey model in practice, public authorities do not exist in a vacuum. Rather, like any other unit of government, once created, authorities are subject to a constantly changing variety of external forces that can dramatically affect them over time. These include actions of state legislatures, the requirements of oversight agencies, and pressures from local politicians, the press, and the public.

State legislatures pass the enabling acts that create public authorities, granting them charters that allow them to exist and operate as public corporations. As "creatures" of the state, public authorities, other special district governments, school districts, and general-purpose governments including cities and counties all remain subject to the actions of the legislature. The state has the power to revoke the charter of any subordinate government, and while this is rare, it is not uncommon for legislatures to amend enabling acts, changing the purposes, duties, powers, governance structures, and jurisdictions of subordinate governments, including authorities.

Indeed, legislatures took more than a passing interest in the four port agencies under discussion, regularly amending their enabling acts to cause both minor operational modifications and major changes in purpose and character to all four. The Florida Legislature granted the Tampa Port Authority the power to license and regulate passenger vessels within the port district, opening the door for the port's entry into the cruise business. California legislators added environmental stewardship and improved water quality to the Port of San Diego's original duties and later stripped it of its airport and aviation powers. The Burton

Act transferred control of the Port of San Francisco to the city, and modifications to its powers and duties have since been a product of negotiations between the port, the city, the Bay Conservation and Development
Commission, the State Lands Commission, and the electorate through
Prop H. Finally, although legislators created the Delaware River Port
Authority to build a single bridge, over the years they expanded its powers and responsibilities to include additional bridges, commuter rail service, ferry service, port planning and reunification, and regional
economic development. Legislators also transferred lands to the four
ports, amplified powers related to the acquisition and disposal of property, and increased the sizes of their jurisdictions. Since the mid-1980s
amendments added new and more detailed requirements for strategic
business plans, master plans, and management audits. Others clarified
policies and procedures such as allowable expenses for board members,
maximum limits for no-bid contracts, and procedures for soliciting and
contracting with economically disadvantaged firms.

Taken together, these kinds of changes had the cumulative effect of
reducing both political insulation and financial independence. Increasingly detailed policies and procedures combined with increased oversight made the port's activities more public, leading to increased
scrutiny and creating a higher profile and more government-like
agency. At the same time, requirements to engage in non-revenue-
generating activities had the effect of hamstringing the finances of nontaxing ports by overburdening other viable revenue-generating projects
and programs. But more generally, the number and frequency of such
changes suggest that these agencies never really had great independence from their superior governments. Rather, their leaders watched
powerlessly as autonomy slipped slowly and inexorably through their
fingers.

As demonstrated in Table 3, three of the ports experienced regular
amendments to their enabling legislation, averaging every two to three
years. But while the Delaware River Port Authority's enabling legislation
was amended with some regularity between 1919 and 1952, after the
1952 amendment there were no others for forty years. Between 1935,
when the bistate commission was first recognized by an act of Congress,
and 1992, there were only six amendments, for an average of one every
ten years. We will return to this unusual pattern in the section on bistate
authorities that follows.

EXECUTIVE, LEGISLATIVE, AND JUDICIAL OVERSIGHT

Authorities are also required to adhere to the laws, rules, regulations,
and policies of superior governments and are subject to investigations by

TABLE 3. LEGISLATIVE ENABLING ACTS AND AMENDMENTS

	Tampa Port Authority	Port of San Francisco	Port of San Diego	Delaware River Port Authority	Averages
Creation year (age in 2006)	1945 (61)	1968 (38)	1962 (44)	1919 (87)	(57.5)
Number of legislative acts	31	11	18	8	17
Average years between acts	2.0	3.4	2.4	10.9	4.7
Longest interval (years)	9 years (1963–72)	13 years (1984–97)	9 years (1965–74)	40 years (1952–92)	17.75

Sources: Enabling acts for the four agencies and all subsequent amendments to the acts through 2006.

independent, executive branch attorneys general and auditors general. States grant these officials the power to conduct investigations into the legality of policies and practices and to conduct performance, management, and financial audits on subordinate units of government. The power of an audit, however, often lies not in enforcement through the auditor or other agencies but rather through its use as a political tool by individual politicians and local legislative delegations seeking to strengthen, weaken, or otherwise modify the functions, governance, and operations of an agency. Civil grand juries may independently choose to investigate the operations of ports and, like audits, grand jury reports are used as tools by legislators and politicians seeking to influence the behavior of authorities. Finally, politicians and authorities themselves sometimes ask the courts to interpret enabling legislation as well as the practices of authorities, their commissioners, and their staff.

In 1989 the Tampa Port Authority filed suit in the Florida Supreme Court seeking clarification on its taxing power, and in 1991 a circuit court judge ruled that the port had the power to levy taxes independently without seeking voter approval. In 1990, and in reaction to concerns over taxation without representation raised by this ruling, the Hillsborough County legislative delegation requested a performance and management audit of the port from the Florida state auditor general. The audit was never completed, but legislation that passed in 1991 addressed this issue by changing the Port Commission's composition for the first time since its creation in 1945. The original commission was comprised of five gubernatorial appointees, but the new legislation reduced this number to three and added the mayor of Tampa and one Hillsborough County commissioner as ex officio commissioners. This change both reduced the governor's influence and created a more representative board that would be more sensitive to local city and county interests. In 2005, the Florida Legislature changed the commission's composition again, adding two more gubernatorial appointees to seats specifically dedicated to qualified representatives of the maritime industry, which had been neglected in port decisions. The combination of court rulings and an audit led in turn to legislative amendments that fundamentally changed the port's institutional character. The Tampa Port Authority's adoption of taxes as a permanent, annual revenue source effectively transformed the authority into a less financially independent taxing district, while its new board composition was more representative of city, county, and maritime interests and therefore less politically insulated.

The Port of San Francisco was a frequent target of grand juries and auditors. Four civil grand jury reports and one management audit between

1983 and 1987 alone focused attention on many of the same issues, including poor financial controls and records, poor rent collection practices, large outstanding receivables, inefficient leasing policies that cost the port money, inability to correlate costs with revenues for individual facilities, general underutilization of property, the lack of a prioritized facilities maintenance plan, and the lack of a land-use plan. A 1986 management audit performed by the Board of Supervisors specifically criticized its investment strategies, including plans to invest in new cranes at cargo facilities that were utilized only 5 percent of the time and for which there were no potential new tenants. In April 1987 the port claimed to be strong financially, but the California state auditor general questioned its ability to meet its future bond obligations based on declining cargo projections. Importantly, California assemblyman Art Agnos sat on the Audit Committee at the same time he was running for the office of mayor of San Francisco. Agnos's purpose in initiating the audit was not to investigate the port but rather to embarrass the Feinstein administration during the run up to the election. In the 1990s the political struggle for control of the port and for control over land use planning in response to Prop H became even more overt. A 1992 grand jury investigated the port because the Board of Supervisors had frozen port funds and requests for new positions as a part of a major reorganization. The grand jury found that port management had the prerogative to reorganize as needed to adapt to change and further criticized the Board of Supervisors for interfering in port management, recommending that it immediately release the funds and approve the proposed new positions. Finally, a 1996 grand jury raised new questions about the port's commitment to maritime uses, suggesting that it had actively discouraged the growth of maritime commerce in favor of real estate development by canceling a major rail improvement project and purposely pushing away shipping lines.

The Port of San Diego was the subject of several grand jury investigations and audits, although unlike San Francisco, the emphasis was on questions of representation, accountability, and poor public image. A 1987 grand jury report found that despite proposals to change the port's commission to an all-elected body, an appointed board was likely to better serve the public good. But the report also determined that a negative public perception of the port was pervasive. A 1998 grand jury report found that the public perception issues identified nearly a decade earlier remained despite efforts by the port to improve its image. The report also found that commissioners and staff favored economic development projects over environmental and water quality duties, recommending that the staff and commission reorder their priorities to address these duties. The report explicitly threatened the port, suggesting that if its recommendations were not implemented local legislators should take measures to amend its enabling legislation to create an all-elected commission. Finally, a highly critical audit completed in 2002 determined that the port had failed to protect the public's interests in port-managed resources. The audit found that it had failed to seek competing proposals for three major hotel projects and offered below-market rent to one hotel. The audit also identified conflicts of interest among its employees and determined that it was doing an inadequate job of properly notifying the public of the business items to be considered in closed session.

Private citizens have had an impact on the Port of San Diego in recent years through the court system. Harvey Furgatch, a wealthy retired land developer and former loyal port commissioner sued the port, alleging that it was flouting the state's sunshine law by regularly conducting public business illegally in closed session and that it was illegally giving public resources to a private developer who was building a new ballpark. Similarly, in 2002, Doug Manchester, the developer of four major hotels on San Diego's waterfront, financed an investigation of Port Commissioner David Malcolm after he began to suspect that Malcolm was engaged in conflicts of interest that were negatively affecting his own projects. Manchester's investigation served as the basis for the subsequent civil and criminal cases, and in 2003 the state convicted Malcolm of felony charges. One outcome of these two lawsuits and the recommendations of the 2002 audit was the Port Commission's adoption of a new code of ethics for employees and commissioners.

The Delaware River Port Authority was the subject of only two direct audits between 1980 and 2003, both initiated by the New Jersey attorney general in response to allegations of fraud and conflict of interest, but neither was ever completed. During this same period the Pennsylvania auditor general and the United States General Accounting Office initiated two other audits investigating discrete port-supported projects. And in response to a suit brought by Tom Ridge, the newly elected governor of Pennsylvania, the state supreme court decided that gubernatorial control over the agency was more important than the ideal of board continuity through overlapping terms, giving the governor the power to replace commissioners before their terms had expired. Yet when compared to the other three ports, the Delaware River Port Authority experienced relatively little oversight despite its size and scope of operations. This relative lack of oversight is another subject we will return to when we discuss bistate agencies.

Local Interference and Other Obstacles to Autonomy

But in all four cases, even legal autonomy did not necessarily translate into practical autonomy and the ideal of financial independence was also more complicated. The San Francisco Board of Supervisors assumed the power to review, comment on, and approve the Port of San Francisco's annual operating and capital budgets despite the Burton Act's requirement that the finances of the port be kept separate from those of the city. The board used this power to influence port hiring and spending decisions and to interfere with management. Former port director Michael Huerta "strongly doubted that the board's assumption of budget review power over the port would have held up in court," but because the port is an enterprise agency of the city, it was not clear who would ever bring such a challenge without putting his or her own job at risk. Over the years the board also increased port costs by charging for city departmental services such as police and fire protection, sanitation, and legal services that many port managers claimed it neither received nor needed. Mayor Willie Brown also filled a number of high-salaried executive staff positions at the port with patronage employees, unnecessarily increasing payroll costs while providing little if any value. Finally, a larger political battle between Brown and the Board of Supervisors played out through the port when the board refused to approve a new, high-paid chief of operations position at the port that the mayor sought to create for another patronage employee. The mayor forced the port director to fire his finance director, an eighteen-year veteran of the agency, to open a slot for the new appointee.[13]

Authorities are often characterized as benefiting from monopoly powers and the discretion to set fees, rates, and rents; however, in practice these powers are often subject to a variety of political and legal constraints. State regulatory agencies dictate allowable land uses on the waterfronts at both California ports, for example. These constraints, in addition to those of Prop H and the Bay Conservation and Development Commission, effectively prohibited the Port of San Francisco from redeveloping its property with revenue-generating uses until 1997. In a more positive example, the Tampa Port Authority began to surrender both political autonomy and financial independence in 1989 when it began to use its taxing power. In response, state legislators added ex officio city and county officials to the board in 1991, and in 1993 the port granted the county the power to review and approve the port's budgets and projects. In exchange, the county agreed to back port-issued revenue bonds with its taxing authority, which instantly improved the port's credit rating, increased its bonding capacity, and lowered borrowing costs. And unlike in San Francisco, the county commissioners did not use this power as a tool to interfere with port decisions and operations. The Tampa Port Authority emerged as a more powerful organization than it was when it had more autonomy on paper but little financial strength.

State and local governments regularly pressured ports to provide financial support in the form of operating and capital grants, grants of land, loan guarantees, and preferred rents for projects that were not self-sustaining or that simply did not match the port's purposes or interests. The California Assembly's 1991 attempt to seize the surplus revenues of the state's largest and wealthiest ports for redistribution throughout the state serves as an extreme example. The Port of San Diego and several other ports in the state joined in a lawsuit challenging the legislation, but more important, rating agencies on Wall Street immediately put all California ports on credit watch, signaling the potential downgrading of bond ratings. The legislation never passed, but the mere rumor of it in the late 1980s caused the Port of San Diego to empty its coffers and pay cash for a $200 million convention center just to ensure that its hard-earned reserves were spent within the region and not elsewhere in the state. After the port financed the new convention center, San Diego's mayor tried unsuccessfully to coerce it into financing a new public library, and the city also tried unsuccessfully to pressure it into financing phases two and three of the convention center. In the early 1990s, the city successfully coerced the Port of San Diego into making an operating grant to cover a municipal budget shortfall during a recession; however, subsequent attempts failed. The cities of Tampa and San Diego both coerced their ports into supporting new waterfront light-rail lines, and the city of Tampa pressured its port into supporting a new aquarium that quickly failed. And the city of San Francisco and the five cities surrounding San Diego Bay all attempted over the years to extract increasingly larger operating charges from their ports, claiming that they were not paying their fair share for the municipal services they received.

Finally, both the Port of San Diego and the Delaware River Port Authority faced additional pressures stemming from their multijurisdictional service areas and governance structures because both redistributed revenues according to formulas that were contested by the individual jurisdictions. Approximately 90 percent of the Port of San Diego's revenues were earned on port land in the city of San Diego, and a large share of the remaining 10 percent was earned at the cargo terminals in National City. But for many years these revenues were redistributed among the five cities in different shares, and indeed the city of Imperial Beach would have gone bankrupt several times if not for the port's contributions. Port leaders argued that this structure benefited the bay overall, but politicians from San Diego and National City resented the loss of revenues earned in their jurisdictions and repeatedly called for the abolishment of the port and the return of the tidelands to the individual cities. The formula at the Delaware River Port Authority was simpler, as all revenues were split 50/50 between the states, but in both cases representatives from individual jurisdictions questioned project spending decisions that reflected not the best uses of resources but rather an arbitrary division of the revenue pie.

Despite previous claims that authorities can operate in relative secrecy, this has become increasingly less so in recent years. Most states now have sunshine laws that apply to all units of local government including authorities and special districts. These laws allow governments to conduct certain types of business such as issues pertaining to personnel, litigation, or real estate transactions in closed session, but routine business must be conducted in meetings that are open to the public and with prior announcement of date, time, location, and agenda.

One outcome of sunshine laws in combination with the public's growing interest in large public agencies is that the press has become more aggressive in demanding all types of public records down to and including, for example, expense reports of authority commissioners and staff. Journalists have published these records, sometimes sensationalizing stories about how authorities and other agencies managed—or mismanaged—public resources, but this increased scrutiny also led to changes in port policies and procedures. The combined efforts of reporters from the *St. Petersburg Times* and the *Tampa Tribune* were influential in causing the Tampa Port Authority to draft and make public its policies and procedures regarding the hiring of economically disadvantaged firms. In the wake of the Port of San Diego's conflict of interest scandals and perennial public image concerns, constant pressure from the *San Diego Union Tribune* contributed in part to the Port Commission's adoption in 2002 of a new code of ethics. Similarly, in 2003, news articles and editorials in the *San Francisco Chronicle* about fraud, waste, and the punishment of a whistle-blower at the Port of San Francisco caused the Board of Supervisors to initiate an audit of the port. And in 2003, the *Philadelphia Inquirer* and the University of Pennsylvania jointly sponsored a number of public events including panel discussions, focus groups, and design exercises to provide a venue through which the public could influence the outcome of the latest proposed project at Penn's Landing.

Citizens also took a more active role in attempting to influence port development decisions in the four cities through both direct political pressure and the activities of nonprofit organizations. The effectiveness of neighborhood activism varied from city to city, as there were great differences in age and proximity to the port of nearby neighborhoods. Because San Francisco's neighborhoods were old, dense, and close to the waterfront, the correspondingly rich and mature network of neighborhood interest groups that developed over many years was successful in passing Prop H. Indeed, the process that flowed from Prop H through the Citizen's Advisory Committee gave these groups a formal voice in planning for the first time, but once the plan was completed this voice became institutionalized. Even after the port's open process led to a well-received plan and good development outcomes, the community still didn't trust it, and it soon found itself in the position of having to seek input from community groups on such simple decisions as entering into a lease for a permitted use.

By comparison, the Port of San Diego had no neighbors until the 1990s, but urban residential living began to grow rapidly, and within a decade new neighborhood groups could claim to have influenced the location of a new Hyatt hotel on the waterfront. Like San Francisco, Philadelphia had several old and dense neighborhoods near the waterfront, and the efforts of the University of Pennsylvania and the *Philadelphia Inquirer* led to the creation of a neighborhood coalition, increased interest from the local district councilman, and the mayor's creation of the broad-based Delaware Waterfront Advisory Group in 2006. Finally, the small group of organized and vocal citizens that resided in Tampa's new Channel District struggled to become a major influence in port land-use decisions. In 2003, the city officially took interest in this new neighborhood by recognizing it as a community development area and guarantying infrastructure improvements through the creation of a new tax increment financing district.

By the 1980s all four ports were in a state of constant change, responding to a combination of legislative changes, superior government oversight, and pressure from the media and the public. Over just two decades, these forces had dramatic effects as autonomy eroded and each port began to devolve, changing slowly into a more representative type of government institution. One of the most important effects of this change was the diversification and activation of the board.

Shifting Winds of Governance

THE NEW, DIVERSIFIED, ACTIVIST BOARD

Between 1962 and 1990 only two females and one nonwhite male served on the San Diego Port Commission. San Diego journalist Dana Wilkie recalled that "there was a time when the port commission mattered mostly to developers who were getting rich off the waterfront, and one didn't see housewives or Sierra Club-ers appealing to commissioners who looked and behaved like some corporate board of directors." However, according to Wilkie, as people came to realize that the port controlled a valuable public asset, "the faces at commission hearings started to change. With the wealthy and well-connected came black men who wanted port contracts, environmentalists who wanted a clean harbor, officeholders who wanted their cities to share port wealth, and citizens who wanted to see their bay beyond the high-rises."[14]

As in San Diego, middle-aged white businessmen and professionals dominated the other three agencies for many years, but in the 1980s the composition of all four boards began to change in several important ways. The ports each trumpeted the appointment of their first female and minority commission members and continued to promote the growing diversity of their commissions.

Another trend was the emergence of a new, more politicized type of board member who viewed a seat on the commission as a stepping-stone to higher political office. This was most noticeable in San Diego, beginning with Maureen O'Connor, who after serving on the Port Commission was elected mayor of San Diego in 1984. Other commissioners have since run for elective office in San Diego, and both the port's 2003 commission secretary, Peter Q. Davis, and San Diego county commissioner and former port commissioner Ron Roberts ran for mayor in 2004 and again in 2006.

Port commissions also added representatives of neighborhoods as well as other communities and constituencies. San Francisco in particular had a history of including commissioners who also served on the boards of local neighborhood groups and other nonprofits interested in limiting development, increasing public access, and preserving the environment. And while the progressive ideal explicitly eschewed labor representatives in favor of businessmen, local union leaders held two of the five seats on the San Francisco Port Commission during Willie Brown's administration, and labor also enjoyed a constant presence on the Delaware River Port Authority Board.

Representation also increased through the addition of ex officio directors to several boards. The purpose of the 1991 legislation adding the Tampa mayor and one county commissioner to the Port Commission was to increase representation and improve relations between the port and the city and county. But former Tampa mayor Sandy Freedman, who also served on the Port Commission, found that "ex officio commissioners are subject to countervailing political pressures." Freedman herself "pushed for the aquarium," and she believed that her successor, Mayor Dick Greco, "favored Ybor City, his administration's primary urban redevelopment initiative, impeding the development of the Channelside Shops project to the detriment of the port." Greco's administration also spearheaded the development of the new waterfront trolley line that connected Channelside and Ybor City and for which the city pressured the port into providing operating grants. At the Delaware River Port Authority, the New Jersey governor appoints all eight New Jersey commissioners, but the Pennsylvania governor appoints only six. The

TABLE 4. BOARD DIVERSITY

	Tampa Port Authority	Port of San Francisco	Port of San Diego	Delaware River Port Authority	Total Avg. (%)	% of Total
White male	4	1	4	9	18	55
Minority male	1	1	2	4	8	24
White female	1	1	—	1	3	9
Minority female	1	1	1	1	4	12
Total	7	4*	7	15*	33	100
% diversity	43	75	43	40	45	—

Sources: 2007 port websites, accessed 9 May 2007; interviews.

*One seat vacant.

remaining two seats are filled ex officio by two elected state officials, the auditor general and the treasurer. Throughout the 1990s these two directors and their alternates, particularly Senator Vincent Fumo, succeeded in dividing the board and reducing the influence of the governor over it. By the end of the decade a unified New Jersey delegation had successfully concentrated its spending on the Camden waterfront while Pennsylvania's fragmented delegation divvied up the pot and dispersed its spending throughout the region to less effect.[15]

WHOSE BOARD? WHOSE INTERESTS?

The combination of increased diversity, politicization, and representation on the board fundamentally altered the character of the board as a governing body when compared with the Port Authority of New York and New Jersey model. First, in addition to reputation and success in business, qualities such as gender, race, and affiliations with other interest groups were also considered when commissioners were being recruited. Second, boards of the past were not as apolitical and disinterested as was ideally hoped for, but they were more cohesive and less fragmented because the commissioners generally had more affinities and common interests.

As commissions started to become more diverse in the 1980s, however, those who expressed loyalty to other groups in addition to the port were more likely to promote different, individualized agendas. Some commissioners sought to ensure that members of the minority communities they represented won more port contracts while others advocated for limiting development and spending on non-revenue-generating projects such as parks, public art, and the environment. Political careerists used their positions on the board as a platform for attracting public attention and preparing for a run for office. Their comments, votes, and public pronouncements were skewed toward popular opinion at the moment rather than the long-term interests of the port. In San Diego, port commissioner and mayoral candidate Peter Q. Davis was particularly vocal in expressing contrary views on the port's plans for one waterfront redevelopment project and the future of cargo, garnering an extraordinary amount of press attention in his run-up to the spring 2004 election. In Tampa, ex officio commissioners were torn between competing interests and agendas and did not always act in the port's best interest. And in general, as trustees and fiduciaries of the port, commissioners who acted on behalf of other groups while serving were, in effect, regularly engaged in conflicts of interest both large and small, as their goals were not always in the best interests of the port but rather of some other group or organization altogether.

Not surprisingly, all four ports experienced scandals and conflicts of interest involving commissioners. Traditionally, a board makes policy while the paid administration is responsible for implementing it; however, in all four cases the line between governance and administration moved and became blurrier, with conflicts occurring at this shifting border. Until the 1980s the boards of all four agencies were disengaged from administration, but they also had limited say over policy setting as strong leadership from the executive director and staff-generated reports and proposals shaped the agenda. But like a pendulum swinging to the other extreme, all four commissions began to assume larger roles in both policy setting and implementation. Individual commissioners also involved themselves much more in day-to-day operations, actively negotiating big real estate deals and contracts. Former San Diego port commissioner Frank Urtasun noticed that some commissioners seemed to relish the opportunity to "run with the big dogs and play the part of the 'deal-maker,' a role that they may not have had the opportunity to play in their regular jobs."[16]

A management audit of the Delaware River Port Authority in the early 1990s concluded that individual commissioners were too involved in agency operations, and as a result, the executive director was given greater power and independence. In the wake of David Malcolm's indictment, the Port of San Diego's 2002 commission chair, Steve Cushman, announced publicly that the days of commissioners doing real estate deals were over and that this responsibility would return to the staff. Joseph Valenti, Tampa's former port director, believed that rather than increasing representation, "the primary reason why the Florida Legislature changed the board's composition in 1991 was to rein in a commission that had become too independent, regularly acting against staff recommendations and engaging in activities that were clearly conflicts of interest." Finally, Mayor Willie Brown selected the developers for two major projects on the waterfront by coercing his commissioners into voting against better designed, better funded, and more popular proposals.[17]

In all four cases a more divided and fragmented board comprised of activist commissioners with individual agendas developed an "every-man-for-himself" culture that increased the potential opportunity for self-dealing that, once exposed, led only to embarrassment, increased scrutiny, and distraction for the port. Further, while the amount of board debate clearly increased beginning in the 1980s, it had the effect of fundamentally transforming the character of the board and reducing unity. In fact the debate itself moved from the commission room to a broader public realm as more interests discovered avenues through which to have their voices heard and more directors came to represent

TABLE 5. EXECUTIVE DIRECTOR TENURE

	Tampa Port Authority	Port of San Francisco	Port of San Diego	Delaware River Port Authority
Last long tenure	(1980–90)	(1983–87)	(1966–95)	(1980–88)
Director 1	11*	5	30*	8*
Director 2	5*	1*	3	4
Director 3	3*	3	3	2
Director 4	5	1	5*	9
Director 5	1*	3		4
Director 6	2	8		
Director 7		3		
Average recent tenures (2–7)	3.2	3.2	3.7	4.8

Sources: Press releases, media accounts, and interviews. As of December 2006.
*Insider who was promoted.

multiple interests, which was sometimes in conflict with their responsibilities to the port as trustees and fiduciaries. But the increased diversification and activist tendencies of the four boards also contributed to
another important trend: the politicization of the port director's job.

"IT'S A POLITICAL JOB"

As discussed in the previous chapter, the qualifications of executive
directors at the four ports changed significantly beginning in the 1980s
as the position became both more entrepreneurial and more political.
In 1977 the American Association of Port Authorities began to identify
a new trend as port administrations suffered from unprecedented political attacks and a record number of port directors lost their jobs for political reasons. As illustrated in Table 5, of the eighteen executive directors
that served at the four ports from 1987 to 2006, only four served for
more than four years, as compared with Don Nay, who helmed the Port
of San Diego for nearly thirty years, or Emmett Lee, who led the Tampa
Port Authority for eleven.[18]

Port Commissions also curtailed the powers of executive directors, further reducing their autonomy and freedom to act. Attempts to place
greater controls on San Diego port director Don Nay began in 1981
when the Port Commission created an executive committee of three in
an attempt to wrest control of the agenda from their director. The port's
original enabling legislation gave the executive director the power to
hire his own staff, but legislation passed in 1996 added another constraint, requiring board approval of all executive staff hires. However,

common practice is often equally as important as laws governing author-ity actions. For example, although the Tampa Port Authority Commis-sion grants the executive director discretion in the hiring of executive staff, in practice directors usually seek the informal blessing of the com-mission prior to making important hires. The Delaware River Port Authority broadened the powers of its director in the early 1990s, but in 2003 the pendulum started to swing the other way as the commission modified its bylaws, reducing the executive director's power to let con-tracts and hire staff without commission approval. In 2004 the Port Com-mission tightened its rules for donating money to community groups, reducing the executive director's discretion once again.

Finally, job security is not what it once was either. The port directors in Tampa and San Diego worked under contract to their commissions, and although their positions became more political, their fortunes were not tied directly to individual elected politicians. This is not the case at the other two ports. The Delaware River Port Authority's executive direc-tor is typically replaced when there is a change in administration in Trenton, and in San Francisco, according to former port director Vello Kiisk, "it's a political job and no matter what you do, when the next Mayor comes in, you're out."[19]

As in the case of the Port Authority of New York and New Jersey, board unity based on shared affinities and interests was central to the success of all four of these ports for many years, as was a powerful executive director who led a relatively disengaged board and served a long tenure, preserving the stability of the agency's single-purpose agenda. But in just twenty years these qualities all but vanished at three of the ports as boards diversified and the executive director's position became ever more political. But what really changed at these ports? How could auton-omy have eroded away so quickly after so many years of stability, and why didn't it happen to the same degree at the Delaware River Port Authority?

The Bistate Authority as Outlier

POLITICAL INSULATION, FINANCIAL INDEPENDENCE, AND A UNIQUE FORM OF AUTONOMY

A bistate authority is different from other authorities for two very impor-tant reasons: it is very hard to create, and it is much harder to change once it has been created. A single state legislature usually creates an authority, but as with the Port Authority of New York and New Jersey, it took years of cross-border cooperation to create the Delaware River Port Authority. Once mirror legislation had been drafted and passed by both state houses, it still required the approval of both governors before the United States Congress would give its consent to a compact between the two states and the president of the United States would sign the compact into law. Amending the compact requires the same arduous process. So while legislators amended the enabling acts of the other three ports an average of once every two years or so, they amended the Delaware River Port Authority's enabling act an average of once every five years until 1952, and then only once after that. This last amendment was the product of a costly and concentrated four-year effort on the part of three governors, numerous legislators, and the entire executive staff of the port. And because such an extraordinary effort is required to amend its enabling legislation, the Delaware River Port Authority benefits from an additional, very thick layer of political insulation that other authorities lack.

By comparison, the other three ports were regular subjects of legislation that modified their duties and powers and changed their policies and practices. The differences become even more apparent when the cost in time, money, and political capital of increasing the Delaware River Port Authority's powers in 1992 is compared with California senator Steve Peace's single-handed takeover of San Diego's airport, which took only eleven days to pass through the California Assembly. Nor is this example a regional anomaly. In 2001, Pennsylvania senator John Perzel seized control of the Philadelphia Parking Authority from the city of Philadelphia, and in 2002 he did the same with the Pennsylvania Convention Center Authority. In each case the senator simply added passages to other pieces of legislation that changed the board composition and appointment powers at both agencies. These slight changes had a powerful impact, shifting from a majority of city Democratic appointees to a majority of state Senate and congressional Republican appointees on both boards. Pennsylvania's Republican governor signed both changes into law before Philadelphia mayor John Street was even aware they had been drafted. The fact that single-state authorities are so vulnerable to such political attacks and takeovers makes a mockery of the concept of political insulation.

Sometimes referred to as the region's eight-hundred-pound gorilla, the Delaware River Port Authority was rarely subject to audits, grand jury reports, court decisions, and their use by politicians as levers to force changes in agency policies and practice. Arguably, this lack of critical oversight could have been because the port was more professionally governed and managed. A different explanation, however, is that it was no more professionally run than other ports, but rather it simply fell into oversight cracks between the two states and between the states and the federal government. In the same way that they gave careful consider-

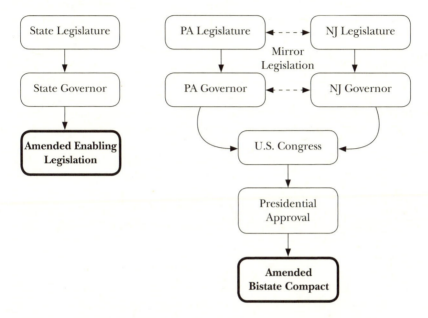

Tampa Port Authority

Port of San Francisco

 Port of San Diego

Delaware River Port Authority

Figure 8.1. Approvals required for the amendment of enabling legislation.
Diagram by Whitney Parks.

ation to an attempt to amend the bistate port's enabling legislation, federal, state, and local politicians might have also decided that the costs of oversight and enforcement were too high for such a large, powerful, and autonomous agency, while hoping at the same time that someone else was watching over it.

One characteristic attributed to public authorities is that they have discretion to set tolls, rates, and charges, but toll increases are actually a very political issue and often fall well outside of the discretion of an agency. At the Delaware River Port Authority the common wisdom is that both governors must agree to a toll increase in the first or second year of their second terms if an increase is to occur. Neither governor is willing to endure the political pressure caused by toll increases in his first term, but a termed-out governor who increases tolls in his second term has influence over the new projects and contracts that will flow from the increased bonding capacity that follows the increase. New Jersey state elections occur one year before those in Pennsylvania. This means there must be two governors tracking together, so that the two governors must agree to raise tolls in the New Jersey governor's sixth year and the Pennsylvania governor's fifth year. Following this informal eight-year cycle, bridge tolls were increased in 1992 when one-way tolls were initiated and PATCO commuter rail fares were increased at the same time. Tolls were increased again in 2000, and in 2007 quiet discussions about an increase in the coming year were beginning to take place on both sides of the river.

Local political pressures influenced the governors on both sides of the river. New Jersey politicians sought to keep both tolls and commuter fares low because their residents used them to commute to their jobs in Philadelphia. Conversely, Philadelphia politicians sought increases because they believed exceptionally low tolls and fares accelerated flight from the city to the New Jersey suburbs because commuting was so cheap. This tension, combined with the constraints of the bistate gubernatorial politics described earlier, led to mortal deadlock, ensuring that tolls and fares would go unchanged for many years, ultimately causing financial stress for the port as costs increased with inflation while revenues remained flat.

But while the Delaware River Port Authority lacked financial independence in the form of discretion to set rates, the balance of power and tension between the two states over tolls ensured a form of stability that did not exist at other authorities that were chartered by a single government and whose behaviors could be more easily modified through simple legislation.

BISTATE GOVERNANCE

Bistate structures also present a different set of challenges and opportunities for governance and administration. One important difference between the Delaware River Port Authority and the other three agencies is that its board is comprised of two equal delegations, one led by the chair and the other by the vice chair, that often act more like two individuals, each representing its delegation and each with equal power.

The resulting dynamic can best be understood by the way in which board meetings play out in public. Sunshine laws require all four agencies to hold their commission meetings in public, but the Delaware River Port Authority's two delegations meet separately and in private in their own dedicated caucus rooms prior to each commission meeting. Most issues within the delegation are usually resolved out of the public's view, and the public meeting serves as a perfunctory event where, in effect, there are only two votes being cast by the two delegations. Further, the unwritten rule that dictates that spending will be split evenly between the two states also encourages the two delegations to support one another's proposals, the only caveat being that neither delegation should attempt a project that could bring embarrassment to the other or to the organization as a whole. Unlike the other three agencies, while factionalism exists on each side of the river, the division of the board into two even delegations results in a remarkably stable form of governance. Indeed, Pennsylvania governor Rendell's dramatic eighteen-month-long shutdown of the commission prompted by New Jersey's resistance to a proposed dredging project serves as an object lesson in how neither state on its own has the power or leverage to seize control of the port. This kind of stability only enhances the tremendous autonomy that the Delaware River Port Authority enjoys by virtue of its being a bistate entity that is more insulated from legislative change and interference from either side of the river.

AN IDIOSYNCRATIC PRECEDENT

There are only a few bistate authorities in the country, and only three port authorities, all of which are in the Northeast: the Port Authority of New York and New Jersey, the Delaware River Port Authority, and the Delaware River and Bay Authority, between New Jersey and Delaware. So why, if they are so rare, has one of them come to serve as the archetypal public authority? As demonstrated earlier, the Delaware River Port Authority and other bistate authorities all benefit from a thicker layer of political insulation that is a product of the high cost of amending their enabling legislation and that shields them from executive, legislative, and judicial oversight and interference. So they are not only rare but also structurally different from other authorities. Further, a commission comprised of two equal delegations ensures that factionalism is dampened within the caucus rooms and out of sight of the public, adding more stable governance to the increased political insulation. The complicated politics of raising tolls has the effect of reducing the port's financial independence somewhat, but the implicit 50/50 spending rule leads to logrolling between the two delegations that actually unifies them and creates a high degree of independence with respect to spending. In short, bistate authorities do operate with a high degree of political autonomy, but many thousands of other, more typical authorities do not. Instead, these authorities are subject to regular modification, interference, and oversight by their sponsoring governments and characterized by a lack of financial independence in terms of both revenue collection and spending policies.

Bistate authorities do enjoy a higher degree of autonomy, and because they do they are more impervious to external influences when they engage in new functions. Unlike other authorities they are also less likely to change dramatically as institutions when they do so. Conversely, it was diversification that eventually exposed the weaknesses inherent in the three single-state port authorities. For while these appeared autonomous for many years, when they expanded into new lines of business the true lack of political insulation and financial independence that was built into their enabling legislation became apparent. An understanding of these differences helps to shed new light on how both bistate and single-jurisdiction authorities evolve as institutions as they engage in new functions. More important, because they evolve in different ways and at different rates, their ability to succeed in new functional areas is based specifically on their type. Thus a bistate authority may be able to engage in new functions with relative ease while the typical authority is subject to many greater and more powerful forces when it attempts to do the same thing.

The Devolution of the Port

Despite prevailing theories of financial autonomy and political insulation, in practice all four authorities were buffeted throughout their individual histories by a variety of external pressures and forces. From legislative amendments designed to modify their powers to audits that politicians used to justify changes in operating practices, none of these agencies was impervious to external political influence. More important, the four authorities were relatively stable and autonomous when they confined themselves to their original purposes, but when they diversified they were subject to greater, often countervailing forces that reduced their autonomy. Because competing units of government, political leaders, and other public and private interests contested their new waterfront redevelopment aspirations, these authorities remained constantly exposed to a greater level of interference and their loss of autonomy became permanent. Politicians, administrators, bureaucrats, and scholars long viewed the public authority as the ideal tool for the implementation of large, costly projects with long time frames such as waterfront redevelopment. But as these four ports attempted to implement waterfront redevelopment in the face of diminishing autonomy, they faced limited chances for success. In two cases legislation formalized this loss of autonomy by changing the port's basic institutional structure, from an authority to a taxing district in Tampa, and to an increasingly representative city enterprise department in San Francisco.

This loss of autonomy also led to a fundamental change in the character of governance and administration. All four commissions became more diverse, more fragmented, and less unified, airing commission debates in public more so than ever before. At the same time, commissions and individual commissioners became less willing to be led passively by a powerful executive director. Many commissioners involved themselves more actively in administration, in some cases crossing the line and engaging in conflicts of interest that only brought increased oversight, scrutiny, and embarrassment to the port while unnecessarily distracting it from its mission.

Despite their increased political skills, executive directors continued to face a much broader and more complicated series of pressures than their predecessors, and as a result, the rate of executive director turnover at all four agencies increased. Gone forever were the mandarins who retained power by virtue of long tenure and Machiavellian-like control over disengaged, consensus- and unity-oriented boards that benefited from shared interests and minimal debate.

Finally, these changes suggest that the Port Authority of New York and New Jersey governance model was never a relevant template for single-state agencies. Board homogeneity, a lack of debate, and a skillful and controlling executive director serving a long tenure may not seem individually important, but the Port Authority of New York and New Jersey required all three for stability. At three of the ports these qualities all vanished. Fragmented boards lacked the unity that comes from the socialization of directors with similar backgrounds and interests, and they were less likely to agree on authority direction and policy over the long term. So when board seats turned over, the direction of the agency was more likely to change than in the past. Consensus over large-scale plans and projects with long time frames disappeared, ensuring a piecemeal rather than comprehensive approach to planning and development. This trend was only exacerbated when the port diversified into many new and often competing lines of business.

The Port Authority of New York and New Jersey has been and will remain for years to come an important source for the study of both authorities and ports, but it is time to place it in a different context by fully recognizing not only how extraordinary but also how idiosyncratic it is. A bistate authority with a congressional compact benefits from a unique structural advantage that ensures political insulation, financial independence, and autonomy. Amending the enabling legislation of a bistate authority requires six major approvals rather than the two required of an authority chartered by one state. The amount of time, capital, and political will required to make an amendment to the legislation of a bistate authority is significantly greater than that required for other authorities, and not surprisingly, it happens very infrequently. So a bistate authority really does have enormous political autonomy in the form of protection from legislative changes and interference, but most other authorities do not. Further, bistate authority governance is characterized by tension between two delegations, but this tension also minimizes public debate and produces stability and a balance of power that other boards lack. In short, the Port Authority of New York and New Jersey's long and largely successful history as an autonomous and businesslike authority was the result of a combination of unique qualities where the whole was greater than the sum of the parts and the linchpin was a bi-state structure.

As these four ports engaged in new and more public-serving lines of business, they became more visible. Politicians, the public, and the press applied greater scrutiny as did legislators who expanded and curtailed their port's powers, duties, and jurisdictions. In response to these pressures they evolved as business organizations, as demonstrated in Chapter 7, but they devolved as institutions, becoming less autonomous, less independent, more representative, and more like a general-purpose government, subject to the pressures of the voters and legislators, in practice if not in legal structure. The autonomy that these ports relied on to implement major waterfront redevelopment programs was, paradoxically, diminished by their diversification into this new line of business, reducing the chances of success. More generally, rather than being autonomous and highly stable institutions, in practice all four of these ports proved to be fluid and ever-changing works in progress that were constantly reacting and adapting to a broad array of internal and external forces and pressures.

Chapter 9
The Price of Diversification

Changing Waterfronts, Changing Organizations, and Changing Institutions

Over a period of just twenty years the ports of Tampa, San Francisco, San Diego, and Philadelphia and Camden were all forced to reevaluate the very purposes for which they were created and to move beyond their past functions as single-purpose industrial maritime and transportation operations. In response, each charted a different course, creating strategies and tactics designed to capitalize on its own unique strengths as it sought to rebuild itself as a business organization and as a government institution while playing a lead role in redeveloping its city's urban waterfront.

But while there are differences among these four stories, common themes emerge. All four waterfronts were faced with the decline of traditional businesses such as cargo and shipbuilding, leading them to search for new and different uses for waterfront property and new sources of revenues to replace lost maritime rents. Ongoing maritime operations and pride in their port city heritage exacerbated conflicts between traditional port users and potential new commercial and public uses. As urban living became more popular and neighborhoods grew and matured next door to ports, citizens and politicians began demanding an ever-increasing role in waterfront land use and development decision-making processes. In all four cities the public sought to increase access to the waterfront and to limit development that obstructed views. The public also increasingly questioned the autonomy of port agencies and their power to control discrete jurisdictions, resorting to grassroots opposition and political processes to blur or erase what many perceived to be arbitrary boundaries in attempts to knit their cities back together and extend the urban fabric to the water's edge.

These forces dramatically changed the four ports as business organizations. Each sought to expand and diversify its revenue base and to redefine the meaning of "maritime use" while at the same time expanding into nonmaritime lines of business. The combination of diversification and increased public scrutiny led to changes in the composition and character of port commissions, the qualifications and backgrounds of commissioners, the qualifications, backgrounds, and tenures of the executive directors and senior staff, and the overall organizational structures of the agencies. The decline in importance of traditional maritime functions relative to new and growing functions and the rise of entirely new departments such as real estate, planning, development, public relations, communications, and governmental relations together changed the shape of the white-collar work force at each agency. Increased pressure to engage in non-income-generating activities such as parks, historic preservation, water quality, habitat restoration, light rail, and public art required the ports to develop more sophisticated financial strategies as they sought to match the costs of these activities with revenues from other lines of business and from new projects and programs. Finally, as their profiles grew throughout these changes, each port was required to redefine itself and craft an entirely new public image that better reflected the increasingly broad and diverse set of interest groups and constituencies that it had come to serve.

These same forces changed the agencies as institutions as well. Politicians, nonprofit citizens groups, the press, local grand juries, superior government budget reviews, state audits, and state and federal legislation forced changes in duties, powers, governance, operations, and finances at all four ports. Further, while legislators may have designed these agencies based on an abstract public authority template, the Port of San Diego and the Delaware River Port Authority were atypical to begin with, and the four ports have since evolved further. Finally, all four port agencies lost both financial independence and political autonomy, and as a result, all but the Delaware River Port Authority effectively evolved into different types of governmental institutions entirely because of these changes.

But if diversification was the only path forward, then what was its price, and what can be learned from the experiences of these four ports? The findings in this book point to ten lessons for port commissioners and administrators, policy makers, politicians, planners and related design professionals, developers, and urban scholars.

Ten Lessons

ONE: STAY CLOSE TO THE WATER

A port has the ability to innovate and successfully enter new lines of business, but there are limits, some of which are beyond its direct control. First, a port's reputation precedes it, and maritime interests, politicians, and the public may not accept the prerogatives of the port when it attempts to engage in activities that seem only distantly related to its original purposes. At the same time resistance from inside the agency and from traditional stakeholders may also prove to be a barrier to innovation and diversification, and it may take years for old cultures, attitudes, and operating styles to change.

Port leaders should therefore think carefully about which new lines of business they will enter, proposing projects and programs that are more closely related to existing activities and that are in keeping with the maritime character of the waterfront. Project choices that represent a logical extension of the port's existing powers and past operations will receive more support from the public while dampening criticism from maritime interests and discouraging incursions from other governments and politicians. As members of the Delaware River Port Authority Commission used to say when discussing programs and projects behind closed doors, "we're ok when we stay close to the river."

But ports must also help politicians and the public better understand the need for a mix of revenue- and non-revenue-generating projects. While the public will demand parks, preservation, and public art, the port will require higher density residential, commercial, and retail development if it is to generate the revenues required to pay for these things. In short, for a port to succeed, it must develop a comprehensive and self-financing program of projects and initiatives that will build on the existing maritime character, which underscores another major challenge.

Two: Face the Structural Financial Problem

Port leaders should recognize that waterfront redevelopment is not a financial panacea that will quickly replace lost revenues from declines in cargo. Even under the best of circumstances individual projects often take years longer to complete than expected, and it will take several decades to completely redevelop an entire waterfront. Ports should therefore not rely on the private sector to finance the infrastructure required for major new redevelopment projects but rather plan to finance improvements incrementally and on a project-by-project basis, at least in the beginning. Only after a few projects have been completed can a port rely on new rents to finance further improvements that will, in turn, stimulate more development.

But more fundamentally, most ports face a serious structural financial problem related to the recapitalization of decayed waterfront infrastructure. When a port has gone decades without the revenues required to keep its piers, pilings, and bulkheads in good condition, the costs of restoring this infrastructure skyrockets beyond the level of infrastructure costs associated with a traditional development project. Some ports solve this problem by bootstrapping themselves, funding the infrastructure for the first few projects and sometimes offering discounted rents to developers who finance a share of it themselves. The rents from each new project represent a net increase in revenues to the port and can be used to help pay for the next project's improvements, while future streams of rents guaranteed by leases will increase the port's cash flow, its credit rating, and its ability to issue debt for yet more improvements.

But the port must be able to dig itself out of this hole first, preferably with its own scarce resources, but more likely with access to general obligation debt through tax revenues, revenue bond debt, grants, and other sources of funds such as tax increment financing. Asking private developers to finance infrastructure improvements in exchange for discounted rent will help to stimulate more development, but this is only a short-term fix because it leaves the port where it was, with inadequate revenues. Only when state and local politicians and the public understand the port's revenue limitations and this structural financial problem will they begin to grant it the latitude it needs to succeed financially as an organization and to effectively implement development on the diversified waterfront. Which leads to the next lesson.

THREE: OPEN UP THE PORT

Port leaders must recognize that the price of diversification is increased scrutiny, which in turn will cause the port to change rapidly, both as a business organization and as a government institution. As the port's new activities affect or become more relevant to a larger and broader set of often conflicting interest groups, political and media pressures will increase. These pressures will force the port to review and modify operating policies and procedures that might have worked previously but that are no longer adequate. Port leaders should expect to respond to more sunshine laws and demands for broader and more open distribution of contracts, commission seats, and patronage jobs. Leaders should also anticipate solicited and unsolicited legislative changes to the port's governance structure, powers, and duties. As the port's profile rises in the eyes of the public, politicians will seek to adjust the port's course, sometimes in ways that are helpful and sometimes in ways that are not. Finally, as politicians and the public challenge the port's prerogatives, port leaders should expect oversight from independent auditors and the courts to increase in proportion to how much the port is perceived to be overreaching its mission and purposes.

Diversification will place the port on the horns of a dilemma between attempting to maintain a measure of power and autonomy and opening itself to input and influence from a broader set of interests. While the first course is alluring, as ports will want to retain independence and the ability to act unfettered for as long as possible, it will also lead to struggles, strife, and mistrust between the port, other governments, local politicians, and the public. More important, in the end, this is a false choice because a diversifying port will be unable to resist the forces of increased scrutiny that will flow from its forays into new, nontraditional activities. But while there will be rough sailing at first, the port stands to develop better relationships with other units of state and local government, politicians, and the public if it exposes its corporate and financial weaknesses while at the same time demonstrating how, with broad support, it can use its own unique powers, skills, and assets to help remake the city. With the right political support and good local relations, some ports will also gain access to needed tax revenues or other sources of funds that are more valuable to the health of the organization than an abstract and idealized autonomy that is likely to diminish anyway. Ultimately, each port must determine how much to open itself up, based on its own unique corporate structure, financial situation, operating conditions, and local political context, but no port will survive diversification without the support and participation of a much broader local constituency.

FOUR: NO MORE COMMISSIONERS DOING DEALS

With the diversification of the port comes activation of the board, a product of the trend toward increased public participation and diversity, the demands of underrepresented groups to earn more opportunities, and the port's involvement in a broader array of activities. Unlike their more unified and stable predecessors, today's activist boards are comprised of more independent-minded commissioners who often see themselves as serving not just the interests of the port but also those of other constituencies such as underrepresented minority groups and neighborhood and environmental groups. Ex officio directors represent other units of government, sometimes contrary to the port's best interests, and some directors view the port as a steppingstone toward higher public office.

But commissioners must always remember that as fiduciaries they are required to act in the best interests of the port first and foremost, not in the interests of other organizations and constituencies. They should stick to making policy and avoid getting involved in operations, clearly articulating port priorities and then allowing the executive director and paid staff to implement them. Only by clearly separating its responsibility as a policy-making body from the day-to-day duties of the staff can the commission ensure that the port's programs will be carried out in a consistent fashion. More important, this clear separation of duties will dramatically reduce the potential for unwanted conflicts of interest that can only cause distraction, embarrassment, and damage to the port's reputation.

Indeed, the activist commission has a positive role to play by increasing the amount and quality of debate on the board and ensuring that more viewpoints are heard and a broader set of interests are represented. But while there will be more debate in the boardroom, there may be less agreement on port priorities, increasing the potential for inefficiencies as some projects and programs rise and fall in importance. Activist commissions and increased debate, however, have also fundamentally changed the job of the executive director.

Five: It's a Political Job

The diversification of the port and the activation of the commission together result in a more politicized organization that can be more difficult to manage than it was in the past. Port directors will face greater challenges building and maintaining relationships with individual commissioners who bring a diverse range of interests and expectations to the port. Those who are hired from outside the agency and the region because they bring new skills and experience will face even greater risks, as they will lack, at least initially, both local support and an understanding of the local political context. As a result, they will also have a harder time guiding the port and exerting control over a commission whose membership and priorities are more fluid than they once were. They may also have to fend off commissioners who attempt to involve themselves in day-to-day operations.

One result is that tenures of port directors will become shorter, and continuity of vision and efficiency in day-to-day operations will be reduced as each new director reorganizes the port's structure and staff and reinterprets strategic plans and goals to reflect his or her own background, skills, and interests. While their predecessors enjoyed great autonomy, stability, and job security and made lifelong careers out of running a single agency, today's port directors must recognize that their job is more akin to that of an appointee in a general-purpose government rather than that of a CEO, despite the increasingly private sector appearance of the port. They must strive more than ever before to build constituencies and support among commissioners and staff within the organization and with state and local politicians, other governments, the maritime community, and the public. Directors who do not balance these multiparty interests are unlikely to last, and even under the best of conditions no director should assume job security for more than a few years. And at a more personal level, because the political side of the position has grown so much in importance, directors must assess where their strengths lie and then back themselves up with capable staff in other areas, as they will find it more challenging than ever to do a good and thorough job of both external relations and internal management.

Job security is related not only to the local political environment and the individual port's appointment process but also to how diversified the port really is and how difficult it is to satisfy all stakeholders at any one time with any single strategic plan or mission. At highly diversified ports, a director with multiple skill sets and experience in some combination of civil engineering, maritime law, real estate development, and the cargo and cruise industries stands the best chance, but even then shifting priorities will be difficult to keep in balance. As the pendulum swings, from cruise to containers to real estate, for example, a port director's strengths may no longer serve him or her as well as they once did. Port directors must accept that their position is no longer a long-term career opportunity with significant autonomy and job security. Rather, their job is a political one; they have been hired at a certain time for certain reasons, and, like their public sector counterparts, they should tailor their goals and objectives to match the reality of a three- to five-year tenure.

Six: Seek Authenticity on the Maritime Waterfront

Waterfronts take decades to redevelop, and most begin, for better or worse, with a rough form of opportunism. Once the early, idealistic, port-created master plan fails to attract investors, a more realistic and opportunistic attitude prevails, typically leading to the development of a large, windowless box on the waterfront. Attracted by significant parcels of cheap land in the urban core, convention centers, aquariums, ballparks, arenas, and other major attractions derive little benefit from their waterfront settings, yet they invariably jump-start investment in the waterfront, leading to better planned and higher quality development over the decades to come.

Ports still stand to benefit from drafting master plans for their urban waterfronts, and the best of these efforts focus on incremental approaches that incorporate existing maritime uses while allowing for flexibility and changes in market demand, technological innovation, design tastes, and consumer fashion over long periods. But the most difficult and challenging task facing port leaders and planners is the development of a cohesive and broadly agreed-upon theme for the waterfront—tourism, residential areas, recreation, commercial development, or more likely some combination—that also accommodates the interests of as many different users as possible. At the same time, planners must remember that the local residents, tourists, and other visitors to the waterfront prefer uses that relate to maritime origins rather than simply the highest revenue-generating proposal available.

Yet despite the best laid plans, waterfronts will develop opportunistically as ports and cities seek sites for marketable projects and the contracts, rents, and taxes that flow from them. But this is not all bad, as market cycles and changing tastes can lead to a more diversified and authentic type of environment on the waterfront. Mega-projects may fail, but over time, a combination of entertainment, office, retail, and housing will develop as market cycles come and go and demand increases or decreases for different real estate products. The outcome will be a place that offers a better urban experience for the broadest possible group of users during the week, on weekends, and around the clock, rather than a tourist bubble that serves only out-of-towners for a few days a week.

SEVEN: PLAN FOR IMPLEMENTATION—AND FOR POLITICS

Integral to the planning process and perhaps even more important is the creation of implementation plans and new systems and processes that will be used by the agency in the selection and development of projects. Planners within ports and other government agencies should seek to remove bureaucratic barriers to development, mitigate external political influences, and create the most efficient and effective developer-selection processes possible within government. For example, for all but the largest projects most politicians are disinclined to challenge detailed technical rankings and recommendations from staff for projects when they are shared publicly and with the media and perceived to be the product of a fair and objective process.

Port planners must ensure that more individual projects of higher quality are initiated when the development window is still open and completed before the market turns down. At the same time, they must resist the urge to push all projects through at once, instead staggering projects. This reduces the risk of overburdening staff, which slows down all projects and causes them to miss the market. It also helps to avoid the problem of putting too many projects on the market at once, risking oversupply. By phasing projects, planners and port leaders can cause more and better individual developments to be completed before other external actors become frustrated with lack of progress and begin to make political incursions that further hamstring the process. In short, planners must do all they can to improve delivery of entitled sites for viable projects on a reasonable schedule if they are to reduce approval risk and ensure that development efforts mesh with market cycles.

EIGHT: WATERFRONT REDEVELOPMENT AS A LABOR OF LOVE

For developers, the risks of getting involved in development projects on waterfront sites are not insignificant, and the rewards are often more modest than those that might flow from other, less complicated work. For while ports have become better at managing waterfront redevelopment, they still are not very skillful when it comes to delivering entitled sites in a reasonable time frame. This is in large part because they no longer have full control over their own land, and they are not always able to resist political incursions that can lead to costly delays or, worse, spell the demise of a project. So developers and their planners and architects must acquaint themselves not only with existing zoning and land-use plans and building codes but also with the whole framework of laws, policies, rules, and regulations that influence development in a city—particularly selection, contracting, and procurement policies. Even more important, because all cities and waterfronts are different, they must become very familiar with the politics of waterfront redevelopment in the specific city they are working in.

When working on waterfront projects, developers run a unique gauntlet of risks. First, projects on waterfront property are subject to potentially high and unpredictable cost shocks stemming from unknown conditions related to the restoration and repair of waterfront infrastructure such as piers, pilings, and bulkheads. On top of hidden costs is increased approval risk resulting from the port's inability to quickly deliver fully approved sites. A long and unpredictable approvals process in turn delays timing to market and increases the risk that a project will miss the market cycle. Finally, major waterfront redevelopment projects, particularly early ones, run the additional risk of coming to market well before their time. The developers of such projects must have a clear-eyed understanding that while theirs may stimulate future development and enrich the developers that follow them after the waterfront has become a recognized destination, in the short run they are taking a bigger risk. For these types of high-risk projects, large developers may indeed stand a better chance of succeeding. But more important, when it comes to the waterfront, the old real estate adage about the importance of location loses its relevance, and the three most important attributes of a project become "timing, timing, and timing."

Waterfront redevelopment is indeed a labor of love, and while there are profits to be realized, developers should only attempt it if they hope to receive rewards beyond the purely financial, for example, the pride of putting an old blighted historic building back into use or creating a new public attraction in a beautiful location. Similarly, ports and local politicians may want to revise their selection criteria to consider developers with both a substantial balance sheet and a track record of taking on—and successfully completing—large, complicated, urban redevelopment projects that require a level of dedication beyond the average strip retail center or speculative office building. Only these developers are likely to have the skilled staff, the interest, and the commitment to deliver a high-quality development despite the risks.

Nine: What Do You Want, What Do I Want, and How Can We Agree?

City officials, civic groups, citizen advisory committees, and individuals would do well to try to understand the unique role their port plays in their city and, specifically, how it is structured corporately, what kind of land it owns or controls, its powers, and its finances. Ports have for many years been viewed as the rich insular agency that refuses to share its largesse with the city, as the arrogant, eight-hundred-pound gorilla that thinks it can do whatever it wants on the public's waterfront, or as the bumbling bureaucracy that cannot seem to make money even as it sits on the most valuable real estate in the city. But these impressions are misleading, as most ports are powerfully constrained in terms of what they can and cannot do, how they are allowed to generate revenues, and how prohibitively costly it is to put their decayed waterfront property back into service.

Indeed, many ports were in severe fiscal distress for decades beginning in the 1960s and 1970s, and some are still facing serious financial hardship. The reason for this chicken and egg dilemma is that ports cannot rent a property to a developer without first improving it at great cost, but they do not have access to the resources needed to improve the property to a level required to turn it into a usable parcel that will generate the rents needed to fund improvements. Because ports typically do not have access to tax revenues, they must engage in activities that will generate revenues from other rents and charges if they are to pay for ongoing operations. They must also earn enough revenues to maintain good credit ratings and the capacity to bond over the costs of capital improvement programs. So as ports begin to open up and try to help cities to better understand their predicament, cities too must begin to move beyond the old reputations, stereotypes, and rhetoric and make a concerted attempt to fully understand the finances of their ports.

Cities can then begin to view their ports as partners and work to understand how the port's powers and limits can be integrated with those of the city and other private and public sector organizations to ensure the best outcome on the waterfront. Officials in some cities will ask whether or not there is still a need for the port, but they must accept that as long as there is maritime activity, even if it is diminished, port authorities created with specific maritime purposes, powers, and land will remain important institutions on the waterfront for decades to come. At the same time, city officials should also understand that attempts to administratively hamstring, politically punish, revenue-raid, asset-strip, or dismantle their ports will only injure the ongoing maritime operations that politicians and the public care so much about and reduce the potential for success in the creation of successful, vibrant, diversified waterfronts.

Finally, politicians will be torn between competing public and private sector interests and their own visions for the waterfront, but they must balance their urge to exert influence and control over their port's plans and projects with their desire to see redevelopment progress on the waterfront. They must also recognize that too much interference will stymie development and limit potential increases in city tax revenues in both the short and the long run. Most important, they should accept that in some cases they might have to give something up—money, power, or contracts—to get something in return.

TEN: ON THE WATERFRONT, THE ONLY CONSTANT IS CHANGE

Changes in trade, technology, and geography have influenced ports, waterfronts, and cities for centuries and will continue to do so into the future. Globalization and population growth, ever-increasing numbers and sizes of ships, and changing attitudes about the best uses for coastal land will combine to influence one another and shape the urban waterfront in important ways.

As trade and the number of ships continue to increase, larger ports will become increasingly congested and secondary ports will begin to exploit new opportunities by developing niche cargo businesses that serve their own growing population centers while also serving as relievers for their larger siblings. This trend will be reinforced through increasing intergovernmental coordination as the federal, state, and city governments and the ports all work together to improve and maximize the efficiency of the multimodal infrastructure systems that connect ports with the hinterlands they serve. Cities such as San Diego, which once thought its days as a port were numbered because of shallow waters, will continue to expand as car transports and other shallow-draft vessels find new uses for them as relief ports. Maritime interests in these and other cities that in the past sounded shrill in their cries to protect scarce port land with deepwater access are already being proven right as the pendulum has started to swing in the other direction and secondary ports that once appeared to have limited futures have started to grow again.

As ship design and manufacturing technologies improve, the size of cargo and cruise ships—length, beam, draft, and air-draft—will continue to grow, with no end in sight. Despite the shorter route offered by the Panama Canal, shipping lines invested in "Post-Panamax" ships that were too big to fit through the canal's existing locks (new, larger locks are in development), with the operating assumption that the cost in time of taking the long way around South America is offset by the efficiencies that come with using a larger boat. Indeed, the most important thing to remember about the maritime industry is that the capital is in the ships—which are moveable—while the landside facilities represent a relatively minor cost that is easily written off and abandoned. In an example of the power of movable capital, the events of 11 September 2001 led the cruise lines to temporarily retask their ships to take advantage of the drive-to markets offered by larger population centers. Some cruise lines later adopted this as a permanent strategy, leading to an expansion in the cruise business at seasonal ports such as Boston, Philadelphia, and Newport News, while new homeports blossomed in Houston, Galveston, New Orleans, and Mobile, serving the population centers of Houston, Birmingham, and Atlanta with western Caribbean itineraries. And should federal legislators ever succumb to the pressures of globalization and modify the Passenger Services Act of 1886, populations and ships would shift from Vancouver to Seattle and from Ensenada to San Diego. Finally, perceptions of security and rising fuel prices will also continue to influence where both cruise ships and cargo ships call in the future.

The value of waterfront property for both maritime and nonmaritime uses will continue to rise at all ports, but as the real estate market cycles up and down every decade or so, incremental redevelopment will continue to be the norm. Real estate trends—such as the commercial office expansion of the 1980s and the residential boom of the mid-2000s—will come and go with these cycles, and over time a mix of residential, commercial, retail, entertainment, and parks will come to populate diversified waterfronts everywhere alongside traditional maritime uses. Ports and maritime businesses will have to continue working with the interests that gained a foothold on the waterfront beginning in the 1970s, collaborating on ways to live side by side with new residents, office workers, tourists, and park users. But at the same time, in the rush to continue redeveloping the waterfront, public officials will no longer be able to dismiss the scarcity of port land and the value of their region's enormous capital investment in its maritime infrastructure over time. A port is a large and complex integration of channels, navigation systems, bridges, land with hardened edge and deepwater access, and road and rail service, and while the urge to place the latest non-water-dependent use on the waterfront may be hard to resist, once it has occurred, this valuable port land and infrastructure cannot easily be replaced.

As the forces of trade, technology, and geography continue to influence one another in fluid ways, ports will continue to gamble on new markets and technologies as they compete regionally, nationally, and internationally for increasing shares of the ever-expanding global trade business. At the same time, port commissions and industrial maritime interests will continue to wrestle over the best use of land and resources, local politicians and other governments will keep trying to influence port plans and projects, private developers will continue to seek new opportunities, and these tensions will ebb and flow along with market cycles.

Finally, Mother Nature herself will continue to shape ports and waterfronts as coastlines shift and channels continue to move and silt up. In an ironic example, the San Francisco Bay Conservation and Development Commission was originally created specifically to preserve and enlarge the size of the bay by fending off inappropriate fill and development activities, but it recently became the region's voice on rising sea levels. For the first time since its creation, the commission is confronting an entirely new and different problem as the bay is beginning to grow—rather than shrink—in size.

Do Authorities Really Matter Anymore?

This book offers new insights into how public authorities as organizations change and evolve as they engage in new functions and new lines of business. It also adds to a growing body of literature that explores the similarities and differences between governance and administration in private and public sector organizations. More important, it calls into question prevailing views of public authorities as financially independent, politically insulated, and highly autonomous government agencies. And while prevailing theories suggest that mature authorities remain relatively stable, this book demonstrates how they devolve over time, becoming more representative of a broader group of interests and changing in character from an authority to a less autonomous form of government.

As they become more visible, public authorities are subject to increasing pressures and controls from legislators, the public, and the media. As a result, they also become more politicized and therefore less autonomous and flexible. For these reasons, an older authority that has already diversified may not be very useful as a potential redevelopment tool. As Mayor Ed Koch of New York City suggested, politicians like authorities because they offer a "path of least resistance" around old general-purpose governments that have become ossified and bureaucratized and are no longer useful for certain types of tasks. Yet as demonstrated in this book, old authorities may become similarly less useful over time, devolving and becoming more like representative general-purpose governments that have difficulty taking on new and different types of tasks. When this happens legislators must either make do with these authorities or create fresh, new ones. But this book also demonstrates that, once created, authorities often take on lives of their own that may be quite different from those originally intended by their makers, casting doubt on the simple notion that whenever we have a problem we can simply create an authority to solve it.

More generally, this book calls into question the value of trying to distinguish between public authorities and other special purpose governments. As these cases demonstrate, the criteria traditionally used to make the distinction are not nearly as black and white in practice as they seem in print. Indeed, rather than considering them a discrete type of government that is distinguished by a handful of key characteristics, the findings in this book suggest that it is not only difficult but also misleading to attempt to differentiate public authorities from other special district governments. These conclusions also suggest that research into the forces that act on existing authorities may also benefit from a shift in viewpoint and that it might be more useful to think in terms of how public authorities change as institutions in response to these forces, sometimes remaining authorities in name only.

Public authorities have for many years captured the minds of urban scholars, but their influence may be diminishing both as an ideal form of government institution and in terms of practical application. If this is so, now may be time to begin refocusing scholarly efforts on developing a new theoretical construct that better reflects the state of special purpose government in the United States today.

Notes

Chapter 1

1. The United States Census Bureau's *Census of Governments* classifies special district governments as "independent, special-purpose governmental units (other than school district governments), that exist as separate entities with substantial administrative and fiscal independence from general-purpose governments." United States Census Bureau, Economics and Statistics Administration, United States Department of Commerce, *2002 Census of Governments: Finances of Special District Governments*, vol. 4, no. 2, *Government Finances* (Washington, D.C.: United States Census Bureau, June 2005), v.

2. United States Census Bureau, Economics and Statistics Administration, United States Department of Commerce, *2002 Census of Governments*, vol. 1, *Government Organization* (Washington, D.C.: United States Census Bureau, December 2002), 6, table 5. Estimating the number of public authorities in existence is problematic. The *Census of Governments* does not distinguish them as a type of special district government, although in the past the *Census* differentiated between taxing and nontaxing special districts. The estimate of authority numbers comes from sources including Gail Radford and Jerry Mitchell and is conservative, particularly when compared with Axelrod's more liberal estimate of more than thirty thousand (Axelrod is surely including all special districts). See Gail Radford, "William Gibbs McAdoo, the Emergency Fleet Corporation, and the Origins of the Public-Authority Model of Government Action," *Journal of Policy History* 11:1 (1999): 59–88, at 59 and 84, n. 1; Jerry Mitchell, "The Policy Activities of Public Authorities," *Policy Studies Journal* 18.4 (Summer 1990): 928–42. For an explication of the difficulties of counting authorities, see Annmarie Hauck Walsh, "Appendix: Statistical Measures of Government Corporations," *The Public's Business: The Politics and Practices of Government Corporations* (Boston: MIT Press, 1978), 353–56.

3. Port Authority of New York and New Jersey, *Comprehensive Annual Financial Report for the Year Ended December 31, 2005* (New York: Port Authority of New York and New Jersey, 2006), 33; Port of Seattle, *Comprehensive Annual Financial Report for the Year Ended December 31, 2005* (Seattle, Wash.: Port of Seattle, 2006), 10; Port of Los Angeles, *Annual Financial Statements, 2005, for the Fiscal Year Ending June 30, 2005* (Los Angeles: Port of Los Angeles, 2005), 13.

4. Michael N. Danielson and Jameson W. Doig, *New York: The Politics of Urban Regional Development* (Berkeley: University of California Press, 1982), 154–62.

5. Commonwealth of Pennsylvania, *Municipal Authorities in Pennsylvania*, 7th ed. (Harrisburg, Pa.: Bureau of Local Government Services, Department of Community Affairs, May 1994), 2.

6. Ibid.

7. Ibid.

8. Ibid., 2–3.

9. Annmarie Hauck Walsh, "Public Authorities and the Shape of Decision Making," in *Urban Politics: New York Style*, ed. Jewel Bellush and Dick Netzer (Armonk, N.Y.: M. E. Sharpe, 1990), 188–219, at 189, 196–97, 213–14; Rina Cutler, Executive Director, Philadelphia Parking Authority, 1994–2000, interview by the author, 17 November 2000, Philadelphia.

10. Walsh, "Public Authorities and the Shape of Decision Making," 189, 196, 212–14.

11. For more detail on these and other examples of authorities expanding the scope of their operations, see Jerry Mitchell, ed., *Public Authorities and Public Policy: The Business of Government* (New York: Greenwood Press, 1992).

12. Brian Hoyle, "Development Dynamics at the Port-City Interface," in *Revitalising the Waterfront: International Dimensions of Dockland Redevelopment*, ed. B. S. Hoyle, D. A. Pinder, and M. S. Husain (London: Bellhaven, 1988), 3–19 at 7–9.

13. Ibid., 9–12.

14. Ibid., 13.

15. Ibid., 14–16.

16. David L. A. Gordon, "Financing Urban Waterfront Redevelopment," *APA Journal* (Spring 1997): 244–65.

17. David L. A. Gordon, "Architecture: How Not to Build a City— Implementation at Battery Park City," *Landscape and Urban Planning* 26 (1993): 35–54.

18. The case-based research begins in the 1970s and is dominated by Annmarie Hauck Walsh, Jameson Doig, Jerry Mitchell, and Donald Axelrod. Erwin Bard, Robert Caro, and Robert Smith have also made important contributions. The case studies represent only a small fraction of the approximately ten thousand authorities that are in operation today, however. Furthermore, because case studies focus on a handful of very large public authorities in the Northeast, primarily in the New York metropolitan area, they do not represent the average authority in the United States. Caro's biographical treatment of Robert Moses and the Triborough Bridge Authority and Bard's account of the Port Authority of New York and New Jersey featured two of the largest, oldest, and most prominent authorities in the country. Indeed, no authority has been studied as thoroughly as the Port Authority of New York and New Jersey. In *Empire on the Hudson* and numerous articles Doig has explored themes of entrepreneurial leadership, technological innovation, and the role of autonomy in the port's success. Walsh described the archetypal governance and administration structure of the port and the proliferation of this structure as a template that many new authorities have since copied. And Smith examined the port's development of the Newark Legal and Communications Center while Deborah Wathan Finn studied its attempts to address the homeless problem in its facilities. Similarly, Peter Hall, Susan Fainstein, Susan Tannenbaum, William Eimicke, David L. A. Gordon, and others have studied the Battery Park City Authority. In addition to the northeastern United States and New York City biases in case research, a bias also persists toward very large port, transportation, and redevelopment authorities, presumably because they are located in big cities and are old, visible, influential, financially significant, and just more interesting. Walsh, *Public's Business*; Jameson W. Doig, *Empire on the Hudson: Entrepreneurial Vision and Political Power at the Port of New York Authority* (New York: Columbia University Press, 2001); Jerry Mitchell, "Policy Functions and Issues for Public Authorities," in *Public Authorities and Public Policy: The Business of Government*, ed. Mitchell, 1–14; Donald Axelrod, *Shadow*

Government: The Hidden World of Public Authorities and How They Control $1 Trillion of Your Money (New York: John Wiley & Sons, 1992); Erwin W. Bard, *The Port of New York Authority* (New York: Columbia University Press, 1942; repr., New York: AMS Press, 1968); Robert A. Caro, *The Power Broker: Robert Moses and the Fall of New York* (New York: Random House, 1975); Robert G. Smith, "The Changing Role of Funding in Authority Policy Implementation," in *Public Authorities and Public Policy: The Business of Government*, ed. Mitchell, 83–95; Deborah Wathan Finn, "Public Authorities and Social Problems: The Port Authority of New York and New Jersey Addresses the Homeless Problem in Its Facilities," in *Public Authorities and Public Policy: The Business of Government*, ed. Mitchell, 129–36; Sir Peter G. Hall, *Cities in Civilization* (New York: Pantheon Books, 1998), 888–931; Susan S. Fainstein, *The City Builders: Property Development in New York and London, 1980–2000*, 2nd ed. rev. (Lawrence: University of Kansas Press, 2001), 160–96; Susan Tannenbaum, "The Progressive Legacy and the Public Corporation: Entrepreneurship and Public Virtue," *Journal of Policy History* 3.3 (1991): 309–30; William B. Eimicke, "Housing New York: The Creation and Development of the Battery Park City Authority," in *Public Authorities and Public Policy: The Business of Government*, ed. Mitchell, 119–27; David L. A. Gordon, *Battery Park City: Politics and Planning on the New York Waterfront* (Amsterdam: Gordon and Breach, 1997).

A different authority case subtype might be called "the great authority disaster." Leigland and Lamb's case study of the Washington Public Power Supply System, also known as WPP$$ or "Whoops," sought to identify the causes of the agency's catastrophic financial collapse by investigating its creation, governance, and administration. Caro's *Power Broker* offered a historical and biographical account of how a hunger for political power ultimately brought down both Robert Moses and the authority he created. Finally, journalist Diane Henriques offered a sensationalized treatment of thirty different authorities in *Machinery of Greed*, which focused on graft, corruption, and mismanagement of authorities. Henriques concluded that the remedy to authority mismanagement is additional controls of the sort that the authority was designed to avoid. Walsh, however, pointed out that no quantitative empirical evidence exists to suggest that public authorities are any more or less corrupt than other units of government and private sector companies. James Leigland and Robert Lamb, *WPP$$: Who Is to Blame for the WPPSS Disaster?* (Cambridge, Mass.: Ballinger, 1986); Caro, *Power Broker*; Diana Henriques, *The Machinery of Greed: Public Authority Abuse and What to Do about It* (Lexington, Mass.: Lexington Books, 1986); Walsh, "Public Authorities and the Shape of Decision Making," 188–219.

19. In a case study of Port Canaveral, Bradley Braun employed economic impact analysis to measure the impact of the port on the surrounding regional economy. Herman Boschken investigated organizational design in a book based on case studies of six West Coast ports competing for cargo trade. Boschken's is the only major study other than the present one that relied on a comparison of case studies of multiple ports. Finally, a survey by Rex Sherman of the American Association of Port Authorities demonstrated that in 2002 only 29 percent of port agencies in the country were based on the public authority model and that these were located primarily in the Northeast. Another 43 percent of ports were special districts, and the rest were other types of agencies. Thus the emphasis in research on the Port Authority of New York and New Jersey also distorts the understanding of port agencies throughout the country by concentrating on a type that is less common and prevalent only in the Northeast. Bradley Braun,

"Economic Benefits of Public Authorities: An Impact Analysis of Florida's Port Canaveral," in *Public Authorities and Public Policy: The Business of Government*, ed. Mitchell, 155–66; Herman L. Boschken, *Strategic Design and Organizational Change* (Tuscaloosa: University of Alabama Press, 1988); Rexford B. Sherman, *Public Seaport Agencies in the United States and Canada* (Alexandria, Va.: American Association of Port Authorities, 2000).

20. Edited collections by Brian Hoyle and Mark Hershman took a geographer's view in examining the spatial, technological, and economic forces underlying the decline of cargo and the rise of waterfront redevelopment. Together, Peter Hall's study of the London Docklands Development Corporation and Susan Fainstein's study of the London Docklands Development Corporation and the Battery Park City Authority offered a perspective on the politics of public-private urban redevelopment in the new global economy. And finally, David Gordon considered these two examples plus those of Toronto and Boston in a series of articles that offered the only comprehensive study to date of the challenges associated with implementing waterfront redevelopment in terms of politics, design, and finances. Brian Hoyle, D. A. Pinder and M. S. Husain, eds., *Revitalising the Waterfront: International Dimensions of Dockland Redevelopment* (London: Bellhaven, 1988); Mark J. Hershman, *Urban Ports and Harbor Management: Responding to Change along U.S. Waterfronts* (New York: Taylor and Francis, 1988); Hall, *Cities in Civilization*; Fainstein, *City Builders*; and Gordon, "Architecture, 35–54; "Managing the Changing Political Environment in Urban Waterfront Redevelopment," *Urban Studies* 34:1 (1997): 61–83; "Financing Urban Waterfront Redevelopment," 244–65; and *Battery Park City*.

Finally, there has been an increase in another type of book targeted toward architects, planners, and real estate developers that consolidates short, concise, image-rich case studies of numerous waterfronts around the world. See, for example, Urban Land Institute (ULI), *Remaking the Urban Waterfront* (Washington, D.C.: ULI, 2004); Ann Breen and Dick Rigby, *The New Waterfront: A Worldwide Urban Success Story* (New York: McGraw-Hill, 1996); and Ann Breen and Dick Rigby, *Urban Waterfronts: Cities Reclaim Their Edge* (New York: McGraw-Hill, 1994).

21. With the exception of Gordon's treatment of the redevelopment of the Charlestown Navy Yard by the Boston Redevelopment Authority, the emphasis has been on redevelopment agencies created specifically for the task. There have been no case studies of waterfront redevelopment by port authorities. Furthermore, as in the study of ports, there remains a bias toward very large, significant waterfronts in world cities as well as waterfronts where redevelopment is complete or nearly so. There have been few studies of how smaller cities redevelop their waterfronts despite the fact that in the postmodern era tourism has become a common form of economic development and nearly every city with any body of water in its urban core has sought to redevelop its waterfront. Finally, because of the emphasis on world cities such as London, Boston, New York, and Toronto, all of which have generally grown economically during the past half-century, there have been few studies of waterfront redevelopment in cities with economies that grew more slowly or that contracted.

22. Dennis R. Judd, "Constructing the Tourist Bubble," in *The Tourist City*, ed. Dennis R. Judd and Susan S. Fainstein (New Haven: Yale University Press, 1999), 35–53, at 39; Bernard J. Frieden and Lynne B. Sagalyn, *Downtown, Inc.: How America Rebuilds Cities* (Cambridge, Mass.: MIT Press, 1989), 259–60.

Chapter 2

1. Emmett Lee, port director, Tampa Port Authority, 1980–90, interview by author, 4 March 2003, Tampa, Fla.

2. Ibid.

3. Ibid.; Joseph Garcia, former director and board chair, Tampa Port Authority, 1983–90, 1993–2000, interview by author, 3 March 2003, Tampa, Fla.

4. Emmett Lee interview; Cooper Carry & Associates and Prime Interests, *Garrison Seaport Center: The Seaport District Plan, for the Tampa Port Authority* (Tampa, Fla.: Prime Interests, 1 June 1994), A1 (hereafter cited as *Seaport District Plan*).

5. *Seaport District Plan*, A2; Prime Interests, Inc., and Frederic R. Harris, Inc., *The Strategic Plan Update: Prepared for the Tampa Port Authority* (Tampa, Fla.: Prime Interests, 1 November 1991), Authorization, 1; Richard E. Gehring, principal, Prime Interests, interview by author, 5 March 2003, Tampa, Fla.

6. *Seaport District Plan*, A1.

7. Ibid.; Richard E. Gehring interview.

8. Joseph Garcia interview.

9. Ibid.

10. Charles Towsley, port director, Port of Miami, 1998–2006, managing director, Tampa Port Authority, 1991–98, telephone interview by author, 18 March 2003; Joseph Valenti, port director, Tampa Port Authority, 1990–95, telephone interview by author, 19 February 2003.

11. Tampa Port Authority, *Comprehensive Annual Financial report for Fiscal Year Ended September 30, 2002* (Tampa, Fla.: Tampa Port Authority, 2003); Joseph Garcia, telephone interview by author, 15 March 2007.

12. Arthur R. Savage, president and CEO, A. R. Savage & Son, Inc., interview by author, 4 March 2003, Tampa, Fla.

13. Ibid.

14. Joseph Garcia interview, 15 March 2007.

Chapter 3

1. Mayors Agnos, Jordan, and Brown all asked some version of the same question, although Brown, who promoted himself as "Da Maritime Mayor" during his election campaign, dropped it within his first year in office when he came to better understand the city's maritime future.

2. Agnos described the decision to tear down the Embarcadero Freeway as "the single best decision I made in my entire public career." Agnos also claimed, "I won by only one vote in the Board of Supervisors, which no one remembers today, and no one would support putting it back now." Agnos believes, as do many others, that the earthquake and the demolishing of the Embarcadero Freeway were the most important events to affect the waterfront, "opening it up from Broadway to South Beach, where people are now building million dollar condos next to low-income housing." Art Agnos, mayor of San Francisco, 1987–91, California state assemblyman, 1975–87, telephone interview by author, 1 April 2003.

3. Martha Groves, "San Francisco Port Maps Out Plan for Future economy: The Underused Facility Calls for Large Investments in Cargo Container and

Fish-Handling Capabilities," *Los Angeles Times*, 20 April 1990, D1; Jim Doyle, "SF Port Plans Expansion over Next 25 Years," *San Francisco Chronicle*, 20 April 1990, A4.

4. City and County of San Francisco Municipal Code, Planning Code, volume 1, section 263.2, Special Exceptions, North of the Ferry Building, and section 263.3, Special Exceptions, South of the Ferry Building (added by Ord. 234-72, App. 8/18/72).

5. According to Vello Kiisk, in earlier times, everything south of the Ferry Building was considered maritime. Vello B. Kiisk, Port of San Francisco, interim port director, 1988–89, chief harbor engineer, 1979–88, telephone interview by author, 28 March 2003; Michael P. Huerta, executive director, Port of San Francisco, 1989–93, telephone interview by author, 1 April 2003; Paul Osmundson, director of real estate, director of planning and development, Port of San Francisco, 1989–2000, interview by author, 10 April 2003, San Francisco.

6. Will Travis, president, San Francisco Bay Conservation and Development Commission, interview by author, 9 April 2003, San Francisco; Kristen Bole, "Shipping Out: S.F. Port Director Dennis Bouey Answers His Critics," *San Francisco Business Times*, 23 December 1996, available from http://sanfrancisco.biz journals.com/sanfrancisco/stories/1996/12/23/story6.html (accessed 14 August 2002).

7. Edward Epstein, "Waterfront Plan Lost in Shuffle, S.F. Ballpark Buzz Clouds Discussion of Other Uses," *San Francisco Chronicle*, 4 March 1996, A13.

8. Jenny Strasburg, "S.F. Port Decision Questioned: Developer Asks for Vote Records," *San Francisco Chronicle*, 20 April 2001, A4.

9. Ben Kutnick, deputy director of finance and administration, Port of San Francisco, 1982–2001, interview by author, 6 July 2007, Minneapolis.

10. Alec Bash, planner, Port of San Francisco, 1997–2001, planner, San Francisco Planning Department, 1971–97, interview by author, 7 April 2003, San Francisco.

11. Dean Macris, director, San Francisco City Planning Department, 1980–92, San Francisco Community Development director, 1972–76; Deputy Director, San Francisco City Planning Department, 1968–72; telephone interview by author, 19 April 2003.

12. Robert Selna, "New Plan to Finance Pier Improvements," *San Francisco Chronicle*, 25 October 2006, B1.

Chapter 4

1. United States Navy, *Navy Region Southwest: San Diego Statistics*, http://www .cnrsw.navy.mil/Facts/SDStats.html (accessed 18 February 2006); U.S. Census Bureau, *State and County QuickFacts: San Diego County, California* (U.S. Bureau of the Census, last revised Friday, 7 May 2007, 09:33:44 EDT, available from http:// quickfacts.census.gov/qfd/states/06/06073.html; (accessed 10 May 2007).

2. San Diegans associated with the port often use the term "cul-de-sac" when describing their city's location and situation.

3. Roger Showley, "Port District Zealously Guards S.D.'s Jewel, and Its Pot of Gold," *San Diego Union*, 9 March 1980, B1.

4. California Assembly, "San Diego Unified Port District Act: An Act to Provide for the Establishment of the San Diego Unified Port District; to Provide for the Calling of Municipal Elections Therefore; Describing the Powers, Duties,

and Functions Thereof; Authorizing the District to Borrow Money and Issue Bonds for District Purposes; to Provide Means of Raising Revenues for the Operation, Maintenance, and Bond Redemption of the District; and to Provide for the Transfer to Such District of Tidelands and Lands Lying under Inland Navigable Waters," *Statutes of California*, chap. 67 (1962): 362–82, at 362, 365.

5. Peter Litrenta, former executive director, San Diego Port Tenants Association, interview by author, 13 May 2003, San Diego.

6. J. Michael McDade, port commissioner, Port of San Diego, 1993–99, interview by author, 12 May 2003, San Diego.

7. Peter Q. Davis, port commissioner, Port of San Diego, interview by author, 8 May 2003, San Diego; Francisco Urtasun, port commissioner, Port of San Diego, 1992–2002, interview by author, 13 May 2003, San Diego.

8. J. Michael McDade interview; Lawrence M. Killeen, executive director, Port of San Diego, 1996–99, interview by author, May 2003, San Diego.

9. Lawrence M. Killeen interview.

10. Ibid.

11. Dwight C. Daniels, "Official Wants His City to Quit Port District," *San Diego Union*, 31 August 1991, B5–6; J. Michael McDade interview.

Chapter 5

1. Delaware River Joint Commission, *Report of the Delaware River Joint Commission of Pennsylvania and New Jersey to the Legislators of the Commonwealth of Pennsylvania and the State of New Jersey and the Council of the City of Philadelphia* (Philadelphia: Delaware River Joint Commission, 31 December 1931), Appendix A, Agreement Between the Commonwealth of Pennsylvania and the State of New Jersey Creating the Delaware River Joint Commission as a Body Corporate and Politic and Defining its Powers and Duties, signed 1 July 1931, 21–22.

2. Eugene J. McCaffrey Sr., executive director, Delaware River Port Authority, 1989–93, interview by author, 3 September 2002, Woodbury, N.J.

3. Peter J. Burke Jr., commission vice-chair, Delaware River Port Authority, 1991–95, "History of the Delaware River Port Authority and the Struggle for Port Unification" (unpublished paper dated 10 February 1997), 14, 26–29, 34; "Let's Sail, Governor: Jersey Needs to Move Ahead on a Unified Port Plan," editorial, *Philadelphia Inquirer*, 8 May 1997, A22.

4. Jonathan A. Saidel, former city controller, Philadelphia, interview by author, 12 September 2002, Philadelphia.

5. James J. Cuorato, director of commerce, Philadelphia, 2000–2004, executive vice president, Penn's Landing Corporation, 1997–2000, vice president of finance and development, Penn's Landing Corporation, 1994–97, interview by author, 3 September 2002, Philadelphia; Thomas P. Corcoran, president and CEO, Cooper's Ferry Development Association, 1983–present, business administrator, Camden, 1975–83, interview by author, 9 September 2002, Philadelphia.

6. F. Joseph Loeper, Republican state senator, Commonwealth of Pennsylvania, 1978–2000, Senate majority leader, 1988–2000, interview by author, 11 September 2002, Philadelphia; William P. Hankowsky, president, Philadelphia Industrial Development Corporation, 1988–2000, interview by author, 20 September 2002, Philadelphia.

7. William P. Hankowsky interview; Jack Shannon, first deputy director of commerce, Philadelphia, 1994–97, business administrator (managing director),

Camden, 1994, staff, Cooper's Ferry Development Association, 1986–94, interview by author, 9 September 2002, Philadelphia.

8. Frederick L. Voigt, executive director, Committee of Seventy, interview by author, 15 August 2002, Philadelphia.

9. Craig R. McCoy, Elisa Ung, and Mario F. Cattabiani, "Fumo Deal with DRPA Nets Group $40 Million: The Agency Financed a Fund That Aided Projects the Senator Favored," *Philadelphia Inquirer,* 14 March 2004, A01; Craig R. McCoy and John Shiffman, "The Case against Fumo," *Philadelphia Inquirer,* 7 February 2007, A01.

10. Charles Bohnenberger, governor's liaison to the Delaware River Port Authority, 1998–2001, director of Governor Ridge's Philadelphia regional office, interview by author, 16 September 2002, Philadelphia; William P. Hankowsky interview.

11. Thomas P. Corcoran interview.

12. Eugene J. McCaffrey Sr. interview; Paul Drayton, chief executive officer, Delaware River Port Authority, 1993–2003, interview by author, 7 November 2002, Camden.

Chapter 6

1. Peter H. Brown and Peter V. Hall, "Ports and Waterfronts," in *Infrastructure Planning and Finance: A Guide for Local Officials,* ed. Vicki Elmer and Adam Liegland (Point Arena, Calif.: Solano Press, forthcoming).

2. Ray Riley and Louis Shurmer-Smith, "Global Imperatives, Local Forces, and Waterfront Redevelopment," in *Revitalising the Waterfront: International Dimensions of Dockland Redevelopment,* ed. Hoyle, Pinder, and Hussain, 38.

3. Ibid., 39–42.

4. Ibid., 42–44.

5. Ibid., 44–47.

6. Paul E. Peterson, *City Limits* (Chicago: University of Chicago Press, 1981), 22, 41–43, 131–33; John R. Logan and Harvey L. Molotch, *Urban Fortunes: The Political Economy of Place* (Berkeley: University of California Press, 1987), 1–2, 33.

7. Stephen L. Elkin, *City and Regime in the American Republic* (Chicago: University of Chicago Press, 1987), 33–35; Clarence N. Stone, *Regime Politics: Governing Atlanta, 1946–1988* (Lawrence: University Press of Kansas, 1989), 4–5, 133, 187, 193.

8. Alan A. Altshuler and David E. Luberoff, *Mega-Projects: The Changing Politics of Urban Political Investment* (Washington, D.C.: Brookings Institution, 2003), 267.

9. Ibid., 265–66.

10. Ibid., 267.

11. Ibid., 268.

12. Gordon, "Managing the Changing Political Environment in Urban Waterfront Redevelopment," 61–83, at 64–66, 68, 70, 72–74, 78.

13. Ibid., 68–70.

14. Gordon, "Architecture," 35–54, at 50–53.

15. Gordon, "Financing Urban Waterfront Redevelopment," 244–65, at 261–262.

16. David L. A. Gordon, interview by author, 31 January 2002, Philadelphia.

17. Maurice Cococcia, former vice president, Real Estate Solutions, Lend Lease, interview by author, 8 April 2003, San Francisco; Jesse Blout, director,

Mayor's Office of Economic and Job Development, interview by author, 9 April 2003, San Francisco; Paul Osmundson, director of real estate, director of planning and development, Port of San Francisco, 1989–2000, personal e-mail, 23 March 2007.

18. Jennifer Clary, president, San Francisco Tomorrow, program associate, Clean Water Action, interview by author, 4 April 2003, San Francisco.

19. Dean Macris interview; Toby Rosenblatt, chair, San Francisco City Planning Commission, 1976–88, telephone interview by author, 1 April 2003.

20. Maurice Cococcia interview; Jesse Blout interview.

21. S. Gail Goldberg, former director, Planning Department, San Diego, interview by author, 15 May 2003, San Diego.

22. Lawrence M. Killeen interview.

23. Maurice Cococcia interview; David Kitchens, principal, Cooper Carry Architects, telephone interview by author, 11 March 2003.

24. David Kitchens interview; Maurice Cococcia interview.

25. Susan Golding, mayor, San Diego, 1992–2000, interview by author, 16 May 2003, San Diego; Jim Chappell, president, San Francisco Planning and Urban Research Association, interview by author, 9 April 2003, San Francisco; Jonathan A. Saidel interview.

26. David Kitchens interview.

27. Arthur W. Jones, architect and principal, Bower Lewis Thrower Architects, interview by author, 20 September 2002, Philadelphia.

28. Inga Saffron, "A Quartet of Fantasies: Four New Penn's Landing Development Plans Seem to Ignore the Site's Reality," *Philadelphia Inquirer*, 14 September, 2003, C1.

29. Michael D. Hogan, chairman and CEO, Hogan Group, interview by the author, 4 March 2003, Tampa, Fla.

30. Ben Kutnick.

Chapter 7

1. The authors claim that this process mimics the biological evolution of species, and, indeed, they found the theories in Charles Darwin's *Origin of Species* to be more useful than many textbooks on corporate strategic planning. James C. Collins and Jerry I. Porras, *Built to Last: Successful Habits of Visionary Companies* (New York: HarperCollins, 1997), 9, 214.

2. James Q. Wilson, *Bureaucracy: What Government Agencies Do and Why They Do It* (New York: Basic Books, Inc., 1989), 182–83, 192, 195, 221–22, 334, 232.

3. Collins and Porras, *Built to Last*, xxiv, 31–34, 297 (table A.8, Backup Data, "CEO Statistics: 1806–1992").

4. Jameson W. Doig and Erwin C. Hargrove, "Leadership and Political Analysis," in *Leadership and Innovation: Entrepreneurs in Government*, abridged ed., Jameson W. Doig and Erwin C. Hargrove (Baltimore: Johns Hopkins University Press, 1990), 1–22, at 3–4, 7–8, 12–16; James G. March, "How We Talk and How We Act: Administrative Theory and Administrative Life," in *Leadership and Organizational Culture*, ed. Thomas J Sergiovanni and John E. Corbally (Urbana: University of Illinois Press, 1981), 28–29, 33; Wilson, *Bureaucracy*, 202–3.

5. Graham T. Allison, "Public and Private Management: Are They Fundamentally Alike in All Unimportant Respects?" in *Classics of Public Administration*,

4th ed., ed. Jay M. Shafritz and Albert C. Hyde (Orlando, Fla.: Harcourt Brace & Company, 1997), 383–400, at 386–89.

6. Walsh, *Public's Business*, 209–11.

7. Danielson and Doig, *New York*, 154–62, 333–38.

8. This is just a portion of the projects listed in the Tampa Port Authority's enabling legislation, and the other three enabling acts offer very similar lists. Legislature of Florida, "Chapter 23338-(No. 824), Senate Bill No. 804, An Act, Creating, Establishing and Organizing a Port District in the County of Hillsborough, State of Florida, to be Known and Designated as the Hillsborough County Port District," *Laws of Florida*, reg. sess. 1945, Special Acts (and the extraordinary session following), April 3 to and including June 1, 1945, and June 2 to July 24, 1945, vol. 2, 475–92 (1945), 477.

9. Richard E. Gehring, *Cruise Industry Overview*, undated PowerPoint presentation to the American Association of Port Authorities 2003 annual conference.

10. Ibid.

11. Ben Kutnick interview.

12. Eugene J. McCaffrey Sr. interview.

13. Ibid.

14. Richard E. Gehring interview.

15. Lori Musser, former manager of public relations, Tampa Port Authority, interview by author, 28 February 2003, Tampa, Fla.

Chapter 8

1. Walsh, *Public's Business*, 210.

2. Mitchell, "Policy Functions and Issues for Public Authorities," 5; Walsh, *Public's Business*, 171–72.

3. Walsh, *Public's Business*, 172–76; Mitchell, "Policy Functions and Issues for Public Authorities," 7, table 1.3; Jerry Mitchell, "Education and Skills for Public Authority Management," *Public Administration Review* 51.5 (September/October 1991): 429–37.

4. Jerry Mitchell, "Representation in Government Boards and Commissions," *Public Administration Review* 57.2 (March/April 1997): 160–67.

5. Walsh, *Public's Business*, 209–11; Mitchell, "Policy Functions and Issues for Public Authorities," 5–7.

6. For an excellent history of the start-up and early decades of the Port of New York Authority, see Bard, *Port of New York Authority*, 5–16.

7. Ibid., 16–26.

8. Ibid., 27–34.

9. Walsh, *Public's Business*, 173–75.

10. Ibid., 175, 180–83.

11. Ibid., 181, 183.

12. Ibid., 172–74.

13. Michael P. Huerta interview.

14. Dana Wilkie, "Many Want More Say on Port Board: Critics Renew Call Urging Election of Commissioners," *San Diego Tribune*, 24 August 1990, A1.

15. Sandy Freedman, mayor, Tampa, 1987–95, interview by author, 6 March 2003, Tampa, Fla.

16. Francisco Urtasun interview.

17. Joseph Valenti interview.

18. Alan Schoedel, "Speakers at the 66 Annual Convention of American Association of Port Authorities Note Port Administrations Currently Face Increasing Political Pressure and Insurance Crisis," *Journal of Commerce*, 26 October 1977, 1; Walsh, *Public's Business*, 210–11.

19. Vello B. Kiisk interview.

Index

Acknowledgments

My thanks go first to Genie Birch, who indulged my interest in public authorities and, more important, encouraged me to write the proposal that led to this book. Gary Hack pushed me to develop and compare multiple cases rather than relying on just one, which resulted in a study that is much more powerful and robust than it otherwise would have been. Seymour Mandelbaum offered thoughtful and penetrating criticism on the theoretical framework that underlies this work. I owe thanks to the University of Pennsylvania for granting me a University Fellowship and to Penn Design's Grosser Research Fund for a grant that financed my research in the four cities.

Thanks also to Ann Forsyth for reading and commenting on the manuscript not once but twice, for providing me with an intellectual home at the University of Minnesota's Metropolitan Design Center, and for offering ongoing advice, technical assistance, and moral support as I tried mightily to balance my professional and academic careers. Ann also provided me with the services of Whitney Parks, to whom I owe thanks for organizing the illustrations and designing the beautiful maps and diagrams that grace this book. A handful of terrific friends and colleagues read the entire manuscript at one point or another, so thanks to David Gordon, Peter Hall, Lorlene Hoyt, Ben Kutnick, Denise Martinez, John Mulhern, Rex Sherman, and one anonymous reader, all of whom offered invaluable criticism and suggestions for improvement.

Most important, I owe an enormous debt of gratitude to the more than 150 people whom I interviewed for this book and who gave generously of their time, energy, and ideas. Some of these people also read parts of the manuscript, often several times, and offered helpful comments and insights while catching numerous errors of fact and interpretation, several quite ghastly. Thanks to Tom Corcoran, Jim Cuorato, Joe Garcia, Richard Gehring, Jenny Greenberg, Anne Halsted, Arthur Jones, Joe Myers, Paul Osmundson, Ron Roberts, Arthur Savage, Will Travis, and Frank Urtasun. Larry Killeen, a former port director in San Diego who passed away in 2007, told me that "a port is like an object of intense desire—it starts possessing your mind." This is certainly true for all of the people with whom I spoke, who enthusiastically shared their interest in and recollections about the ports, waterfronts, and cities for which they have such passion. Without their help this book would not have been possible, and while they may not all agree with my conclusions, I can only hope that each feels that I have been fair.

At the University of Pennsylvania Press, Peter Agree, Chris Hu, and Erica Ginsburg were a delight to work with and made the mysterious publishing process a smooth and enjoyable experience while at the same time helping me to produce the best book possible. I thank them for making me look good.

Finally, thanks to my lovely and brilliant wife, Anna Larsson, who listened to my ideas, challenged my arguments, helped me to refine my thinking, and in the process gained a better understanding of ports and waterfronts than she could have ever possibly hoped for. This book is dedicated to our son, Magnus, who brought us both great joy arriving as he did, just as I was completing the manuscript.